JOHN MONAGHAN

SON OF AN ORPHAN FATHER

ISBN: 9798412977232

www.john-monaghan.co.uk

Contents

Prologue

In February, 1929, an illegitimate child is born in London to an Irish hotel maid, Kathleen Monaghan.

With no named father and no prospect of Kathleen being able to provide for her baby boy, he is taken into the care of a London orphanage.

An Irish farming couple, Mr and Mrs David Jones, quickly adopt baby Maurice, named by Kathleen, and sail back to Ireland with their new son.

As soon as Maurice is old enough, he is set to work on the farm. The work is relentless for this young child.

Maurice grows up with no experience of a mother's love or affection, and times are hard in 1930s Ireland.

He has no shoes or socks and he's poorly clothed; the best time of year is Easter, as he can eat as many boiled eggs as he likes, but for that day only.

As an adult, in the late 1950s, he sails to England to find work and escape poverty for good.

He meets and marries an Irish girl, Nancy Lynch, and in 1958 they are blessed with their first child, a daughter they name Anita.

Two years on, in 1960, their second child is born, a son they name John.

I am that second child and this is my story.

1

Through the eyes of a child

It's 9 November 1960, the day that I am born at the Hammersmith Hospital in London. President Kennedy has just been elected.

As a newly born infant, I have already felt the strong bond, warmth, and encompassing love that only a caring mother can give to her child. But I'm yet to endure a childhood living with my father, whose distorted and confusing idea of love ranges from being a great provider – taking us on holidays, buying sweets and toys – to what some would describe as child abuse. In the years to come, as I grow, I will be singled out from my brother and sister to take my mother's place as his metaphoric punchbag for everything that has and will go wrong in his life. But, unlike my mother, for me it will be physical as well as mental. Why he does this will only become clear to me near the end of my childhood.

My earliest memories will not start until I'm three years old. The family, my dad, Maurice, my mum, Nancy, my sister, Anita, and I are living at 148 Fennycroft Road, Hemel Hempstead.

The year is 1964. I'm three years old, too young to know what season this is, but I think it's autumn. I'm sitting alone inside the open front door of our house. It's the middle of the day and I think Anita's at school and Mum's talking to one of the neighbours.

I'm picking up the dried tree leaves that have been blown into the porch area by the front door and examining them, trying to understand what they are and how they got there. I'll wait here until Mum calls me. Suddenly there's a gust of wind and the leaves are blown from the ground, startling me for a second. *How did they leave the ground, fly into the air, then land on me, unless they're alive? Well, there's nobody around to ask and it's stopped, so I'll wait for Mum and ask her.*

It's the weekend, early morning, and the sun's shining through my bedroom window. Lying on my bed, I can see rays of sunlight filled with glittering dust. The dust sparkles as it floats around in the beam of light. I move my hand around in it to see if I can make patterns with it. I can hear a dog barking in the distance and the voices of my family downstairs; they're laughing and they sound so happy.

I think today's my birthday. Mum and Dad tell me they have a nice surprise planned for me. We're all going somewhere in the car. As we sit around the kitchen table having tea and toast, I feel my excitement building; I have no idea where we could be going.

The wait for everyone to get ready and get into the car seems like an eternity, but eventually we do and we're on our way. After a short drive, we slow down and Dad parks the car outside a toy shop. He tells us to wait in the car, and runs in on his own.

He walks out of the shop, carrying a blue metal pedal car. I cannot believe my eyes. Has he really bought that for me? He opens the car door and shows it to me. With his voice almost drowned out by the passing traffic, he asks me, "What do you think?"

"It's brilliant!" I reply, boiling over with excitement.

I can't take my eyes off the shiny blue paintwork, with the white wheels and matching white steering wheel. It's like a real car made especially for me and we're taking it home; it's a dream come true!

He puts it straight into the boot; he looks pleased. As soon as we arrive home, he takes it out of the boot and immediately I'm pedalling down the alleyway behind our house. It's like a road made for my pedal car. After going up and down the alleyway a thousand times, I decide I need to figure out how it works. I've found some pieces of wood and have raised it off the ground by putting the wood under the wheels, like grownups do with their ramps when they're fixing real cars. I'm lying under the pedals, examining everything – it's amazing, and it actually works.

Some weeks pass and I go back to my old three-wheel bike. I've always had this one; I don't remember getting it anyway.

There's a boy about my age, who lives in the last house on our block, and he has a three-wheel bike, too; he's riding up and down the alleyway. He asks me to ride with him. I have to ask my mum and away we go. We're racing down the alleyway and around the block. His bike has pump-up tyres, but mine are solid rubber. His tyres are making his bike faster and he's in front of me. I wish I had those tyres! He's gone ahead of me, but he's stopped outside his house. I'm right behind and he's just around the corner. I'm pedalling as fast as I can when I notice he's there, but it's too late. My brakes aren't good and I run my bike straight into the back of his, crashing into his back tyre on the righthand side. Straight away, I notice a big bubble coming out of his tyre. Oh no … I must has caused that.

He sees it too and says, "Oh no, look what you've done! What do I do now?"

I have to come up with an idea, so I tell him, "I know, go and get a pin."

He rushes into his house and asks his mum for a pin, then comes out and hands it to me. I have everything I need to fix it now – it's all up to me. I'll stick it in the bubble and it'll go back into his tyre. I'm pushing quite hard and then "POP", it's gone back in. Wow! Job done! It worked. At this moment, his dad walks out and asks, "What are you doing?"

I'm so proud of myself, I reply, "It's okay, it's fixed now."

The boy tells him what I did. He looks at me as if he wants to kill me for some reason. Some people are so ungrateful!

It's a new day and I've woken up early this morning. It's cold and wet outside, and I'm not sure where Mum is, as it's early. She's either still in bed, or down in the kitchen. Anyway, I don't feel like staying in my bed, so I get up and go out to the top of the stairs. It's daylight and I can hear Dad getting ready for work. There's a window halfway down the stairs. I climb onto the windowsill. Looking through the window, I can see across the green at the back of our house and the grass is almost white with dew. It's misty and the sound is muffled by the mist. I'm daydreaming and watching all the movement outside, when I hear the back door close – it's Dad leaving for work. I watch him walk across the green to get to his car and he's wearing his black donkey jacket and work boots. As he walks away, I'm thinking, *He's doing that for us, the whole family, because he loves us.* He works hard and he's out in the cold all day; I feel sorry for him. I stay on the windowsill for a while and watch him disappear into the mist. The green seems huge to me. It's not long before Anita's up and my peace is broken. She's going to school.

Mum and I walk Anita into school and on the way home we stop at the local shops to buy food for the week. Along the precinct path, there's a wall between the shops and the car park. It's quite a long wall and Mum's walking ahead of me. I decide to walk on the wall, because she can't see what I'm doing. In fact, I'm not just going to walk on the wall – I'm going to walk along it backwards, without looking. I've walked backwards for a long way, when suddenly I'm at the end. I fall back and feel a crack to my head. Everything's gone blurred and I'm lying on the steps down to the car park. I hear a scream. It's Mum – she's holding me in her arms and looking down at me. I feel calm and glad to see her. I think I must have knocked myself out. I get up and walk a bit, before Mum asks, "Are you okay now?"

"Yes, I'm okay," I reply.

We continue the walk home, but I still feel sick and shocked.

I won't be doing that again!

Some weeks pass; it's morning and it's cold outside. Mum tells me, "We're going down to the town to do some shopping now."

We arrive in town and I look up at all the buildings in amazement. This place is full of people walking around all over the place. The most amazing thing is the glass bridge that goes from the upstairs of one building, then across the road to the upstairs of another building. It has a green stripe all along the side of it. I'm asking my mum, "Are we going on the bridge?"

"Maybe," she replies.

We stop at a lot of shops and Mum's reading out the prices, "Three pounds, seven and eleven."

I ask, "What does that mean?"

"Three pounds, seven shillings and eleven pence," she replies.

That sounds like a whole lot to me, but then anything more than this one-penny piece that I have is a lot to me.

After a while, to my elation, we go across the glass bridge. Further down the road, I can see the zebra crossing with the flashing beacons. I love this place – it's all brand new, clean and shiny. I love walking around here, especially with Mum.

"Come on!" Mum says. "We're going to the market."

Before I know it, we're walking around all the market stalls. Mum's buying groceries and she's talking about prices again.

Suddenly, I look around and she's gone. I call for her, "Mum … Mum …" But she doesn't answer.

I start walking, but I can only see legs and hands everywhere. I'm trying to see the faces of the people around me, but they don't look down to me. They're all rushing around and trying not to trip over me. I still can't see her and it's going on for ages. I'm getting scared now. I pull a lady's hand and say, "I can't find my mum!"

She grabs my hand and pulls me through the crowd of people. She finds her. Mum grabs my hand and says, "John, why did you walk off like that?"

I don't mind her telling me off; I'm glad that I'm back with her.

We've walked for miles and Mum has tons of shopping. We're waiting at the bus stop; I'm cold and tired. I keep asking, "Can we go home now?"

Mum has stopped answering me.

Shortly, a nice man comes in his car and gives us a lift home.

Thank God for that!

Mum says, "Don't tell your daddy that the man gave us a lift home, will you?"

"No, I won't," I reply.

I wonder why Dad shouldn't know about it, but as Mum's told me not to say anything, I won't.

It's spring, 1965; the days are getting much warmer. Anita's at school again and Dad's at work, so it's just Mum and me at home. We're both in the kitchen and Mum's by the sink washing up. I'm lying on the black-and-white chequered tiled floor and the radio is on, playing a song by Petula Clark, called "Downtown". That song reminds me of when Mum and I go to the town.

While I'm lying on the floor, I'm thinking. I'm wondering why my mum's belly's getting so big. I ask her, "Why's your belly getting so big, Mum?"

She laughs and tells me, "It's because I have a baby in there."

"What? How did that happen?" I ask, horrified.

She explains to me, "When a man and a woman get married, they have babies and that's where you came from."

"I came from your belly because you got married?" I ask her in shock.

"Yes, your daddy gave me a seed," she replies.

"Where does he get those seeds from and where does he keep them?" I ask.

Mum doesn't answer that question. I don't know why, because even if I knew where they were, I wouldn't touch them. She must think I would go around planting babies everywhere. He probably keeps them in his pocket anyway.

I'm thinking deeply about this and how it's all so strange. Everything in this world seems to be well organised and planned out. I've learned a lot about the world in my time here already. Married people have babies who grow into children like me.

We all have a mum and dad and we all live in houses. We all get bigger and go to school. We have ambulances in case we die and they come and make us alive again. We have police who are nice people who look after us and make sure that we're safe. We have firemen who put out house fires, because they're good people, too. I like this world. It really is a perfect place.

Anita's home from school. She runs in, telling Mum about her day. She keeps talking about her class.

She seems excited about it. There's no chance for me to ask her what a class is. I think she must mean glass, but I've never seen a glass big enough to stand in. I'm imagining Anita standing in a giant glass. Well, class sounds like glass, so maybe that's what she means. One day I'll find out for myself.

It's the weekend, so Dad and Anita are at home. It's warm and sunny outside and there are some boys outside the front of the house on the green; they're squirting one another with water pistols. The water pistols are in the shape of a space rocket and they're transparent. I want one, too. I run with excitement to Mum and ask if I can have one. She replies, "No way, you're not having one of those so you can behave like those little brats."

Well, it's Sunday now, the following day, and I'm still sad I can't have a water pistol. Mum says we can all go for a walk in the woods to pick bluebells. The woods are just across the green at the back of the house, so it's very close.

We all get ready and walk to the woods: Mum, Dad, Anita, and me. When we arrive there, Anita runs ahead and starts picking flowers. It's a beautiful place. The sun's shining through the trees and the ground is a sea of blue from all the bluebells. I've never seen such natural colour, and being with my family in this place is like heaven.

We pick plenty of flowers – Anita picks the most. I give mine to Mum and tell her that she can have them.

We arrive home and Dad starts searching for his door keys, but he can't find them. He says, "It's okay, the bathroom window's open. I'll borrow a ladder from one of the neighbours."

We all wait by the house and he comes back with a huge long ladder. The house is three storeys high and the bathroom window is on the top floor. He puts the ladder up against the house next to the bathroom window and says, "The window's too small for me to fit through. John, you'll have to climb the ladder and get inside. Once you're in the house, come down the stairs and open the door."

"Okay," I reply.

I put my right foot on the first rung of the ladder, then look up to see where the window is. Oh God! I can barely see the end of it, it's so far up in the sky that it's much smaller that end than this.

"Go on, hurry up," Dad says.

I look over at Mum, but she say's nothing. She looks scared and upset. I grasp the ladder with both hands and step by step I climb, getting more scared the higher I am. As I approach the small window without looking down, I become more aware of how high up I am. I'm at the window; I'm feeling dizzy and shaky. I know what'll happen if I fall and there's nobody to help me up here. I don't want to let go to climb in.

"Go on, climb in the window, John!" Dad's shouting up to me.

I need one more step to be high enough. I push myself up, then put my head through the window and slide on my front with a crash, as I smash Mum's ornaments and fall head first to the floor.

"Jesus, Mary, and Joseph!" I can hear Dad shouting.

Still shaken, I run downstairs and open the door for them. I don't feel safe with him any more.

The weekend's over and it's the start of another day. Dad's gone to work and Anita has gone to school. It's just Mum and me again. She tells me she has to go somewhere without me today, so she's going to leave me with Nell down the road. Being left with Nell is one of the worst places for me. I don't like her, because she's ugly and she makes me blow my nose. Also, she has a son about my age and there's something wrong with him. When he comes to my house, he throws my toys around and won't play properly. Last time he was there, I had all my cars lined up in a traffic jam and he swiped his hand through them and messed them all up. When I put them all away and refused to play with him, his mum said there must be something wrong with me. I don't like him – his name's Paul Townsend and he's really stupid.

Anyway, we've had our tea and toast and Mum says in a fluster, "Come on, John, we have to go."

I walk along the pavement towards their house with her with a sick feeling in my stomach, knowing where I'm going and what to expect.

We arrive at Nell's house and she opens the front door.

"Oh, come in," she says.

But Mum replies, "Sorry, I have to go. I'm late," as she starts walking away.

Nell grabs my hand and pulls me into her house. Mum says, "Bye, have a good day."

I'm waving goodbye, wishing she wouldn't leave me here.

Nell calls Paul and says, "Look, Paul, John's here to play with you."

Out on the green at the front of their house, Nell's set up a tent for us to play in. "Come on now, both of you, let's go out to the tent," she says cheerfully.

She takes both of us by the hand and pulls us along. I go inside it and there are cushions, plates, cups, drinks, and food in there. I sit inside it, while Paul's outside on the green, picking up dog's poo and throwing it at the tent with his bare hands. After a while of doing that, he comes inside and starts eating food with dog's poo on his hands. He doesn't say anything. He eats some food and then starts shouting and throwing the plates around, almost hitting me with the cups, knives, and anything he can get his hands on.

I have to get out of here, away from this nutcase! I walk out, but Nell comes out and shouts, "Stay in the tent!"

"But Paul's throwing things," I reply.

"You shouldn't tell tales!" she says as she pushes her hanky against my face. "Blow your nose now."

I can't blow my nose, because she's squeezing it so tightly.

Why does Mum leave me with these crazy people?

She looks into the tent and sees all the broken plates and cups and says, "Oh no, what have you two been doing?"

I wish Mum would hurry up and come and get me.

Finally, after a day full of things like this, Mum knocks on the front door. Nell lets her in and the first thing Mum says is, "Has he been good?"

Nell replies, "Well, we did have a little trouble, but he hasn't been too bad."

I don't like this crazy woman, or her son, and I never want to see them again. The only one in their family who's okay is Stan and he's Paul's dad.

He has a Ford Consul. It's black and sometimes he takes us to the sweet shop in it to get sweets. It has four doors, so I can get in through a door of my own without having to push the front seat forwards.

In Dad's car, I have to tip the front seat up to get into the back. Actually, the last time we went in Stan's car, I asked him if we could get sweets and he said, "No, because you asked, you can't have any." So, he didn't get us any. He's horrible as well. They're all horrible.

It's a new day and the sun's shining. It's warm and Mum's inside the house in the kitchen, which is on the first floor in our house. There's a flat on the ground floor, beneath the house, where an old lady, called Mrs Surridge, lives. On our ground floor, all we have is a hallway and the staircase.

I'm riding my trike up and down the alleyway and Mum's watching me out of the kitchen window while she's doing the washing up. There are some other boys in the garden next door and they start calling me.

I ride up to them and we start talking. One minute this boy is talking to me, and the next, he starts punching me. His punches are not hurting me much. I don't think he's that strong. I don't want to hit him back, because I don't want to hurt him, but he catches me out and pushes me off my bike.

He climbs onto it and says, "I'm taking this."

The thought of someone taking my bike is unbearable. I stand in front of it and tell him, "Get off it!"

But he won't. He keeps saying, "Make me."

Holding the handlebars tightly to stop him from riding away, I shout one last time, "Get off my bike!"

He says again, "Make me."

I feel fury inside me. Who does he think he is?

I grab the front wheel and pull it up high above my head. The boy falls back and hits his head hard on the ground – he's screaming. I don't care. I think he deserved that!

Suddenly, I hear Mum shout to me, "Good for you, John!"

She must have been watching the whole time.

Time has moved on and the days are getting much warmer. There are flowers growing everywhere and the birds are singing. Today's not the same as usual and I know something's wrong. Mum's lying on the settee – she looks sad and not well. Dad is at home and he's rushing in and out of the house with things to bring to the car. I ask Mum, "What's wrong Mum, why are you so sad, are you not well?"

She looks at me with tears in her eyes and hugs me, then lies back down, and I can see the tears running down her face.

"Why are you crying?" I ask.

"Because I don't want to leave you," she replies with a forced smile.

I feel a knot in my stomach. I ask, "Why do you have to leave me?"

"I don't want to leave you and Anita, but I have to go into hospital and stay there," she replies.

I step back in shock. My mind's racing.

"I have to go into hospital, but I'll be coming back with a baby," she adds with a giggle.

Confused, I ask, "But if you're coming back with a baby, then why are you crying? We'll have a baby here with us."

"I don't want to go," she whispers, with a tearful smile.

I feel scared; I feel like there's something she's not telling me. Mum's then taken to hospital and soon enough she's back with a baby boy. His name's James.

James is born on 16 May 1965.

"What do you think of him?" Mum asks me, proudly.

"He's smashing to bits; he's my baby brother," I reply.

Some weeks pass and Mum's always busy with James. I spend a lot more time playing alone or with Sooty, our little black dog. I feel like I'm not needed any more. When I'm not playing, I sit on a windowsill and watch what's going on outside. At the moment, I'm watching Dad trying to get his car started. He uses this funny handle thing that he pushes through a hole in the front of his car. I think he's trying to wind it up, but it's not working. Nobody else has to wind their cars up, just my dad.

A few months pass and the summer is coming to an end. It's getting dark early in the evening now. Our funny black car is gone. Anita always called it "Blacky the Elephant" for some reason, but I've never seen a black elephant. I suppose there must be some somewhere, because she knows a lot of things that I don't.

Instead of our black car, Dad has bought a blue Anglia Van. He never liked Anita calling our old car Blacky the Elephant.

This blue Anglia Van has a sad face; some of the Anglia cars have a smiley face. Well, the front grill part makes it look like that. The van has seats in the front and a bench seat in the back for Anita and me. James has to sit on Mum's lap.

When Dad drives off fast, the seat that Anita and I sit on tips up and we both fall back and hit our heads. We've started to go and see Granny and Grandad almost every weekend in this van. They live on Plympton Road, Kilburn, in London. Dad always drives fast and he overtakes a few cars in a row going down Brockley Hill in Edgware.

It's a long hill and he swerves in at the last minute, avoiding the cars coming the other way. I'm always scared of that part of the journey and I'm glad when it's over. We're on our way there again today. We go through Edgware to get to Kilburn and he's angry again. He shouts and swears about the other drivers. He says, "Look at him trying to get it front, just because he has a great big bloody Jag."

Somehow, we arrive at Granny and Grandad's. Their house is an old Victorian London house and it's five storeys high, with a big black wooden front door – it's massive. We go in through the front door and there isn't any carpet, just tiles and an old black phone on a shelf with a metal dial.

Granny takes us all down to the back of the house, where there's an old farmhouse-style table and chairs. The kitchen's just an old sink and a couple of 1950s units. There's also a settee in the room where Grandad's sitting, smoking his pipe.

The room's full of smoke and he blows it at his cat's face, but the cat doesn't like it.

Grandad tells me to come and sit on his knee. He always grips his hands around my knees and squeezes them so hard. His hands are strong. I think he could crush anything. Granny cooks Grandad a steak for his dinner and then he cuts off a piece and pushes it towards me, saying, "Go on, have a suck on that." He's a very tough and abrupt man.

Granny's warm and loving. I sit on her lap, playing with the ends of her fingers. It's funny, because when I push the end of her fingers, they stay flat, and when I squeeze them the end pops out again. I could do this for ages; it's fun.

Anita and I run around this big house, while Mum and Dad talk to Granny and Grandad. It's like an adventure, because the house is so big. There are stairs, then rooms, then more stairs, then more rooms, then more stairs and even more rooms. Until you get to the top, where there's one last door, but it's locked.

Outside the door, the sun shines brightly through the landing window, because we are so high up. In the opposite direction of this door, you can walk out onto the roof, where there's a roof garden.

After a while, we go downstairs. In the hallway there's a door that leads to the cellar. We decide to go through the door and down the steps – it's dark and dusty. There's a tiny ray of light shining through a vent down at the end of the cellar. I find a lot of old tobacco tins with screws and nails inside; further on there's Grandad's old black metal tools.

This place is spooky and smells musty. There are spider's webs everywhere. Anita tries to scare me, "Ah, look there's a ghost down there!" She screams.

That's spooked me. I'm going back up to see Granny.

After a while, it's time to go home. Granny and Grandad come to the front door to wave goodbye to us as we leave. We all get into the van. Anita and I take up our positions kneeling on the back seat to wave goodbye through the two small back windows.

Dad accelerates, the back seat tips up and we both whack our faces on the floor of the van. This kind of thing is normal for us.

On the journey home, Dad drives through a red traffic light and we get chased by a police car. The policeman stops us and he's looking through Dad's window. Dad had a Murray mint in his mouth and he took it out and put it on the dashboard. Maybe he thought it was illegal to eat Murray mints when driving?

He winds his window down and the policeman says, "Why did you drive through the red traffic light?"

"They were amber," Dad replies.

"They were red," the policeman replies.

He writes on a piece of paper, then hands it to Dad saying, "Look, you have your kids in the back of your van, so you need to drive more carefully."

I think the policeman cares more about us than Dad does. I'm glad he's been told off; maybe he won't drive like a maniac on the way home now.

This weekend we're going to see Aunty Mary. She lives at 1 Tiverton Road, Queensbury, just past Edgware. We have to go down Brockley Hill again to get there and I start to brace myself.

At the top of the hill, Dad's already driving close to the car in front, then his indicator goes on to start overtaking. He accelerates and we zoom down the hill at speed, overtaking all the cars. I feel my stomach flip with fear. Will we make it without a crash? At the last minute, again he swerves in.

Phew, we made it.

We turn into Tiverton Road and park outside. Anita and I run up to the front door and wait. Mum rings the doorbell and Uncle Liam lets us in.

Aunty Mary's in the kitchen; she makes tea for everyone. I like her – she's lovely. She reaches up to a cupboard and takes out a massive tray full of fairy cakes and butterfly cupcakes, then places it on the table. My eyes pop out of my head. She's just made them and they look great. Straight away, everyone's asking for one. We all have one each and then I ask, "Can I have another one please?"

"Yes, just take one," she replies in her lovely soft Irish accent.

They taste so sweet and creamy and they just melt in my mouth.

"Can I have another one, please, Aunty Mary?" I ask.

"Oh, you are a greedy boy, aren't you?" she replies.

I realise she's right. I am greedy. I look down to the floor, shamed.

"Go on, then, have another one, but that's it, no more," she says.

I cagily take another cake, eating it more slowly and staying quiet.

When the cakes are all gone, we go down the alleyway and I play catch with my cousin Eyvon.

As we leave, my uncle Liam is talking to Dad about his Wolsey. It's a big car and has tail fins. It looks green and white to me but I can't tell.

We leave to go and see my aunty Kathleen; she lives a few miles away in Harrow.

When we arrive, my uncle Eddie opens the door and we all go in. My cousins Stephen and Gavin are in the garden. They have an electric pedal car and they let me have a go on it. It's brilliant – it has a black switch on its dashboard and you switch it up to go forwards and down to go back.

All around their back garden, there are paths like roads that I can drive on. I love this car. They're so lucky. I never want to get out of it.

But before long, the battery has gone flat and we go inside.

Uncle Eddie's very posh. He's a bank manager and he's the only English uncle I have, as all the rest are Irish. He doesn't talk much to Dad, mostly to Mum.

Soon it's time to go home. It's been a long day and I'm tired. We have the journey home yet and Dad's been drinking again.

I hope we get home safely!

It's a weekday. Mum's cleaning a lady's flat today; she's taken James and me with her. We have to stay quiet while she works.

James is asleep and I'm sitting on the floor near the window in the living room. It's a very posh flat and the carpet is thick and spongy. I can squash it down with my hands. It's cold outside, but where the sunlight is on the carpet, it makes it warm to touch. It's funny how one part of the carpet is warm, but the part in the shade is cold. Mum finishes her work and quickly gets James ready to leave.

"Come on, John, hurry up and stay quiet on the way out. You're not supposed to be here with me," she says.

The next day, we're going to work with Mum again, but this time it's at the bowling alley. I don't know what she does there – maybe cleaning the balls? Anita's not at school today, so she's coming, too. We both have the same jumpers.

They're brown with a zigzag pattern in white across our chests and around our backs.

We arrive early and there's nobody around, so Mum lets us have a game of bowling. I always follow the ball down the lane and Anita laughs at me. It's warm in here and we're getting too hot, so we both take our jumpers off.

Mum calls us, "Come on, it's time to go home."

We can't tell whose jumper is whose. Anita smells both jumpers and says, "This one's mine – yours smells of coffee and mine smells of tea."

"Why does mine smell of coffee?" I ask.

"Because you drink coffee and I drink tea," she replies cheerfully.

I've never even tasted coffee before, but she must be right because she knows more than I do. I accept what she says and I put on the jumper that she gave me. We all go home and it was a lot of fun.

It's a cold January morning in 1965. I'm looking through my bedroom window and I can't believe my eyes. Everything's completely white with snow and it's still snowing. I look through the landing window and the snow is up as high as the dustbin lid. I run to look through the front room window and I can't see the difference between the road, the green, or the pavement. It's all flat and completely white.

I look across to the garages and all of the cars are stuck in the snow. People are pushing them and Dad, who seems to be in charge of everything, is digging a car out with his shovel.

He shouts, "Go on, go now," to a man in his car.

But the man's got stuck again and Dad's shouting, "Jesus, Mary, and Joseph!"

He digs it out again and the man drives off, sliding all over the place. He's shouting to the other drivers, but his voice sounds muffled. Is the snow causing that? Finally, he digs his own van out and drives off to work.

2

Into the system

It's early September, 1965, and it's my first day at school. I'm going to Blessed Cuthbert Main School in Hemel Hempstead. Mum's taken Anita and me into school today. I've been looking forward to this day, because now I'll find out what Anita does every day.

I'm led into a large room, along with a lot of other children, and the first thing I notice is lots of tables, chairs and massive glass windows that go almost all the way down to the ground. There are toys, a sandpit, posters and boards on the walls. There are lots of coat hangers, which is where we are told to hang our coats.

There's a lady who's in charge of us all; she must be a teacher. She tells all of us to sit down on the floor and cross our legs. I don't know why I have to sit like this, but everyone does it, so I do as I'm told.

The lady says that she is going to call out our names and we are to answer "Yes, Miss".

She starts calling out lots of names and the other children answer, "Yes, Miss".

I'm waiting for her to call out my name. "John Maurice," but she doesn't. Then she calls out, "John Monaghan."

Well, as far as I know, my name is John Maurice, as nobody told me otherwise. I stay quiet. The teacher seems distressed and calls in another lady. She says, "John Monaghan's missing, but we have John Maurice in the classroom!"

The other lady dashes out of the classroom and a few minutes later she comes back with Anita.

Anita's pointing at me saying, "That's my brother there."

The teacher says, "No, that's John Maurice."

"No, it's my brother, John Monaghan," Anita replies.

"Are you John Maurice or John Monaghan?" the teacher asks me.

"I'm John Maurice," I reply.

"Is this your sister?" she asks.

"Yes," I reply.

"Well, then you're John Monaghan," she says.

Anita goes back to her class and now I feel stupid. I'm not John Monaghan. I'm John Maurice Monaghan then.

As the day goes on, somebody comes in with a crate of small milk bottles. They're glass with a foil top and some have milk in them and others have orange juice in them. I'm given a bottle of milk and told to drink it.

I like the sandpit, because there are cars in it that I can push around in the sand.

We all sit around the teacher after a while of playing and she reads us a story. I'm not sure about this place – hopefully I won't have to come here every day.

After a day that seems to go on for a long time, Mum comes to take us home. It's funny, because Anita's been here all day as well, but the only time I saw her was when she came in to point me out to the teacher.

On the way home, Mum asks me, "Why did you say you were John Maurice?"

Anita gives Mum a full report of what happened and now I feel really stupid again.

The next day, I'm back at school again. I have a new school uniform on today: grey short trousers, a white shirt and a cap with a badge on it – it's the school badge.

After the teacher talks for a while, she tells us that we can all go around, talk to one another and play with the toys.

Today I don't feel like mixing or playing with the toys, because I miss being with Mum.

On the wall there's a huge picture of a town. It has a main road with traffic lights, buses, cars, and a zebra crossing. The zebra crossing has flashing beacons, just like our town; it's reminding me of when I go down to the town with Mum.

I feel extremely sad inside as I stare at this picture and a song seems to play in my head. "Downtown" by Petula Clark, the one that Mum always has on the radio. I don't know if I'll ever be allowed to go to the town with her again.

I wonder if she's gone there today on her own, without me. I can feel tears in my eyes. I don't want to be here. I want to be with Mum.

A week or so passes and I'm more used to the idea of going to school each day, because at least I'll be home each evening and every weekend.

I'm at school again today and it's play time. All the children are out on the playground and they're all playing in different groups. There are a few boys who I'm with, but I don't know them well yet and I'm not sure if I like them or not. They're all sitting talking and I'm looking around to see what the other children are doing. I notice a girl who's walking around with her friends. I think she looks really pretty. I feel like I want to get her attention. I need to think of a way to do it. I can't just walk over and start talking to her, because that would be really stupid. Boys don't talk to girls, because they're not like us. They're strange – they like skipping and playing hop scotch.

I've come up with a plan. If I can get all the boys who are with me to form a circle by holding hands, the boy to my right can open the gate to this circle by letting go of my hand. We can then go around the playground, trapping people in the circle. Of course, the pretty girl will be the first one to capture and let go.

All the boys agree that it sounds like a good game. We form the circle and I guide everyone towards this girl. We trap her, but it doesn't go to plan. Instead of me getting her attention, everyone's pulling in all directions. She's knocked over and cuts her lip on the ground. A teacher rushes over, looks at her, and says, "Whose idea was this?"

A couple of the boys point at me.

The teacher shouts at me, saying, "Go and stand facing the wall at the edge of the playground!"

I feel so stupid. I never thought she'd get hurt.

I don't say anything to the teacher. She wouldn't understand. I walk across the playground with my head facing down in shame. She told me to face the wall, but there isn't a wall; there's just a low hedge.

I feel stupid with my back to the playground, looking over the hedge like a donkey. Especially as there's an alleyway on the other side of the hedge, people are walking down the alleyway, staring at me like I'm a nutcase or something. I've been standing here for a while now and, to my horror, I can see Mum walking down the alleyway.

Oh my God! What am I going to do now? She's walking up to me, looking confused.

"John, what are you doing?" she asks.

I wish I could disappear right now.

"Nothing," I reply.

I can hear the other kids playing and laughing behind me. Mum asks, "Why aren't you playing with the other children?"

It's too complicated for me to explain, so I tell her, "I've been naughty."

"What did you do?" she asks.

"I kicked another boy," I reply.

"Oh, John, you shouldn't do things like that," she replies.

Now that the shock of Mum seeing me like this is over, I'm glad to see her.

"Can I go home with you?" I ask.

"You can't come with me now, but I'll be picking you up soon," she replies.

I look down at the ground and back up to her. I want to go home with her so much.

She tries to distract me. "Look what I've just bought," she says excitedly. She pulls out a light blue metal alarm clock from a carrier bag and holds it up for me to see.

"It looks really nice," I reply, smiling.

She seems really happy. She has the warmest smile and I always feel loved by her.

She makes everything seem okay.

The whistle's blown and all of the others start lining up to go back into class. The teacher calls me. I say bye to Mum and run over to the others, then we all go single file back into class.

I hope Mum doesn't tell Dad, because I don't want to be told off by him, as well, or even smacked.

It's Saturday morning and I'm playing with my cars in the living room. We have a dark brown swirly patterned carpet in our living room. The pattern looks like roads for my matchbox cars.

Suddenly, Dad bounces in the front door downstairs and shouts out, "Nancy! Anita and John, come and look at the new car!"

We all rush downstairs and across the green to the garages. Parked by the kerb is Dad's new Ford Anglia. It's spruce green and it has a white stripe down each side with chrome trim; it's an Anglia Super.

This Anglia Super has a smiley-face grill, unlike our Anglia van that had a sad-face grill.

Dad tells us to look inside. I can see it's all shiny and new and it has tightly fitted clear plastic on the seats. Anita's excited. She's jumping up and down.

I can't believe we have a brand-new car, with a back window that slopes the wrong way and nice new seats that won't tip up when we drive off. The only bad thing is, I still haven't got my own door to get in like in Stan's car. I have to tip the front seat up to get in the back.

One year passes and it's now the summer of 1967. I'm six years old. I'm very used to school now and I have friends there. My best friend's called Richard Fulham.

It's the summer holidays and I have seven weeks off school. Today we're leaving in our new car to go on holiday to Ireland. It's a long journey and we have to go on the ferry across the sea.

Finally, after a long drive to Holyhead, we're getting on the ferry. It's very busy and there are people everywhere.

We all get out of the car when we are told to and go upstairs to the deck. We have suitcases with us, and Dad takes one up with him. As the ferry leaves the Holyhead port, the cool wind blows across the deck. The crowd of people are sitting on their suitcases, including Dad. Anita and I go over to the railings to look over the edge to see the sea. There's all this white stuff in the sea. It looks like cream. I ask Mum, "What's all the white stuff in the sea?"

"It's salt," she replies.

"Salt?" I ask. "Who put salt in the sea?"

"There's always been salt in the sea," she replies.

I look again and it really doesn't look like salt, but Mum said it is, so she must be right.

After a long time on the ferry, we finally arrive in Dublin. The first thing I notice is all of the number plates on the cars: they're different to ours. They're white, while ours are black and silver, or black and white. As we drive through Dublin and out into the country, it starts to get dark and misty. We're heading for Uncle Terry's house in Cavan. He's Mum's brother.

After more hours of driving, we're all getting tired and it's turning dark and foggy. There are no lights on the road at all and hardly any other cars. All we can see through the car's windscreen is two beams of light from our headlights, and they're just lighting up the thick fog.

I'm not scared, because Dad's driving slowly for a change.

Finally, after a slow and boring journey, we arrive at the house quite late. It's pitch-black outside, and when Dad turns off the car's lights, I can't see anything at all. I'm standing between our car and the front door, with my eyes wide open, but it's like they're shut or I'm blind. Uncle Terry opens the front door with a candle on a plate. I can't believe he has no electricity. I ask Mum, "Has there been a power cut?"

"Shh, they have never had electricity here," Mum replies.

We all walk inside quietly. Everyone in the house is asleep. Mum's given a candle and we all go to bed in the same room.

I don't like it being this dark. I whisper to Mum, "Mum, can I leave the candle burning for a while?"

"So long as you blow it out before you go to sleep," she says.

I am lying in bed, watching the candle flicker; it's hypnotising. I'm exhausted, and eventually I drop off to sleep.

The following morning, I'm woken up by Mum saying, "John, I told you to blow the candle out before you went to sleep. Look what you've done to the chest of drawers. It's all burned from the candle!"

I jump up, rubbing my eyes to see. There's a big black mark where the candle was.

"I didn't mean to fall asleep and not blow it out!"

Mum shouts at me, "You could have burned the house down!"

I feel stupid now.

Mum goes into the living room with Dad. They're talking to Uncle Terry. Mum tells me, "Go with your cousin Peggy to the well to get a pail of water!"

I look around, but I can't see any taps. There's no kitchen either, just a turf range in the living room.

There are only three rooms in the whole house.

This is weird. I start walking down the driveway with Peggy and out onto the lane where we seem to walk for miles. I've been checking either side of the road for a well, but can't see one. Then Peggy calls out, "Here it is!"

She's reaching down at the side of the lane.

"Where's the well?" I ask her.

"This is the well," she replies in her Irish accent.

"It's just a hole in the ground?" I ask.

She looks at me with a confused expression.

I was expecting a proper well with a tiled roof and a bucket on a rope. I look down into the hole and I can see water. Peggy pulls the bucket up from the ground and it's full of clear water.

"Come on," she says, "hold the other side of the pail."

I do as she asks and we carry the pail all the way back to the house.

When we get back, everyone scoops some water from the pail using their tea cups, then they all start brushing their teeth. This pail of water is used for everything: Uncle Terry's shaving, washing, and even tea.

But the worst thing of all is, there's no toilet and I need to go. I ask Mum, "Where can I go for a wee?"

"You'll have to go in the hedge at the end of the garden," she says.

I run out to the hedge. I'm desperate and I make it just in time. I'm worried now – if this is where they go for a wee, then where do they go for a poo? I'll have to ask Mum. I rush back in and breakfast is being dished up. I've got sausage, egg and bacon, with fried bread the same as everyone else, except Dad, who's eating black pudding as well. He tells us he wants to go and visit Uncle David today.

Uncle David is a farmer and he's my dad's step-dad, because Dad was an orphan. It's a nice sunny day. We all get into the car to start our journey to see this man, whom I have never seen before. When we arrive, Dad turns into a long concrete driveway; it has cow dung everywhere all over it.

He drives all the way down to the end and opens a big wide iron farm gate, then drives the car through and closes the gate. He parks up next to the house and I can see part of the roof has collapsed. They can't be living there, surely?

Dad opens the car door and tells us to get out. I step out of the car straight into some cow dung. It's squashed all over my shoe. This place is horrible.

"Oh no!" I shout.

Closing the driver's door, he says, "Wash it off in a puddle." I do as he tells me, but it stinks.

We go inside the house and it's dark and scruffy. Uncle David and his wife are pleased to see Dad. They're laughing and talking. Suddenly I realise I need a poo.

I'm embarrassed, but I ask Mum anyway, "Where's the toilet?"

Mum tells Dad and he tells Uncle David. But Uncle David starts laughing and looking at me. I wish I could just disappear.

"Go out into the field and make the best of it!" he says.

I can't believe it. Nobody in Ireland has a toilet.

I move closer Mum and ask her, "Can you ask for some toilet paper?"

"Use a dot leaf," Mum replies quietly.

I do as they say and head out into the field next to the house, avoiding all the dollops of cow dung.

I find an area where there are no cows and make my way over to a large oak tree. I squat down on the other side of the tree, so nobody can see me from the house. I'm shielded from the road in front of me by a long hedge row. I have to go as quickly as I can, because I don't want anyone to see me. Luckily, there are dot leaves I can reach for when I've finished. I'm halfway through going, but I can hear a loud diesel engine and someone shouting. I look up and see Uncle David driving past on a tractor, shouting and laughing with his friend. I feel myself panic but I can't do anything. I have to continue and he's waving to me. I wave back as if it's normal; maybe to them it is. Now I really want to go home.

I head back to the house and as soon as I arrive Mum says, "Come on, we're going now."

Thank God for that!

On the way back, Dad seems to be lost. He shouts, "The fecking signposts have been turned by the tinkers. We're going round in circles!"

He slams the brakes on to stop the car, then yanks the handbrake on.

"Calm down," Mum tells him.

But that makes him worse and he starts shouting at her.

Eventually, he does calm down, but then he starts to drive off again and can't release the handbrake. He's pulled it on so hard that it's jammed.

Now he's even more angry, because we're stuck here, unable to move.

"Jesus, Mary, and Joseph," he shouts. "The fecking handbrake is stuck on now!"

After a few minutes of even more shouting, he presses the footbrake and manages to release it. Then he seems completely calm. As he drives off, he says to Mum, "That's a good trick – if ever you get your handbrake stuck on, just press the brake pedal and you can release it easily."

Mum looks away from him.

"What's the matter?" he asks.

"After all that, you want me to talk to you?" she says.

We finally find our way back to Uncle Terry's house and have dinner, but it's late and it's getting dark again. We all sit around the range and my cousins PJ and Peggy are telling ghost stories. Anita asks my aunty Maggie if we can dress up as ghosts. Aunty Maggie then leaves the room and comes back in with three sheets.

"Here, you can use these," she says.

Anita hands Peggy and me a sheet each and we go out into the dark driveway and run around with them over our heads.

"Let's go down the driveway to the road," Peggy calls out. "We can scare all the drivers as they go past."

"Will they really think we're ghosts?" Anita asks.

"In Ireland, everyone believes in ghosts," Peggy tells her.

The three of us run down the driveway to the entrance by the lane. Anita says to me, "Hide behind the hedge and I'll call out when a car comes, then the three of us put the sheets over our heads and stand in the road."

I don't think Mum and Dad know we're doing this, but it's fun.

After a few minutes of waiting and lots of giggling from Anita and Peggy, Anita calls out, "I can see two headlamps coming in our direction!"

We all jump out into the road and the car stops quite a distance away from us.

"They've seen us!" Peggy says.

The driver backs up quickly, turns around and races off back the other way. Anita and Peggy can't stop laughing. The same thing happens two or three times, but the last car doesn't stop. It keeps heading towards us and we all run up the driveway to the house. The car follows us. We all run into the house and the car backs down the drive and goes away.

We all look panic-stricken. Mum asks, "What have you been doing?"

Anita explains and we all get a good telling-off.

It's time for bed and Mum tells me tonight I have to sleep in PJ's room and share his bed. PJ tells me to get into the bed and I'm sleeping next to the window. It's a single bed so there's not much room. He gets into bed next to me, then blows the candle out. It's not quite so dark tonight, as there's a bit of moonlight. But after all the ghost stories and playing at being ghosts, I'm a little bit spooked, but I'm also very tired. I doze off for a while, but I can hear a funny noise and I start to half wake up. It sounds a bit like someone rubbing sand paper up against something. My eyes are barely half open and I'm lying on my side facing the window. There's something white moving up and down outside. I don't know if it's my imagination or not, but then it bangs against the glass. I jump up off the bed and almost out of my skin,

"Ah! PJ, quick!" I shout. "There's a ghost!"

PJ jumps out of the bed as well and shouts, "Where?" "Look at the window!" I shout.

PJ looks at the window and says, "Jesus, Mary, and Joseph, it's the cow licking the water off the glass. They always do that. Now go to sleep!"

He gets back into bed and plumps his pillow up, then starts snoring. I slide back into the bed, still shaking from the shock of it all. At around five am, I feel myself start to wake up again for a minute, not knowing where I am. I quickly realise that PJ has his bare bum pressed against my bare bum and I jump out of the bed with a jolt.

"Jesus, Mary, and Joseph, and all the saints, what the hell's wrong with you now?" PJ asks me.

In disbelief, I reply, "Your bum, PJ. It was stuck against mine!"

He stares at me for a second and mutters, then goes back to sleep. I get back into bed and stuff the sheet between us while PJ's snoring.

Next thing I know, it's morning and we're all having a cooked breakfast. Aunty Maggie's outside, holding the two goats by the horns, because they won't let Dad out of the field to come back into the house after going to the toilet.

The two goats are joined together with a piece of wood with holes in it for their necks to go through. This place seems mad to me. I ask Mum, "Why are the goats handcuffed?"

Everyone just laughs, but nobody tells me why.

Today PJ and I are going out to the potato field to tin the potatoes. Well, that's what PJ told me. Because of his Irish accent, he says "tin" instead of "thin". To "thin" the potatoes is to pull out the weaker, smaller, potato plants to give the larger, stronger, potato plants more room to grow. I don't know anything about farms. I'm very keen to go with him, because I would like to see how they get the potatoes into the tins. Off we both go to "tin" the potatoes. As soon as we arrive at the field, PJ hands me a bucket and says, "Watch what I do."

He starts pulling up small potatoes and throwing them into a bucket. After around ten or fifteen minutes, the bucket is almost full.

I ask him, "Where are the tins?"

PJ looks at me with a confused expression and says, "What tins?"

I reply, "The tins to put the potatoes in?"

PJ replies, "There are no tins."

"Well, how are we going to tin the potatoes then?" I ask.

PJ looks frustrated and says, "This is how we tin the potatoes. We don't put them in tins, Jesus, Mary, and Joseph."

I'm so disappointed, I just want to go. But after what seems like forever picking, or thinning, the potatoes, we make our way back to the house and all have lunch together. We have thickly cut bread, with a lot of butter on it. The butter is so thick that I can see teeth marks where my teeth have bitten through it. It makes my stomach turn when I see that.

When lunch is finished, we all get into the car. PJ, Peggy, Aunty Maggie, and Uncle Terry get into their car. We're going out for the afternoon to a field. I don't understand why, because there are loads of them all around the house. Uncle Terry owns them. We drive for about an hour or so and we arrive at the field. Everyone gets out of both cars and straight away PJ is kicking a football around. There are lines and lines of hay or straw ridges along this field.

Anita says to me, "Let's run and jump over all the ridges of straw."

She starts running and jumping, and I follow. I'm jumping each ridge and watching my feet as I go, paying no attention to the hedge in front of me, beyond the last ridge. I jump straight into the middle of it and it's full of prickles. Beneath it is a ditch full of water. The prickles are sticking into every part of me and I can feel the branches breaking, but I can't move.

I'm calling out, "Help!", to Anita.

"I'll be back in a minute," Anita calls back.

I'm scared – I think I'm going to die here, because I'm sinking and it's hurting. Within minutes, Dad arrives. He reaches down to grab my hand and says, "Stay still and hold my hand."

His hand is a long way up from me. I push my hand through the sharp prickly branches, tearing my skin on the way. I touch his fingertips, then my hand is squashed by his grip. Like lightning, I feel my entire body being dragged through the sharp thorns and the pain is intense. Pulled to my feet, I look at my arms and legs and they're bleeding all over.

Dad says, "You're lucky you didn't drown. That happens in water-logged ditches."

We head back over to the others and I realise Dad has just saved my life. If I had been here on my own, I would never have survived. As we arrive back near the car, PJ kicks his football high into the air and it lands on our car quite hard. Dad goes mad at him and tells him he's scratched it. We all get into the cars and head back to the house. Everyone seems to have had enough of this field.

Back at the house, I ask Mum, "Can I go and play in the quarry next door?"

"Okay, but don't be too long," she replies.

In the quarry, I get bored quite quickly and go for a

walk down the lane. My arms and legs are still stinging. Nobody knows where I am and I'm not realising how far I am from the house. All of a sudden, PJ's coming in the other direction on Auntie Maggie's bike. It's black, with steel mud guards and has a chrome headlamp on it. He rides up next to me and says, "Where are you going?"

"Nowhere," I reply.

"Do you want a lift to nowhere?" he asks.

He brings a smile to my face. "Okay, thanks," I reply.

"Get onto the rack and I'll take you home," he says.

I climb on and all I can think is, Wow! He's going so fast and it feels so solid and stable on this rack.

We're twisting and turning around all the bends down the lane.

I can feel the wind gushing on my face; this is great fun.

This is the best part of the holiday by far.

The holiday comes to an end. We drive off the ferry, back in Holyhead, and I'm glad to be back in my own country, where everything seems more normal. I've missed the green signposts and the roads that I'm used to seeing. But the best thing of all is we have toilets here.

We've finally arrived home. I'm counting up the Irish money I have left. The two-shilling bit I have has a dolphin on it and the one-shilling bit has a bull on it. The coppers have a hare that looks like a rabbit on them. I'll keep these coins, but I'm glad to be back in England.

My seventh birthday comes and goes. In my card from Granny and Grandad, there's a ten-shilling note. I'm so excited to have this much money. Mum lets me spend some of it in the shop on sweets. I have quite a lot of change from it, and the next day I decide to take it to school with me. I feel so rich now that I'm at school with all this money. I want to share how I feel with my friends. I give some money to my friends and it's great to see them so pleased to have money as well. They walk around, showing one another how much they have and I feel happy seeing them happy.

During dinner the same evening, I tell Mum, "Mum, I made everyone happy today at school."

"Oh, that's nice. How did you do that?" she asks.

"I shared out my money with all my friends," I reply.

She looks furious. "Did you hear what he did, Maurice?" she says to Dad.

"Well, that's the last time he'll be allowed to have money then," he says, as he glares at me.

Mum adds "That was a really stupid thing to do!"

I only wanted to make everyone happy.

The following week at school, I'm looking at the wooden numbers. I like them. I wonder if anyone would notice if I slip the number two into my pocket and take it home. I'll give it a try.

Nobody's noticed. I'm looking forward to the end of the day, in case anyone finds out though. The day comes to an end and I've got away with it.

Later that evening, I show Mum and tell her how I got the number two.

Mum tells me off again, "That's stealing. You'll have to take it back to school tomorrow!" she says.

I feel really stupid. I keep doing things wrong.

The next day, I sneak the number two back and nobody notices. Phew!

3

A new home and school

It's summer of 1968 and I'm seven years old. Today we're moving to our new house in Watford: 45 Sandringham Road.

It's so exciting. We're following the removal van all the way to our new house. When we arrive at the house, Dad opens the front door, and the first thing that I do is find the bathroom because I'm desperate for the toilet. But the toilet's blocked.

I call Mum: "Mum, the toilets blocked."

Mum comes in and unblocks it. She says, "This house is filthy!"

Dad dashes in from the back garden and says, "The shed's gone!"

"Oh no," Mum replies.

"I'm calling the estate agent," he says.

He storms around the corner to a phone box and calls the estate agent, then comes back very angry.

Mum asks, "What did they say?"

"He said she said you didn't want the shed," he replies.

Anita and I go around repeating it and laughing. We think Dad sounds funny saying that in his Irish accent. After a while, he goes around the corner to the chip shop to get chips for all of us. When he gets back, he finds he can't get in the front door, because the lock is stuck.

We can't open it from the inside either, so he breaks the glass on the door to reach in to see if he can free the lock, but Sooty bites his hand.

Anita and I laugh, but then we see he's bleeding and he's angry again. I don't know why we left our lovely house in Hemel to come to this old house, because there's so much wrong with it and it's very dirty. From this day on, all Dad ever seems to do is go to work, then come home, sand things down, paint, and wallpaper.

After a couple of days of settling into this house, Mum takes Anita and me to see our new school. It's St Catherine's School in Garston, just off Horseshoe Lane.

There's a long, bendy driveway off Horseshoe Lane that leads up to the school. It's a damp, drizzly morning and Mum is not sure where she's going. We walk across a field and end up in the wrong school, called Francis Comb. The children seem really stupid here: a bit like the boys who lived in Hemel near my old house. The teachers are not very nice to her and so we leave. Eventually we arrive at St Catherine's.

The new school seems nice. It's newer than my old school, and it has woodland on one side and a massive field on the other. There's a big playground and wooden classrooms by the field. It looks really nice, but I'm a bit nervous about starting here, because I'll have to make new friends again. Mum goes inside to talk to the teacher, while we wait outside. Around 20 minutes later, she's back out with a smile. She tells us, "You'll both be going here from now on."

We catch the 347 double-decker bus to go home. On the ride home, I stare through the window, thinking that this is like starting a completely new life.

It's evening and we're all sitting down having dinner. Mum's telling Dad about the new school. He's cutting into his lamb chops and enjoying his dinner, when the end of the table collapses and his dinner ends up all over his lap.

"Stupid fecking table!" he shouts as he picks up bits of his dinner, putting it back on his plate.

Anita and I laugh, but he glares at me as though I set it up to do that.

It's one of those tables from the 1950s that has an extension flap on either end, but the spring that holds it in place just gives way when you push down on it.

A few days pass and it's my first day at my new school. I wake up to Mum calling out, "Come on, time to get up, John and Anita, come on!"

I'm not looking forward to this. I slowly make my way down the stairs to the kitchen where Mum's making tea and toast for all of us.

We all have breakfast and catch the 347 to school. It stops at Horseshoe Lane and we all walk the rest of the way to the school. There are two subways by the bus stop and I would really like to walk under them. They look fun.

When we get into school, Mum says goodbye and the teacher leads me to my new class. I know my name's John Monaghan now, so hopefully I won't look stupid here today.

I sit at my desk and there's an inkwell in it and a groove to stop the pens rolling off when you lift the lid of the desk.

This is really good, because I can put all of my things in it. The teacher calls out, "Quiet, everybody. We have a new boy starting today and his name's John. Can you all say 'Hello' to him, please?"

Oh my God! Everyone's looking at me and saying "Hello", while I have my desk lid up and I'm staring into it. I quickly close it, but I don't know where to look.

After a short while, it's playtime and we all go outside to the playground. All the boys gather around me, asking me things like, "Who do you support?" … "How fast can you run?"

They all seem to worship this boy called Owen Ryan, who they say is the fastest runner in the class. He has a couple of races with two other boys and I think he wants to impress me. On both races, they have to run around the whole school, then back to an oak tree. At the end of those races one boy shouts out, "Here comes Owen!" And, of course, he's first. Owen then comes over to me and asks, "Do you want a race?"

I don't really see the point, but I feel like I have to.

"Okay, then," I reply.

Somebody shouts out, "Ready, steady, go!"

We both start running and I can tell from the start that I'm not going to win, because he loves doing this. I'm not that interested in running. It's the end of the race and Owen's won it, but not by that much. To the other boys, he's still their hero and now I'm just the average new boy. Maybe I should have tried harder.

They're not so interested in me now, but I don't mind it like that.

A week or so passes and everyone gets used to my being around at this school, but they all have their own groups of friends and I feel like I'm just trailing around Owen Ryan's group, not being noticed. I'm fed up following them around; I want to go back to my old school in Hemel with my friends.

Today I'm going to walk around on my own at playtime. It's a sunny day. The tarmac's warm from the sun and I can hear the drone of planes flying over in the sky. I'm walking around the playgrounds and the outside of the school building.

I've never felt as alone as I do today. All the others are playing different games in different groups. I'm the only solitary boy. I feel like I'm a ghost; I don't exist in their worlds. There's a group of boys playing marbles near the wooden classrooms. That looks much more fun than Owen and his stupid group who just run every day. I'm watching to see what they do. They have small marbles and bigger marbles. The first boy rolls one marble and the other has to roll a marble to hit the first boy's marble. If he hits it, he wins it. If it's a big marble, he has to hit it twice to win it.

I want to play this game, but I don't have any marbles. I ask one of the boys, "Where can I get some marbles?"

"You have to buy them," he replies.

I ask the other boy, "Can I play?"

"Got any migs?" he replies.

I guess migs are marbles. "No," I reply.

"Can't play if you ain't got none then, can ya?" he replies.

I continue walking alone around the playground, watching everyone else and wishing for the whistle to blow, so I can go back into class.

4

Meet the school bully

This same evening, Dad's decorating. He's shouting and swearing, because it's going wrong. He's wallpapering and has just got down off his step-ladder and put his foot into the bucket of paste.

"Jesus, Mary, and Joseph, who put the paste there?" he shouts.

I think it's best I don't ask Mum for marbles tonight.

The next day at school seems like a repeat of yesterday, but today is worse, as I've been noticed by the school bully, Francis Burn.

The teacher has sent us all out for playtime, and again I'm walking on my own, when he jumps on me and pushes me to the ground. He's sitting on me and he has his hands around my throat. I'm unable to breathe. He slaps me around the face and says, "I'm gonna get you every single day!"

He gets up, then kicks me and walks off, looking back at me like he's evil. He's much bigger than me and he's older. Now I don't know what to do, because I would never be able to fight him.

The same thing happens for the next three days. I have to tell the teacher. The teacher seems annoyed about it and writes about bullies being cowards on the blackboard, but it carries on every day right through to the next week.

It's Monday morning and I'm back at school. It's about ten minutes before playtime. We're all having our morning milk and I know what's going to happen as soon as the teacher sends us out to the playground. At the door on the way out, I ask a couple of boys, "Who's the toughest boy in the school?"

"Terry Murphy," one boy tells me.

I have a plan. If I can get Terry Murphy to be my friend, Francis Burn won't beat me up any more.

We're all sent out and the first thing I do is find Terry Murphy. I can't see Francis Burn anywhere. Maybe he isn't here today. I ask a few of the others where Terry Murphy is and they point him out to me. He looks miserable. He's not playing, just leaning against a wall. I walk cagily over to him and ask, "Are you Terry Murphy?"

"Yeah, what do you want?" he replies.

"Francis Burn keeps hitting me," I say.

He doesn't even look at me and just replies, "I'll sort him out."

He doesn't seem very friendly, so I thank him and leave him alone. Within one minute, I've been grabbed around the neck and thrown to the ground.

I can feel the weight of someone on top of me and I'm being punched and slapped. It hurts a lot and I can barely breathe.

"I told you I'd get you!" the boy's shouting in my ear.

Suddenly, his weight feels like it's being lifted off me and he's screaming. I look up and see Terry Murphy; he's pulled Francis Burn off me and he's punching and kicking him.

Francis Burn walks off sobbing in pain, but Terry Murphy just calmly strolls away. I don't think he realises what he's done for me. He did it like it was nothing and doesn't expect any thanks.

I get up, still bent over from the pain of being hit, and run over to Terry Murphy.

"Thanks, Terry," I say.

He glances at me and carries on walking. Looking straight ahead, he says, "It's okay, just tell me if he gives you any more trouble."

Everything starts to get better from this day on. At the weekend, Mum buys me some marbles and the following week I start playing with the other boys at school. I'm starting to be happy again.

It's half-term school break. I couldn't sleep last night, so I've got up early. Everyone else is still in bed, except Dad. He's in the kitchen, shaving at the sink. I'm sitting at the table, watching what he does. He has a round mirror on the windowsill in front of him and lots of foam all over his face. He makes funny faces as he pulls the razor across his face, making tracks that looks like clear roads in the snow. He makes a lot of splashing noises when he dips it into the sink to rinse it off. He asks me, "Is that boy still giving you trouble?"

"It's all okay now," I reply.

He drains the water from the sink and puts a towel against his face, dabbing away the foam that's left. He looks at me and says, "You know when I was at school, there was a boy that kept hitting me and do you know what I did?"

"No, what did you do?" I ask with great interest.

"I picked up a great big brick and threw it straight at him."

I stare at him with my mouth open.

"You could have killed him!" I reply.

He looks proud of himself and says, "Well, he never did it again."

I know I couldn't have done that. I wouldn't want to kill someone, even if they were hitting me every day. He must be very different to me.

Dad finishes up and says, "We're going to the funfair today in Harpenden," with a smile.

I'm so excited; I can't wait. The next thing I know, Mum and Anita are up and we're all having tea and toast before we go. On the way there, we stop for petrol and we get a free Esso man each. It's a keyring and it's the oil drip man.

When we arrive at the funfair, Mum and Dad find somewhere to sit on the field and give us five shillings to go on the rides.

Anita's in charge of the money, so she gets to choose what rides we go on. She only chooses the rides she likes and then all the money is gone. We're not allowed any more, but Dad lets us have a go on the bumper cars before we leave and we get a toffee apple. Well, Anita has candyfloss. We've had such a fun day and I wish it were like this every day.

It's 9 November 1968, my eighth birthday. I've just woken up and it's freezing cold in my bedroom. I look over at James to see if he's awake, but he's still asleep.

Sitting on the edge of my bed, it's so cold that I can see my own breath. It looks like I'm breathing smoke. Looking over at the window, I see the curtains are open.

Mum must have been in our room already. I can't believe what the windows look like – they have patterns all over the glass from the ice. It looks like leaves or something, like someone has drawn a picture. I get up and get dressed quickly. I run downstairs to the kitchen and Mum's there making tea and toast.

"Happy Birthday! You're eight years old today!" Mum says cheerfully. "Do you want to see your present?" she asks. "It's in the living-room, go and have a look."

I run into the living room and I'm so happy. It's a real Hornby electric train set.

It has a box made of wood, with lots of different compartments for all the carriages and two steam engines. There's a passenger carriage, coal carriers, and a tanker.

I think it's second-hand, because the box looks like it's homemade. It's not very clean, but that doesn't matter.

I start setting up the track and plug it in. It works.

Anita comes in, just as I finish, and says, "The big locomotive steam engine's mine and the small stumpy one is yours, you know!"

I don't understand why she says that, but I accept it anyway and play with the small stumpy engine. I only need one engine anyway. It comes with oil for the track; there's a signal stand and even change-over tracks.

The transformer is a big metal box, with a round knob on it that has a pointer, so you can change the speed of the train, and if you turn it the other way, it can go backwards. The smell of the oil on the track makes it like a real machine and not a toy. It's not a baby toy; it's real. I'm so lucky. I don't ever want to put this away. This is the happiest day of my life.

Some weeks later, Sooty seems to be getting more and more ill each day and he's losing his hair. Mum called the vet out today and he said that Sooty has developed a mange. He said that he's suffering and would only get well again if he were taken care of day and night seven days a week and it's too much for anyone to do.

He's told Mum it's best just to put him down. Mum has agreed, so the vet gives him an injection right away, puts him in a big black bag, then takes him away. I'm sad about it, but at least he won't suffer any more.

I really like it at school now. We play marbles every day and British bulldog. There's a new boy who's just started. His name's Kevin Lee. He's had to go through the same things as me, starting in a new school, so I've helped him with that and now he's my best friend.

This is my last year in the Infants. Next year I'll be a Junior. I wonder how that feels – I bet it feels really grown up. When you're a Junior you can wear long trousers, like an adult. For now, I'm happy being an Infant, because the work is easy.

It's Christmas morning and I've just woken up. The sun's shining and I'm rubbing my eyes. At the end of my bed, I can see Christmas wrapping paper. I jump up out of my bed with excitement. Father Christmas has been and I didn't hear a thing! There are three presents just for me. Straight away, I shout out, "Mum, Father Christmas has been and left presents for me!"

Mum replies, "Oh, has he?", and she starts to get up.

I dive into unwrapping my presents and I have a game called Dizzy Bug, a spinning top game, and a tin aeroplane.

I don't know which to play with first, because they're all brilliant. Dizzy Bug has two round tin bugs with friction motors that spin around and fall into holes in a plastic arena. The spinning top game is a plastic arena with four spinning tops that you put string around and pull to spin them. There's one in each corner of the arena and they bash each other out of the arena to win. Their names are Desperate Dan, Hurricane Hank, and two others. This game's brilliant, but the plane is a (747) jumbo jet – it's made of tin and it is battery operated.

You put two HP2 batteries in it and it moves around.

When you switch it on, it goes forward until it hits a wall, then it turns itself around until it hits another wall and it has flashing lights on it. This Christmas is the best ever. I run down to the kitchen to show Mum and set it up on the kitchen floor.

Dad's washing the turkey in the sink. He says he's giving it a bath and Mum nearly stands on my plane, so I take it into the living room still in my pyjamas.

It's now the summer of 1969 and everyone's talking about Apollo 11: it's going to the moon. This is the first time a man will land on the moon and it's on the news all the time. We watch it take off on TV and the power of the rocket is unbelievable. Nothing can go wrong, because these people are astronauts and they know what they're doing. Watching it on our black-and-white TV, with the picture going snowy and twisting, doesn't make it look very real, though. I would love to watch it for real, but it's in America. Everything's good in America.

It's the school summer holidays and over the past few weeks I've been learning how to ride a proper bike by rolling down the garden on an old wreck that Dad found. It has no brakes and a broken chain, but at least I can learn how to balance on it.

A week or so later, and Dad's bought new bikes for Anita and me. Anita doesn't use hers, but I'm never off mine. It's everything to me. It's red, with blue mudguards and 20-inch wheels. Dad's even put a dynamo on it for me. He says I should have the headlamp on the front forks, because it looks good when it lights up the spokes. I want it up in the middle of the handlebars, so it looks like a motorbike. During this long and hot school summer holiday, I ride my bike all over the place. Down Clarendon Road, it's all industrial and there are massive puddles like lakes to ride through. I like to see how slow I can go through them without putting my feet down, but they're so deep I get my feet wet anyway.

Because of the astronauts going to the moon and coming back safely, everything seems to be about space and I'm very interested in it as well.

Thunderbirds is my favourite TV programme, because Thunderbird One is a rocket, but I like Thunderbird Two as well. Funny how Thunderbird Three is a rocket, too, except it's white and not grey like the others. There's also *Doctor Who* and *The Daleks*. *The Daleks* are not scary, but I'm having nightmares about the Cybermen. I don't like them at all.

Near the end of the summer holidays, I'm getting a bit bored. There isn't much to do and Mum's just lying in the garden. It's hot and there's nothing to drink but water. I ask her, "Is there anything to eat?"

"Yes, bread and jam," she replies.

All we ever have to eat is bread and jam. I'm fed up with bread and jam, bread and jam, bread and jam. I go and sit in the garden near Mum and say, "I'm bored!"

"Why don't you ride your bike?" Mum replies.

"That's all I ever do!" I say.

I hear a plane go over and stare at it to see if I can see what colour it is, but I can't because of the sun.

Well, soon enough school term comes around and I'm back at school. I have long trousers now and a satchel. I'm catching the 347 into school on my own now and I'm in the Juniors.

I feel really grown-up, but we still play the same things during break. About a week or so into the new term, Kevin, my new best friend, hasn't come into school. It's breaktime and this reminds me of when I first started here, because I'm all on my own again. Kevin and I just hang around together when he's here and we don't bother much with the other kids.

I'm walking around the back of the school, when I'm grabbed around the neck and dragged backwards into the boys' changing rooms. I look around and it's Francis Burn and another boy. Francis Burn has his elbow across my neck saying, "This time I'm really going to kill you!"

His friend is just standing there, watching. Terry Murphy's not at this school any more, because he's gone to senior school, so I'm alone and back in the same situation that I was in when I started. I don't know what to do.

Francis Burn wrenches my tie off and makes a noose out of it, then says, "We're going to hang you now."

With his friend holding my arms behind my back, he ties one end of my tie to a coat hanger, then tells me, "Stand on the bench and put your neck through the hole."

The other boy says nothing as I plead for him not to kill me. Francis Burn is evil and I really do believe I'm going to die today. I'm only eight years old. Why do they want to do this to me? The other boy looks at me, as if he has some pity for me, but then he says, "Just do it!"

Frances Burn just keeps punching me and shouting, "Do it!"

I'm shaking in fear. The tears running down my face fall to the floor by my feet. I'm going to die now and I don't even know what I've done. Francis Burn grabs my hair and pulls my head through the hole in the tie as the other boy lifts me up onto the bench. Then he pulls the tie tight around my neck. I can't breathe; it's getting more and more tight and I can see nothing but blurred light through my tears. The sound of the bench grating on the floor echoes, as it moves under my feet. Then I hear laughter and the door bangs shut.

They've both run out of the changing rooms.

I manage to release my tie from around my neck. My throat's hurting. I'm coughing and gasping for air. I've survived, but my life's not worth living if this is how it's going to be for me. I walk to the sink and wash my face, drink some water, and try to compose myself. Then I walk out of the changing rooms and down the tarmac path, hoping nobody notices I've been crying. As I turn the corner, I notice Frances Burn watching me. He walks towards me and says, "That's not the end of it!"

I can see in his eyes he's not finished with me yet. He grabs me around the neck and tries to wrestle me down to the ground, but he's on his own. His friend is not with him to help him. I can tell he's struggling to get me to the ground. Maybe he isn't as strong as I thought he was. I remember how Terry Murphy beat him up, so I'm going to fight back, because I can't live like this. I throw a punch to his side and I can tell it's hurt him. But he's getting angry; he's punching me back and it hurts a lot.

I don't care how much it hurts any more. I hit him in the stomach and he doubles over. I hit him again and again and again. I'm not going to stop. He's losing. I can't believe it. I'm stronger than him. He's crying like a baby.

At that moment, Anita walks around the corner with her friends and says to him, "Leave my brother alone!" She's too late. I've already won.

As the weeks pass, Francis Burn stays well away from me and I have peace back in my life, but it's a different kind of peace. Nobody's protecting me any more, so I have to protect myself. Word has got round the school about what happened between Frances Burn and me, so now there are kids who come to me if anyone's bullying them. This school seems to be all about fighting, but I'm not that kind of boy. I don't like hurting people.

But I'm strong. I can hold my head up high, and between my best friend, Kevin, and me, we're the toughest boys in the school and nobody will question that. Kevin and I have the occasional fallout and we fight, but when we do, the whole school comes to watch.

My ninth birthday's here and for my present I got a James Bond car – an Aston Martin. It has a shield on the back and an ejector seat a man sits on, so the roof opens and you can fire him through it. I've also got a black Mercedes; it's a dinky toy, with windscreen wipers that work while you push it along. They're great, but Dad has also got me some ball bearings that can be used when we play marbles. Ball bearings are a much better prize than marbles – everyone wants to win one.

Christmas passes and Mum has said she'll get me a guinea pig. I don't know why, because I've never asked for one. She gets me one anyway and I love him. His name's Guinea and Dad's made a hutch for him out of plywood. It has an arched window at the front with wire mesh across it and a door at the side.

It's April, 1970 and we've watched the launch of Apollo 13. It was much the same as Apollo 11, but still exciting. After a few days, it's on the news that Apollo 13 is in trouble and won't be able to land on the moon.

I'm at school one day shortly after that and we're all expecting the return of Apollo 13 to earth. During class, one of the teachers comes into my class and tells us that we must all go to the assembly hall, because they want to watch the astronauts return safely. We all file in and sit cross-legged on the floor, while the teachers put chairs out for themselves at the back of the hall.

Sister Martini, the head teacher, opens the doors on the wooden case of our school television. "Everyone must stay quiet!" she shouts.

The hall is silent as we all stare at the school television, while it switches from reporter to reporter. The next thing we see is the Apollo 13 capsule. It has dropped into the ocean. We hear the communication live: "Odyssey, this is Houston. Do you read? Odyssey, this is Houston. Do you read?"

There's silence in the hall and the reporter says in a solemn voice how concerned everyone is for the astronauts. This seems to go on for a long time and I look over to my teacher. She's a nice lady. There are tears running down her cheeks and she has her hands resting on her neck as she stares at the screen. You could hear a pin drop in this hall, it's so quiet. At this moment, Kevin blows off, but nobody says anything, except a girl, whispering, "Oh, Kevin!"

Still, it carries on.

"Odyssey. Do you read?" He's saying it almost as though he expects no response.

Everyone's still silent.

"Odyssey, this is Houston. Do you read?"

Suddenly, there's a response: "Houston, this is Odyssey. We read you!"

I look around and the teachers are hugging one another, crying, chatting and cheering – it's a relief the astronauts are back safe. There's so much emotion in the hall. Everyone talks about it for the rest of the day.

5

Taking care of James

It's 16 May 1970, James's fifth birthday. My little brother is getting to be more like a little boy now than a baby. It's more fun to have him around, as we play better together now. We play all kinds of games, mostly created by my imagination. One of them being to turn Dad's creeper board into a car, by putting pieces of wood onto it and me wheeling James around the driveway, crashing into things. A really good game that we play is to stand on the grass and throw six darts in the air, then try to jump out of the way before they land on our heads. Well, today it's all about James, because he's five and everyone's making a fuss over him. He has a nice birthday cake and he looks funny with his chubby cheeks when he's blowing out the candles. He has some toy cars and he's got more for his birthday, but he has a long way to go to catch up with my car collection.

Some weeks later, we're playing the best game, throwing darts in the air, but James doesn't move out of the way of all the darts. He falls over and a dart gets stuck in his hand. He screams. I quickly have a look and it's gone in deep. I pull the dart out of his hand and he goes to run in the house, crying. It's important that he doesn't go in and tell Mum what happened, so I have to calm him down in the garden before he goes in. But he seems okay. We go and play a different game. This game involves putting James's teddy bear on the top rung of the ladder up against the house and telling him to go and find it.

We have loads of toys, and now that Dad's working on a demolition site, pushing down old houses with his bulldozer, he finds even more.

He's brought home a tin steam engine for James and me to play with and a few other toys.

The weeks roll on and we are on the way down to Granny and Grandad's. Dad stops at a garage and says we're going to buy a new car. Anita and I are running around the forecourt, looking at all the new cars with prices in their windows, and I notice a red Vauxhall Viva. I want Dad to buy that one, because it has a gold stripe down the side, strange door handles, and it has four doors. Dad doesn't pay any attention to me and he buys a Morris 1100. It's a stupid little car, but at least it has four doors. For the first time ever, we have a door each. From the day he gets this new car, he hates it and goes back to the garage, complaining about it.

He says that the clutch is slipping, but the garage doesn't agree with him. He doesn't keep it very long and trades it in for another new car in Watford where we live. He buys a dark green Ford Cortina. We're back to having just two doors again. The registration is PXC 948E and it's three years old.

It's the school summer holidays and we've gone to Southend-on-Sea. We've walked along the seafront, and Mum has taken

Anita and James to the toilet. Dad and I have walked up to a seafood stall and he's talking to the man.

He asks me, "Do you want a jellied eel?"

Well, I love jelly, especially the jelly Mum makes in her oval glass bowl. She always puts a spoon in the bowl when she pours the hot water in – she says it's to stop the glass from cracking. I even like eating the Rowntree jelly cubes from the packet. The man hands Dad a jellied eel for each of us. I don't know what an eel is, but I know I will love the jelly. Dad eats his straight away and looks as though he enjoys it, then hands mine to me. He puts it straight into my hand, but the jelly has no colour and there's something horrible in the middle of it. It looks like an animal. I'm staring at it in my hand and the jelly's melting and dripping through my fingers.

I'm horrified. "Urgh, I don't want this!" I tell him.

He replies, "Just eat it, John, it's nice."

I take his word for it and taste the jelly, but it's so salty. I can't eat it. I spit it out, as it tastes disgusting, and I'm almost sick. He tells me to throw it in the bin, which I do as quickly as I can. Why would anyone eat that and why would he do that to me? I notice Mum walking towards us with Anita and James. Dad tells Mum all about it and laughs.

As we walk along the seafront, I can hear the seagulls while I'm looking in the shop windows where they sell plastic buckets and spades. Mum goes in to buy one for Anita, because she's asking for one. As we go down towards the beach, Mum tries to pick James up, so he can walk along a wall. She pulls him up by his arm and dislocates it from his shoulder. He's crying so much and I think he's just being a baby, not knowing what's wrong. Mum's worried about his crying, so we all have to go to an emergency doctor. The doctor just grabs his arm and twists it back where it should be and James stops crying straight away. Wow, I think that doctor's brilliant – he made him better just like that.

James seems to go through much more dramatic things than I do, as he has already had a hernia before from Anita and me bouncing him down the stairs. Every night in bed, James starts asking me silly questions.

Just as I'm dozing off, he asks, "Who would win a fight out of a dinosaur and a crocodile?"

I reply, "A dinosaur," impatiently.

Then he asks, "Who would win a fight out of a dinosaur and a dragon?"

I reply, "Dragons aren't real."

"But if they were real, who would win?" he asks.

"James, go to sleep!" I reply.

He asks a few more silly questions before he goes to sleep. As if that's not bad enough, there's another problem. He's still wetting the bed. The doctor's given Mum a sheet that goes under his bed sheet. It's attached to a metal box that has a loud buzzer and a big red light on it that lights up the whole room. I haven't been asleep for more than ten minutes when I'm woken up by a loud buzzing sound. I jump up. "James, you're wetting the bed!" I shout. "Stop wetting the bed!"

James jumps up and says, "What?"

"It's too late now – you've already done it," I say in despair.

A few minutes later, the light is on and Mum's changing his sheets muttering, "That stupid machine. What is the point of it?"

It's Anita's twelfth birthday today and she's got the best present ever. She's got a puppy. It's black and it's a girl dog. She has floppy ears and looks like a Labrador, but she is a mixed breed. Dad opens the top of the cardboard box and there she is. She's so small, nervous, and she's shaking. He takes her out of the box and hands her to Anita. Anita loves her straight away. We all do. She names her Sooty, the same name as our last dog.

The following morning, I'm having a bad day already. I had no clean pyjamas last night and I have no clean clothes today either, because Mum didn't get the washing done in time. I normally come down in my pyjamas, but I have nothing at all. I have to go down and have my breakfast naked. I'm not bothered about it, though, so long as it's just my family around me.

The doorbell rings. Mum goes to answer it and I can hear Maureen Gillett and her daughter, Jane. I hate the way Jane always stares at me. If she comes into the kitchen, it would be my worst nightmare. I start calling to Mum, "Don't let them in!"

But no, Mum's so busy talking to Maureen that she lets her straight in. Jane walks down the hallway and the kitchen door opens, I have nowhere to hide. Oh God! She walks straight in, staring at me and won't look away for me to escape. This is trauma. I wish I could disappear. I'm so annoyed with Mum for doing that.

Later in the day, it gets very hot. The sun's beaming down and Mum's lying in the garden, sunbathing. Anita and James are indoors. It's peaceful; the birds are singing, and there's hardly a cloud in the sky. We have some diluted orange juice but the wasps keep coming towards my cup, trying to land on it. I sit down next to Mum and I can hear a plane go over, making a steady droning sound. That sound always makes me feel relaxed. It's a sound of summer for me now.

The wasps will not stay away from my drink and they're annoying. I decide to go inside and find the fly spray that Mum keeps under the kitchen sink. As Mum sleeps on the lawn, I wander around the garden, hunting them down and spraying them. It works. It kills them! I want to kill every wasp I find in the garden. I'm sneaking from bush to bush, killing all of the them, when Mum looks up and says, "What's that hissing sound?"

"I'm just killing the wasps!" I reply.

Mum looks at me angrily and shouts, "Put that back John, it's expensive and you are wasting it!"

I reluctantly walk back in and put the fly spray back.

It's the end of the summer holidays and we are back at school. This year is much different, though, because I'm in the Juniors and I have to take James with me to school, because he's in the first-year Infants.

All the first-year Infants look so small.

On the way to the bus stop, there's a sweet shop right on the corner of St Albans Road and Balmoral Road. I take James into the shop with me and buy us some Black Jacks and Fruit Salad chews. You get eight for a penny. We carry on to the bus stop to wait for the bus. I normally either have three pence or six pence to spend on sweets. My dream would be to have eight pence, so I could buy a Bounty Bar, but Mum would never give me that much. It's not long before the bus arrives, and for the first time I'm taking my little brother with me to school. He seems too young to go to school, especially as he's carrying his great big panda bear with him. It's almost as big as he is.

My teacher's name is Mr Booth and I'm in one of the wooden classrooms by the field. We arrive at school and I check to see if Mr Booth has arrived, but he's not in the classroom. Before I take James to his class, I tell him to put his big panda bear on Mr Booth's chair, behind the desk, so it looks like his panda is our teacher. James puts his panda on the chair and I take him to his class. Everyone in my class is sitting at their desks and looking at our new teacher, James's panda. A few minutes later, Mr Booth walks in and stares at the panda in his chair.

"I see, and whose panda is this?" he asks.

"It's my brother's, Mr Booth!" I say.

"Okay, well go and ask your brother to come and collect him please," he replies, smiling.

Poor James, he walks into the classroom and picks up his panda from the chair in front of the whole class – he looks so small. He walks towards the door, carrying the huge panda as quickly as he can, and says nothing. Mr Booth watches him with a half-smile on his face. He's a good teacher and he sees the funny side. All the girls are saying, "Aah, he's so cute."

Mr Booth says, "John, I think you had better go with him to make sure he finds his classroom."

I rush out to take him back to his class, then I run back to mine. It's funny being in a wooden classroom. It's like we're all in a massive shed and the floor is bouncy, but it's nice.

The next morning, I'm taking James to school with me again, but when we get to the corner shop, I realise that I haven't got any money at all. I have a really good idea, though. If black jacks and fruit salads are eight for one penny, then that means they're four for ha'penny, so two black jacks can't cost anything, as there's nothing less than half a penny. I decide to go into the shop and ask for two black jacks. The man says, "They're eight for a penny."

"But I only want two," I tell him.

He puts two on the counter and says, "That'll be a ha'penny then."

"But it's four for half a penny, so two must be free," I reply.

He looks very angry and shouts, "No, it's not, so stop wasting my time and get out. Go on, get out!"

I run out of the shop. I feel really stupid, but it was worth a try. James and I head off to the bus stop with no money and no sweets, just our bus passes. James asks, "Did you get any sweets?"

"No," I reply.

His bottom lip starts to quiver.

"Never mind, we'll get some tomorrow," I tell him cheerfully.

Some weeks pass and Dad's bought another Anglia Van for his work, but he's keeping his car. He has to do a lot of work on this van and he seems angry all the time. He wants me to help him work on it. I don't like working with him, because he gets mad at me, then shouts and swears, because it always seems to go wrong.

It's the weekend. He's at home today and I have to help him work on it. He's doing the brakes and I have to pump the brake pedal while he bleeds them. It's not going right, of course, and he's shouting at me, saying, "You're not pumping them right – you're useless!"

I'm doing what he said to do. This goes on for the whole day and I hate it.

The evening draws in and he's decided to paint the van with red lead paint. He's reversed it into the garage in case it rains and he's told me I have to hold the gallon tin of paint up for him, so he can dip his brush into it. I also have to hold his metal lamp to shine it where he's painting.

"Hold that fecking lead lamp straight. You're shining it in my eyes!" he shouts.

He notices a run in the paint and slaps me hard around my head.

"Go into the house. You're useless!" he growls. He always calls me "useless" when I work with him. I walk towards the house with my eyes to the ground and my head throbbing.

As soon as I walk into the living room, I hear his angry voice again: "John, come back out here!"

I turn to walk back out and Mum looks at me but says nothing.

"This time tell me if you see any runs!" he says.

I have my coat on with the hood up to keep warm, so I can't see very well from side to side, because my hood doesn't turn with my head. It's nearly ten pm and I'm very tired.

"You're letting the paint tin drop down too low, hold it up!" he shouts.

My arms are so tired from holding it up that I just can't.

"*Why didn't you see that run?*" he screams and hits me around the head again.

I can't move or even look at him, so I stand there like a punchbag. I feel useless and I just want to go indoors.

I think that one day he might actually kill me. I know it would be accidental. He wouldn't mean for it to happen, but he gets so mad at me and I don't understand why. For most of my life so far, he seems to dislike me and doesn't treat Anita or James this way.

A few more weeks pass and it's my tenth birthday. Dad is at work and Mum walks into my room, smiling and says, "Happy birthday! You're in double figures today. You're ten."

I smile back at her. At least I know she loves me, although she's starting to see me as the stupid child as well, lately. For my birthday, she's bought me a toy slide projector. It takes two HP2 batteries. Tonight, I've taken it to bed and I'm using the only two slides that came with it: Tom and Jerry cartoon comic strips. I'm shining it onto the ceiling and it looks like a cinema screen up there. Ten minutes later, the batteries have gone flat. I know Mum won't buy more, so that's the end of that.

Christmas comes and goes, and it is now January, 1971. It's a school day and I've just woken up. I've never in my life known it to be this cold. My chest feel tight from the cold air and my breath looks like I'm blowing smoke. I can't see through my bedroom window, because it's all patterns of ice and it's frozen on the glass on the inside of the window. I wake James up and encourage him to come downstairs quickly, because Mum's calling us:

"John and James, time to get up!"

We run to the kitchen and Mum has the electric bar fire on in there. We all have to get dressed next to it, as it's the only heat we have in the house, apart from the coal fire, but that's never lit in the morning. We get ready and I take James with me down the road into the corner shop, then on to the bus stop. The snow is still very deep from when it snowed a couple of days ago, but now it's frozen solid. James and I are standing at the bus stop. My fingers and toes are hurting from the cold. I'm very worried about James. His face is red and it looks like he's going to cry. The bus is late because of the bad weather. James has started crying and I feel so sorry for him. I take him into a shop doorway and start to breathe on his hands and rub them to warm them up. Another fifteen minutes later and the bus still hasn't come. I decide that's enough and I tell James, "Come on, I'm taking you home."

I take him by the hand while he's still crying and walk him back home. When we arrive home, Mum seems very angry with me and says, "What are you doing back here?"

"James was too cold. The bus didn't come, so I had to take him home," I reply.

"Oh, John, that's just stupid. Can't I trust you to do anything? I have to go to work," she replies.

I thought I was doing the right thing, because James couldn't stay out any longer in the cold. I don't like to see him suffering.

I'm in the second year of Juniors now and Anita has left and gone to the senior school, St Michael's, just across the field from my school, St Catherine's. It's spring and it's getting much warmer. James and I have been sent to bed for the night, and James has gone through his usual list of questions. But then he says, "John, some boys keep ganging up and picking on me at school."

As soon as he tells me, it brings back bad memories and I start feeling upset. The thought of someone doing that to him is unbearable. I tell him, "Don't worry, I'll deal with it tomorrow."

The next day at school, during breaktime, Kevin and I are outside our wooden classrooms. I spot James on his own and call him over.

"James, come here quickly!"

He runs over to me.

"Can you see the boys who've been picking on you?" I ask.

"Yea, they're over there on that playground," he says, pointing towards them.

"Okay, what I need you to do is to walk out onto that playground so they can see you. Kevin and I will hide around this corner," I tell him.

I can see his bottom lip start to curl up and quiver. "They might get me!" he says.

"Don't worry, I won't let them!" I reply as I hug him.

He looks so scared.

"James, if they come after you just run down to the corner where we're hiding and we'll jump on them." I add.

He doesn't want to do this and I can tell he's scared, but I have to persuade him he'll be safe. It's the only way.

Eventually, he reluctantly walks over, near to where the bullies are, as Kevin and I get into position. We both get ready to jump on them. As I expected, he's noticed, and one of the bullies shouts out, "There he is, let's get him!"

We watch closely. There are three bullies running after him. They're gaining on him.

I mutter quietly to myself, "Come on, James, run faster."

They're about to grab him. As he passes the corner, Kevin and I jump out. We don't ask any questions. We throw punch after punch until they're all crying like babies. They'll never bully my little brother ever again. I turn to James and say, "There you are. I told you I would sort it out."

I know how James is feeling right now. He never has to worry about them again, as they all know now his brother and his friend are the toughest boys in the school.

6

The bully at home

Sadly, my days of being bullied are not over yet. It's still happening to me in a place where I should feel safest of all: at home. Every single day, my own Dad picks on me, telling me I'm "useless". It's like he's entertained by it. "'Useless Eustice,' we should call you," he says.

I've started to notice that Mum's being bullied by him all the time as well. She's weak and seems to accept it. What makes things worse is that she's started calling me stupid and I feel she's saying it to get his approval. He's done such great things, and yet he's gradually become someone I fear rather than love. When I was in the Infants and he told me how he dealt with his bully, I realised I was nothing like him. He doesn't mind hurting people.

It's summer sports day and I've been allowed to bring my bike into school, because I've entered into the slow bicycle race. The idea is that we all start when Mr Booth drops his flag and ride our bikes to the finish banner in a straight line. Nobody's allowed to put their feet down from the pedals, or they'll be disqualified. You have to have good balance to win this race, as the last person across the finish line wins the race.

Mum is at the side line, watching along with all the other parents and teachers.

I know I can win this easily, but I don't want to be the centre of attention, as my confidence is not good any more. We're all on our bikes, waiting for Mr Booth to drop his flag. As he does, the whistle is blown to start the race. The line of bikes moves forwards and I start riding as well. I move just a couple of yards, then slow the pace almost to nothing. I can virtually stay still on my bike without putting a foot down, but I keep moving or else I'll be here all day. But there are no cheers for me and I feel like I have no right to win and spoil it for the other kids and their parents. I'm at the back by quite a long distance, so I'm winning this race.

I can see other kids putting their feet on the ground, but nobody seems to notice. We're getting close to the finish line and I'm still at the back. There are just three of us left now and I can hear the fathers of the other two boys shouting, "Come on, you can do it!" to their kids.

Still, there are no calls for me. I don't want to take this from them, so what's the point? This doesn't matter to me anyway, so I'm going to give the race away. I press down on my pedals and ride fast across the finish line, passing the other two boys on the way. On the other side of the line, I carry on riding and go to lock my bike up, but Mr Booth calls me. He sounds sad. "John, come back. You've come third, so you get a prize. And why did you do that?"

I look up at Mr Booth and just shrug my shoulders. He looks confused, but then the cheers come from the parents of the boy who got first prize.

That same evening, when Dad arrives home from work, Mum tells him that I won the slow bicycle race. He looks around at me, looks me up and down, and says, "Well, he would win that, wouldn't he?"

Mum replies, "Oh, Maurice, it's not easy. They have to have good balance."

Dad just mutters to himself. I don't know what I've done for him to think so little of me. This is why the race didn't matter to me. And I didn't win, anyway. I came third.

It's Friday night and I've woken up in the middle of the night. I keep doing this, because I'm having the same nightmare every night. It's always the same. I'm lying in my bed and I can see the landing light on, but I'm totally alone and can't move. There's a loud thumping sound and it sounds like someone coming up the stairs, but much louder. The thumping starts quietly, then gradually gets louder and louder until it sounds like whoever's coming towards me is almost upon me, but then I wake up. I can't go back to sleep, because it will happen again. The next day, I decide to go on my own down to the park and I sit on the riverbank, watching the water flow. I don't want to go home, because I don't want to have that dream again and I don't feel safe at home. Maybe the thumping sound in my nightmares is Dad coming to get me. But I don't know. Maybe it's something else. He thinks nothing of hitting me these days and it's more often because he's in a bad mood, rather than a punishment for something that I've done wrong. I take comfort in the time that I have when he's at work.

A few days later and I've just got home from school. My favourite programme of all time is *Lost in Space*. It's about the Robinson family, who have a flying saucer type spaceship and they go from planet to planet, meeting all kinds of aliens. It's on TV every Thursday at 4:55pm. It's much more than a kid's show about space ships and space, though. Well, it is to me anyway. It's about a family who are close and they all show respect for one another. They're not perfect, but they're good people. Watching this show, I go into my own little world, imagining I'm Will Robinson, as he's about my age. His dad, John Robinson, sits and talks to him about anything, mostly to educate him. He never hits him and he never tries to scare him. Will has no fear at all of his own family. He only has love for them.

I haven't told anyone this before, but, sometimes when I'm alone in the house, I watch some of the old films on TV. I think maybe there's something wrong with me, because one of my favourites is one where a young couple go out to the country in America and buy a dilapidated old house. They do it up so they can raise their family there. One day, I want to do that. I'll get married to a beautiful girl. I'll buy an old house and make it perfect. Then we'll have children: a boy and a girl. The house will have plenty of room and we'll get a dog. I'll be the best father ever. I'll be just like John Robinson is with his children.

I'll love them, educate them, and teach them right from wrong. They'll feel safe and secure with me and they'll have real love from both their mum and dad. They'll never be scared, because I won't let that happen. When they grow up and finally decide to make their own way in the world, get their own houses, and start their own families, their mum and I will support them all the way through it. They'll want to come and visit their mum and me quite a lot, because their mum, who will be the grandma to their children, will lay on a great Sunday dinner. Then, eventually, my wife and I will grow old together and we'll still love each other just as much as we did when we were first married. In the future, I'm going to make all this happen. I'm going to make a perfect world for my family, just like in the movies and *Lost in Space*, except we'll be on earth and not in space.

It's Sunday morning. Mum and Dad were out last night at Blow and Ox Social Club, having a drink. Mum tells me that they were dropping Mr and Mrs Goldfinch back at the Meriden estate where they live, but when they were going through the traffic lights on Woodmere Avenue and crossing the A41, they collided with another car. Dad's saying to Mum that it was the other man's fault, but I bet he was driving like a maniac again and that's why it happened.

A week or so passes and Dad has bought an old car to use while his car is being fixed at the garage. Mum, Anita, James, and I have just arrived back from the shops, and Dad has this old car in his garage, where he's working on it. He's shouting and swearing, as it's all going wrong as usual. It's a yellow Ford Popular 100E. He instantly orders me over to help him work on it. My heart sinks. Now I must prepare myself to be shouted at, pushed, called "useless", and hit whenever he feels like it.

After going through the usual process of my worst fears, he decides he wants to test the car on the road. For some reason, he's removed the front passenger seat, but I still have to go with him. As he drives the car out of the garage, he shouts to me, "John, watch and make sure I don't hit anything or run any tools over."

I'm holding the garage door out of his way at the same time, so I have to concentrate. If I get it wrong, he'll hit me again. Once the car's out and parked on the road, I close the garage doors and the gates, then get into the car with him to test drive it. As, there's no front passenger seat, I have to get in the back.

He drives the car to the end of the road and then shouts, "I'm going to test the brakes now!" Then he instantly slams them on so hard and I have nothing to hold onto. I'm thrown from the back of the car and I hear a "crack" sound as I hit the side of my head hard on the metal dashboard. Everything's blurred and it hurts.

I hear him saying, "John, are you all right?"

He sounds muffled.

I reply, "Yea, I'm okay." He looks a bit shocked and I say, "It was lucky that I didn't hit the windscreen instead of the dashboard," thinking I may have gone straight through it.

He hugs me and says, "John, don't be silly. I think far more of you than I do of a windscreen."

For the first time in a long time, I feel like he does really care about me, but does he really think I was worried about breaking his windscreen with my head? Is that how worthless he's expecting me to feel? I say nothing, because at least he's being nice to me.

7

Becoming a bully

During the summer holidays I have to think of things that James and I can do together. I've taken him to the North Watford Public Library, so we can get our membership cards. It's really good, because if we don't have any money, we can always go there and get three books completely free, as long as we take them back on time. I always take James to the Infant side, so he can choose his books, and I tell him I'm in the other room, where the books are for the older kids, so he feels safe. I have to keep checking on him to make sure he's okay, but he doesn't see me checking on him. Today I've got a book called *Uncle Cleans Up*. It's a bit babyish on the story side, but it's good for my reading practice and I can read it to James for his bedtime story. It's about an elephant who's known as Uncle and there's also a mouse in it, called Hit Mouse, who's a baddie. Three books are a lot to get through, but we always manage it.

The next day, I take James down to the park. I notice that bulldozers have been over one side of it. They've dug the ground up and made massive mounds of mud. Some other boys arrive and start throwing stones at us.

I tell James, "Stay close to me and do what I do!"

I run over behind one of the two mounds and start throwing stones back at them from behind it. I call to James, "Cover your head because they'll throw stones back."

Straight away we have stones landing all around us. I gather loads of stones quickly and throw them back, one after another. It's like machine-gun fire. They're hiding behind a mound about 30 feet from us. I tell James, "Pass me more stones!"

Then we run from mound to mound, throwing stones as we go. This turns out to be the best fun ever. Instead of making enemies, these boys say they want to be our friends.

The school holidays come to an end and we're back at school. This is my last year at this school, as next year I'll be going to St Michael's. Today we have a late summer school outing and we're going to London Zoo. This is so exciting. We're going on a coach. Mum's done a special packed lunch for me and I've got five shillings to spend. Once we all get on the coach, I check my lunchbox and find a big bag of plums. Wow, I love plums. We've arrived at the zoo and we're all walking along in single file. I'm happily looking around at all the animals and dipping my hand into my bag of plums, eating one after the other. This is a great day. What could be better than this?

Suddenly the teacher calls out, "Come on, now, hurry along all of you, and, John Monaghan, stop eating those plums!"

Oh no, not my plums. I was enjoying them. My favourite animal in this zoo is a baby elephant. Maybe reading the Uncle books has made me feel warm towards elephants, but maybe there are other reasons, too. We have all been allowed to go over and pat this baby elephant and it seems happy to have the attention. Some of the aggressive boys are punching it and the teachers are not noticing.

I shout, "Stop doing that!"

One boy says, "It can't even feel it, because its skin's really thick."

I reply, "So? It's still not good to do that."

Everyone's pushing and shoving to get to the elephant. Then I trip over and I fall underneath it. It wants to turn around and walk, but I'm on the ground underneath it. I can't move, because I'm surrounded by the other kids. It starts to put its foot down on my chest. It feels me under its foot, then lifts its leg back up again and puts it down on the ground to the other side of me. It knew I was there! I thought I was going to be crushed – they must be such gentle creatures. Mum told me weeks ago that elephants never forget and I wonder, *Will this elephant remember me?*

After seeing the animals, we're allowed to go to the shops in the zoo and spend our money. I can't wait to spend my five shillings. I call it five shillings, but they changed our money earlier this year and it's not really five shillings any more – it's 25p now. Five shillings seemed a lot before, but now it doesn't seem that much. It was two half-crowns and they were big coins. They also got rid of our ten-shilling note. Now it's just 50p. All that I get to buy in the shop is a pencil sharpener, a pencil, and some sweets, but I'm happy with them and today has been a great day.

Back at school the following week and I'm really enjoying this year at school. Mr Booth is a great teacher. He does such interesting stuff all the time. He's brought in a big spool-type recording machine that records our lessons and we all get to talk into the microphone. He plays the recordings back to us the following day, then asks us what we all think of our responses. He also does a lot of scientific experiments and we have projects. Mine's about the solar system. We do a lot of practical experiments outside as well, involving building things.

Kevin and I have been assigned the job of planting new trees all along the perimeter fence that separates the school from the A405. Mr Booth is almost like the father I never had. He focuses on the good things I do and tries to encourage me to do great things. While Kevin and I are digging the ground and planting the trees, he stops me and says, "John, one day you'll come back to this school as an adult; you'll look at these great trees and they'll be fully grown. You can think to yourself, 'I planted those trees.'" I wish he was my dad.

I always forget to put the tools back into the tool shed. I leave them lying around the place and then we find them all rusty a few days later. Mr Booth never shouts at me or hits me, though. He just looks disappointed and says, "You would forget your head if it wasn't screwed on." That's enough for me to get my act together, though.

The next day, Kevin and I are down by the long jump sand pit, and there are some Infants playing in the sand there. I look over at the edge of the sand pit and there's a hammer that I must have left out from when we were building an experiment site a few days ago. I pick it up to bring it to the tool shed. But, as soon as I pick it up, this little Infant boy looks at me, petrified. His face looks so funny, and I can't resist going up to him and saying in a silly voice, "I'm going to kill you!"

His face is hilarious. It's almost as though his hair's standing upright on his head. I then go and take the hammer to the shed and when I return there's a girl with the little boy and he's in tears. I've scared him out of his wits.

The girl looks at me and says, "Go away, you bully!"

The word "bully" hits home to me after all I went through. I should know better.

All of the way home on the bus and at night when I'm in bed, I keep thinking about why I did that. I hate myself and I'll never do anything like that again.

But it will not be the last time I bully someone. There's a boy in my class called Tony Mitton. He's skinny and very stuck up. He acts as though he's above everyone else. He's more like a girl than a boy and he has perfectly cut sandwiches in his lunchbox, along with nicely cut pieces of fruit, a KitKat, and an Aero. He always puts his hand up to answer the teacher's questions to show he's the bright one. He puts his hand up with one finger pointing upwards, as well, like the girls do. He has leaky moles on his back and I have to sit with my bare back against his in PE. His backbone sticks out because he's so puny. He always looks down his nose at me, like he's better than me. He never says anything. It's just how he looks at me. I don't like him and he's going to know it.

Four weeks on, Kevin and I pick on him about his lunch box and all his fancy food.

"Give us a piece of your KitKat, Tony," I say to him. "No!" he replies.

Kevin says, "Tony and his shit cat. It's all for him and none for us!"

Eventually he tells the teachers and Mr Booth writes on the blackboard about bullies. This time I know it's about me and I feel bad, but I still hate Tony. It doesn't stop Kevin and me, until one day, during assembly, he tells another teacher.

The lady teacher keeps Kevin, Tony Mitton, and me back when assembly has finished. We all sit around her on chairs and she asks, "Okay, Tony, what's the problem?"

"They're bothering me again," he says.

Even the word "bothering" gets on my nerves, but I have to sit and listen. Eventually, after listening to the teacher, I *really* hate him, but I tell Kevin we have to leave him alone now. I'm ashamed of what I did, but he was giving me looks every day like he didn't approve of me, or he wanted to challenge me. After going through what I've been through myself, I should never have bullied him.

8

A mum in a million

For the past few months I've been telling Mum that my bike's too small for me and I'd love to have the new Raleigh Chopper bike that's just come out. I arrive home from school and Mum's in the kitchen, cleaning. As soon as I walk in, she smiles at me and says, "It's time to go down to Halfords to get your new bike."

"Really?" I say in disbelief.

"Yes, but it's for your birthday and Christmas, combined, because it's so expensive," she replies.

My birthday's not until November and it's late September now, but that's okay. I'm getting a new bike. I'm so happy and excited that I'm jumping up and down. Anita calls Mum and Dad out to the garage and complains, "John's getting a new bike, so I should have one, too."

Dad thinks the world of my sister. He walks out to the garage to look at her old bike. She stands next to it and says, "Look. My bike is so small, it's ridiculous!"

Dad replies, "Yes, I can see what you mean, but we can't afford to buy two bikes." He then turns to Mum and asks, "Do you think we should get Anita a new bike first?"

My God, she's actually going to ruin this for me and she never even uses her bike. I'm never off mine, I love riding it so much.

"No! Anita doesn't use her bike," Mum replies.

Anita says, "I don't use it because it's too small."

"You've never used it, Anita. I've promised John, so we're going to get his bike today," Mum says.

Thank God for my mum. Mum and I head up to Halfords in North Watford on St Albans Road. Walking into the shop, I can smell the polish and rubber from the tyres. All the lovely new bikes are on display.

Mum asks, "Which bike is it that you want?"

"The Raleigh Chopper," I say, thinking I must be dreaming.

"What colour do you want?" she asks.

"Blue's my favourite colour," I reply.

There's a blue one on display in the window and she takes me over to look at it – it's the most beautiful bike I've ever seen. It's light blue with white name stickers and it has a long, comfy seat with chrome tubing. It has three gears on a shift change, like a car, and a black-and-silver gear knob. This is the bike of my dreams and I'm minutes away from owning it.

Mum walks over to the counter to talk to the man. "We would like the blue bike in the window, please," she says.

The man puts his stock book on the counter and says, "Oh, sorry about this, but we only have a red Chopper in stock. Would you like a red one, young man?" he asks me.

"Yes, please, if I can't have the blue one today!" I say.

I can't wait any longer. I'm bursting with excitement. Mum turns to me and says, "No, John. What colour do you *want*?"

"Blue, but they haven't got one," I reply.

Mum frowns and asks the man, "Why can't we buy the display bike?"

"It'd be too much trouble to get it out of the window, because there's so much in the way," he says.

"Okay, leave it then!" Mum replies sharply. She turns towards the door and says angrily, "Come on, John!"

She then walks straight out of the shop. I can't believe it. Why is this happening to me?

"I will have a red one, Mum. It's okay," I say, running behind her.

"No!" she replies angrily. "That man can't be bothered, so we'll go somewhere where they can be!" she adds.

I know there's not enough time to go to the town centre now and if Anita has anything to do with it, I won't be getting my bike. Somehow, I persuade Mum to go back into Halfords and ask them if they can get the blue one out of the window again. She calms down and we go back into Halfords. She talks to man behind the counter for a while and then he agrees to take the blue bike out of the window. I'm sitting on it and I absolutely love it. It's unbelievable.

"Okay then," he says to Mum, "are you buying it on HP finance?"

"Yes," Mum replies abruptly.

He opens a draw and picks out some forms, then hands them to her to fill out. Mum finishes filling the forms out and hands them back to him.

He checks through them and says, "So, if you can just get your husband to come in and sign here, you can take the bike."

Mum looks furious. She says, "Why do I need my husband to sign? I'm paying for it. I'm working!"

The man replies, "It's customary to have the man sign the forms."

Oh no, I can't believe it. Not another problem. This is like torture. I *can* have the bike, then I *can't* have it, three times so far. Eventually the man agrees to accept Mum's signature. I will have this beautiful treasure of a bike out of the shop. Phew! That was close to me losing it.

Wheeling it out through the front door of the shop, I'm in my element. I can't express how happy and grateful I am to Mum. This bike will become my permanent partner. I'll go everywhere on it and I'll never get bored of it.

A week or so later, Dad's getting rid of his yellow Ford Anglia 100E, because his proper car, the Cortina, is repaired now, so he doesn't need the Anglia. Anita called that Anglia the Yellow Submarine, after the Beatles song. It's a silly car, anyway. It only has three gears instead of four and the wipers work off air, instead of electricity, so when you go fast, they go slow and when you go slow, they go fast. As he's getting rid of it, I ask him if I can have the plastic sheet that's stuck in the rear window. It's just there to stop the window from steaming up. He says I can have it, so I remove it to make a windscreen for my new bike. I find some old brackets, screws and washers, and I make holes through the plastic with a big screwdriver. I then bolt it across my handlebars. It looks great. It's a chopper bike with a windscreen. All I need to do now is save up my pocket money and I can buy a speedo. With my windscreen fitted, I go for a ride to test it out. I've got the best bike in the whole of Watford. When I arrive back, Dad's messing around with the old Anglia, taking things that he wants off it. He calls to me, "John, I need you to drive this car forwards a bit."

Is he joking? "But I can't drive," I reply.

He half smirks. "Don't be stupid, John. Just get in. You know what all the pedals are for, don't you?"

"Yea, but I can barely reach them," I reply.

"Just get in," he says again.

He walks around and stands in front of the car.

"Start the engine," he shouts out.

I do as he says.

"The handbrake is already off, so press the clutch down," he says.

Again, I do as he says.

"Now push the gear lever to your left and then forwards," he says.

I push it forwards and it crunches into gear. I'm getting nervous.

"Okay, now press the accelerator," he says.

I press it down, but the engine's screaming.

Then he shouts, "Jesus, Mary, and Joseph, not to the floor. Just a little bit!"

I ease off and press it about halfway.

"Now, slowly let the clutch up," he shouts.

With my hands shaking, I slowly let the clutch up, but the car jolts forwards. I fly back in the seat and then bounce forwards and my foot presses the accelerator to the floor with him standing in front of the car. Then I'm thrown back into the seat while the car lurches straight at him, knocking him over and into the wall of the house. The car crashes into the side of the house and stalls. I'm in total shock.

I think maybe I've killed him, but he gets up and laughs. "Jesus, Mary, and Joseph, are you trying to kill me?" he asks. I'm still trying to catch my breath.

"No," I reply, "I couldn't stop it!"

"Never mind," he says, with smirk on his face. "Go in and tell your mum what you did."

It's a weekday and Mum says it's okay for me to ride my new bike to school. This is great and I have my windscreen now, so if it rains, I won't get too wet. I quickly have my tea and toast, and then I'm on my bike like a bullet. I ride to the end of Sandringham Road, actually on the road stopping at the give-way signs and checking before I cross. When I get to Bushey Mill Lane, I have to go on the pavement, as it's so busy. I turn left onto Bushey Mill Lane, then along St Albans Road. It's even busier when I get to Odhams roundabout, just past the library and the Clocktower, so I get off and walk. I get back on and continue past the bus station until I get to the traffic lights at Horseshoe Lane, but the good thing here is that I can go through the subway. I think this is great fun on my new bike, as I'm changing gear for all the hills.

Arriving at school, I put my bike on its stand outside our wooden classrooms. As I'm early, I sit on the tarmac admiring it. Everyone else arrives and they're all admiring it as well and asking me questions. One boy says, "Wow, it's even got a windscreen!"

Mr Booth also comes over to look at it and asks, "Did you fit that windscreen yourself, John?"

"Yes," I say proudly.

"You made a good job of it, well done," he replies.

On the way home after school, I stop at the bike shop to see if I can get a speedo for it, because then it'll be complete. They have just the one I want, but I don't have enough money yet, so I'll have to save for it. When I finally get home at 4:55pm, I turn the TV on to watch *Lost in Space*, as Mum's not home yet. She's working at Golden Wonder crisps in Imperial Way, Watford. Mum has had all kinds of jobs. She does the accounts at Golden Wonder, where they use these big electric adding machines. Sometimes, I've been waiting with Dad when we collect her from work and I've seen her using the machines. They have a till roll that prints out the calculation. You put all the sums in, and when you press the equals button the machine makes a funny noise and prints out the whole lot. I love playing with those machines. The last job she had was at the Odeon Cinema. She was an ice cream lady and when she took us to work with her, we got to watch the movies completely free. We watched *Chitty Chitty Bang Bang* three or four times when it first came out and *The Yellow Submarine* by The Beatles. During the breaks, the lights in the cinema would come on dimly and then I could see Mum walking down the aisle with her Lyons Maid ice cream tray. It was all lit up and she was selling ice cream to everyone. She did look funny.

My eleventh birthday comes and goes uneventfully, as I already had my great present, my bike. I've saved some money towards my speedo and Mum tells me that she'll give me the rest towards it. Wow!

It's the weekend and off I go to the bike shop, excited and hopeful that it'll still be there. To my relief, the speedo is still on sale there. It must have gone down in price, because I have 50p more than I need. Trying to contain my excitement, I point out the speedometer to the man behind the counter.

"Can I buy that speedo please?" I ask him.

The man hands the speedo to me in its box and I hand him my money. I look inside the box and it looks complicated to put on my bike. I ask the man, "Can you put it on my bike for me, please?"

He looks at me like I'm a nuisance, sighs, and says, "Not really, we're busy and the mechanic is going to lunch now."

I look over at the back of the shop: the mechanic has a bike upside down and he's turning the pedals. "Does that sound healthy?" he asks the man behind the counter.

The man says, "Yes, that's better."

"Well, I'm off to lunch now then," the mechanic replies.

I look up to the mechanic and ask, "Would you fit my speedo for 50p, please?"

The mechanic puts his hands on his hips and replies, "No, I'm off to lunch!"

Then the man at the counter says, "Oh, go on. It won't take you long. Look at him. And you get the 50p."

The mechanic sighs, then replies, "Come on, then, give me the 50p and come back in half an hour."

I'm elated, grinning from ear to ear. He's going to fit it for me. I go for a walk around the shops for what seems like a very long half hour. When I get back to the shop, he's just finishing and testing it. He turns my bike the right way up.

"There you go," he says with a smile. "Clever idea for the windscreen," he adds.

I'm bubbling over. "Thank you," I reply.

From the bike shop, which is on St Albans Road, opposite Bushey Mill Lane, there's a long wide pavement most of the way back to my house in Sandringham Road. It's slightly downhill, so I pedal as fast as I can to see how high my speedo reads and it almost makes 30 miles per hour. But suddenly, out of the blue, the local neighbourhood psycho is standing in front of me, right in the middle of the pavement. It's Wayne Broad. I brake as hard as I can, or I'll ride straight into him. He's never done anything to me, but other people have told me he's totally psycho. He grabs my handlebars with both hands.

"Why are you riding so fast?" he asks.

I tell him calmly what I'm doing, but I'm not sure what he's going to do. He looks at my bike and the speedo. He compliments me on all of it and we part company.

Phew! That could have gone badly, but it didn't, and I won't let it spoil my day. I carry on again, peddling like crazy, while checking my speedo, but I'm going so fast that the front wheel is almost off the ground and I'm losing my steering. I think it's best to slow down and the steering comes back. That only seems to happen with a chopper bike.

Ever since I got my guinea pig, I've been going on my bike once a week to the pet shop and the greengrocers on St Albans Road. I get the hay and dried food from the pet shop and the greengrocer gives me any vegetables I want from the back of his yard. They're just vegetables he would throw away otherwise, but they're fine for my guinea pig – he loves them. Carrots are Guinea's favourite and parsnips come second. He never stops eating; he munches his way through all the food and, when it's all gone, he munches his way through all the hay, until that's gone, and even then he'll start eating the newspaper that I've put in the bottom of the hutch to keep him dry.

Each morning when I get up, I go to check on him outside and fill his bowl with water. As I walk around the corner, I make a noise like a bird and then he knows I'm coming. He squeaks and squeaks, because he's happy that I'm coming; it sounds like he is saying "goody, goody, goody, good". When I open the hutch door, he pokes his head out and licks my hand like a little puppy. Sometimes, he escapes from his hutch and the neighbours have told Mum that they've seen him walking down the road. Mum doesn't believe them, as when she goes back to the house to check, he's gone back into his hutch again. Many times, in the evening while we're all in the living room, watching TV, and it's cold outside, I feel sorry for him being out on his own, so I take him inside with me and he always crawls up my jumper. Sometimes, he pops his head out of the neck of my jumper and starts licking me. He knows who I am and I can tell he loves being with me. When Dad was asleep in his armchair one evening, I put him on his stomach, but then he woke up shouting, "Get him off me. He's a rat!"

I quickly took him off and said, "He's nothing like a rat!"

Dad replied, "Yes, he is. He's a rat with no tail!"

It's late November. I've just woken up and the house is freezing again. The windows are frozen and I can see my breath. It's Saturday, so there's no school today, but I have to get up to go and get Guinea's vegetables, then clean out his hutch. I jump out of bed and get dressed quickly, to avoid getting too cold. I find some newspaper and step out the back door. It's even colder outside and it's foggy.

As I walk around the corner to the patio where Guinea's hutch is, I make my funny bird noise to call him, but this time there's no reply. He doesn't squeak or make any sound at all. I know straight away something's wrong. I peer through the wire mesh on the front of his hutch, while laying down the newspaper and bag of hay on the wall beside me. It's frozen everywhere and inside the hutch I can see the hay I gave him is all gone. He must have eaten it, so maybe I didn't leave him enough food for this cold weather. The newspaper that was on the floor in the hutch has all been torn up. I reach inside the hutch with a horrible feeling in the pit of my stomach. I run my hand through the shredded newspaper to see if he's still asleep underneath it – maybe he's not well, or worse. In the corner, I feel a lump. It's rock hard and ice cold. I put my hand underneath it to pick it up and I'm devastated. He's dead. I'm stunned. I can't even feel the cold any more.

Later in the day, I find an old shoebox and put him in it. I run my fingers through his furry coat one last time before I put the lid on. I get my dad's shovel from the garage and at the end of the garden I dig a deep grave for him, then carefully place the box at the bottom. I fill in his grave and make a little cross for him to mark where he is, then kneel down beside it and pray he didn't suffer. I know he must have suffered, though. I'll never forgive myself and I'll never forget him. He was my little friend. For weeks, I keep having dreams I can hear him squeaking in the garden. It's like he's free and he's telling me he's okay. I miss him so much and I wish he were back with me.

9

He must be mad

It's getting near to Christmas and Mum's working late tonight. It's a week night and we have school in the morning. Dad is with us and he's acting like a maniac, as usual. He's burning a fence post on the open fire in the living room and it's about four feet long. He's lit the fire with smaller pieces of wood and stuck one end of the fence post into the fire, while the other end is resting on the fire tool stand, which is now in the middle of the floor. There are sparks flying everywhere and he's decided he wants to hoover. He doesn't give us a chance to get our toys cleared out of his way. He just gets the hoover out, plugs it in, and starts hoovering.

"Who owns this?" he asks, pointing at a toy in front of the hoover.

"That's mine," I call out over the noise of the hoover.

"Get it off the floor. Anything I find on the floor, I'm going to throw it in the fire!" he says.

We are all rushing around, clearing our toys away before he throws them in the fire, but when the fence post is almost finished burning, he decides to throw my car garage on the fire anyway, because it's made of wood. It's one of my favourite toys and I play with it a lot, but now I have to watch it burn on the fire. Just as my garage is almost burned to nothing, he shouts, "John, go and get some coal from the coal house!"

Still very upset, I take the coal scuttle and walk out to the coal house. I hate doing this job when it's pitch-black outside. Not only can I not see what I'm doing, but opening the door to the dark coal house, I always think a ghost might be in there. I shovel the coal into the scuttle and bring it inside anyway. Dad's sitting in his armchair with his feet up on the mantlepiece and says, "Put some coal on the fire."

I do as he says and go back to sit on the sofa.

"This is rubbish on the television, John. Turn the television over," he says.

To turn our television over is not as simple as it sounds. It has a button on it that you have to press, but it has a funny mechanism. When you press the button, you have to press it with just the right amount of pressure and if you press it too hard, the TV almost falls backwards. If you don't press it hard enough, it turns halfway and gets stuck. It makes a horrible mechanical sound until it gets to the next channel, if you're lucky. I press the button and it makes a nasty noise and gets stuck.

"Jesus, Mary, and Joseph, can't you do anything right?" he shouts with a face like fury. He gets up and messes around with it and it starts working. "God, you know what you want!" he snarls. He normally says that before he hits me. This time he doesn't hit me; he just shouts, "Get to bed! Now!"

I start walking up to bed and James comes with me. Anita follows and says, "There's a list of jobs I've made for you and James to do before you get into bed."

My heart sinks.

She says, "You have to sort out your clothes for school in the morning; tidy up your bedroom; and then I'm going to give you both a bath."

We work through her list, while she's running our bath. When I get in the bath, the water is ice cold. James kicks up and says, "No, I'm not getting in!"

Anita doesn't want to look stupid in front of Dad, but she forgot to put the hot water tank on, so there's no hot water.

"You'd better just get in," she says, as Dad shouts up the stairs,

"What's going on?"

"Nothing! Just getting them bathed!" Anita shouts down.

Both James and I climb into the icy cold bath and try to wash on a cold winter's evening in a house with no heating. We're both shivering while we're washing, but we do it and we go to bed.

It's January, 1972. Christmas came and went quickly and it was good, but not that eventful. We are a couple of weeks back in term time and this morning in assembly Sister Martini says she has an announcement to make to everyone. She gets up on the stage and, as usual, sends a couple of boys to get the slipper or strap for talking. She tells us there has been a terrible accident and that Timothy Clancy has been knocked down by a car and the doctors are fighting for his life. Timothy Clancy is James's friend and he's in his class. I know him well. I've been to his house a few times and they're a nice family. It's a shock and I'm worried James will be upset, but I'm not with him. I know he will hear what's happened. He never really talks about things that upset him, though, unless he knows I can do something about it – and he knows there's nothing I can do about this.

A couple of months pass and Timothy is back at school. He seems like he's recovered completely, but he's not the same, because he had head injuries. He does silly things that he would never have done before. He flashes to the girls, among other things he shouldn't do, but I don't think he gets into trouble for it, because the teachers know what happened to him.

It's Saturday afternoon, the week after Easter, and I've had to help Dad clear all the rubbish from the garage and the garden, because tomorrow we're taking it to the dump.

Sunday morning and he decides he doesn't want to take it to the dump. He wants to take it to a skip that's outside the place where he works as a forklift driver. It's called the Vending Centre. It turns out that he's not allowed to dump rubbish in the skip there, but he's going to do it anyway. I help him put all the rubbish into the boot of the car and there's all kinds of stuff: old pieces of cars; bits of furniture; pieces of plywood and glass things. He tells me to get into the car and he drives to the Vending Centre. As soon as he turns into the industrial area, he starts to behave very differently. He drives very slowly, looking from side to side, as though he's making a crime movie. He mumbles under his breath, "Doesn't look like anyone is here."

Then he reverses the car up to the skip.

"John, help me put the rubbish into the skip, but don't make any noise!"

I get out of the car and close the door as he's untying the boot lid.

"Be quiet!" he says.

I reply, "But I had to close the—"

"Jesus Christ, shut up!" he cuts in on me.

He starts taking the rubbish from the boot, one piece at a time, gently lowering them into the skip in total silence. You could hear a pin drop. I'm taking things out of the boot and passing them to him in silence as well. I dare not even speak. The last few pieces of wood, he places into the skip very gently. I've got some heavy metal strips. I carefully reach over the edge of the skip, but a couple of them slide off the top into the skip, straight through some glass and other noisy steel. It makes the loudest crashing noise I've ever heard.

"Jesus Mary, and Joseph, you fecking idiot. Get in the car!" he shouts. "You'll have me hanged!" he adds, as he runs and jumps into his car like Jack Regan from *The Sweeney*. I've just opened the door on my side and he's shouting, "Get in! Get in! Get in!"

I haven't even closed my door and he's screeching around the corner with me trying to close it.

"God, John, you know what you want!" he's shouting at me, almost all the way home. He's a maniac.

Last year, he took me to work with him when he was working on a building site, driving his bulldozer; he called it his "drott".

It was a Sunday and it had been raining, so the mud was soaking wet and slimy everywhere I walked. His bulldozer wasn't working and he wanted to get it running, ready for Monday morning. When we arrived there early in the morning, he put his wellies on and gave me a pair, too, but they were too big for me. They were adult size. He told me to follow him over to his bulldozer and then he just marched off through all of the slimy mud towards it. I was following him like a clown. With every step I took, the boots got stuck in the mud even more and almost came off my feet when I tried to pull my foot up to take the next step. It was as though they were being sucked into the mud on each step. The boots were so big that the tops of them were most of the way up my thighs, so I could hardly bend my legs. It took me ages to get to him, but eventually I got there.

He decided the battery was no good on his bulldozer and he went to steal one off someone else's. Off he marched to another bulldozer and told me to come with him. Again, he was there in a couple of seconds. I followed him again, sludge, sludge, sludge, sludge, until eventually I got to him. He didn't seem to notice how long it took for me to arrive, because he was so engrossed in what he was doing. He got the battery off quickly and marched back to his bulldozer.

"Come on!" he called to me.

I thought, *No, not again*, but I followed him, sludge, sludge, sludge, sludge, and again he didn't notice how long I took. He was almost finished fitting the stolen battery to his bulldozer by the time I arrived, when he said, "Oh no, I left the milk bottle of water on the other drott. John, go and get it."

I turned around again, sludge, sludge, sludge, and I picked up the bottle of water off the other bulldozer. On the way back to him, the mud was getting more and more stuck on my wellies and they were getting heavy. Each step towards him was becoming slower, as I had to pull my feet up out of the sticky mud with the boots gathering so much mud that they were almost twice the size they were to start with. Slowly, I made my way through with the milk bottle, sludge, sludge, sludge, sludge, sludge.

He glanced at me. He was worried that someone was going to turn up and notice he'd stolen their battery. I looked towards him, worried, knowing he would go mad at me for taking so long.

"Jesus Christ! Hurry up!" he shouted at me,

I was around ten feet from him, sludge, sludge, but then, just as I arrived by the big metal tracks of the bulldozer, I tried to lift up my left leg, but the boot was firmly stuck in the mud. I couldn't pull my foot out and fell towards the track of the bulldozer, trying not to let go of the glass bottle. It smashed against the track and cut my right wrist deeply. Blood was gushing out everywhere.

"Jesus Christ! Can't you do anything right?!" he shouted.

Then he saw how badly I was bleeding and took me to the builder's hut. The cut was three quarters of an inch long and it was wide open.

He looked at it and said, "Yeah, it's a bad cut, all right." He found some bandages in a first aid kit and bandaged it up for me. "Wait here. I'm going to sort the drott out," he said. When he returned, he asked, "Do you want to go to the hospital?"

"No, it's okay," I replied, because I didn't want to cause him any more trouble.

We got into the car and he drove me home. When we arrived home, Mum asked me, "Why have you got a bandage on your arm?"

"He cut himself," Dad replied for me.

Mum opened the bandage and looked horrified.

"For God's sake, Maurice! Why didn't you take him to the hospital?" she said. "Take him now. He needs to go."

"He didn't want to go!" Dad replied.

"Take him now!" Mum shouted.

Her face was red with anger. I'd never seen Mum as angry as that before. I thought Dad was always the boss. He drove me straight down to the Peace Memorial Hospital.

The nurse looked at it and said, "It's going to need stitches." She cleaned it up and it looked horrible. Then she got her needle and thread out, and just started stitching it up as though my arm were an old sock. When she'd finished, she said to me, "You're going to have a scar there, you know?"

"How long for?" I asked.

"Forever, I should say," she replied.

I wasn't too bothered about that – at least I didn't bleed to death.

The man Dad works for is Mr Collins. Collins Plant Hire was the company name. I went with him to Collins's house one day and he had a Jack Russell dog. While Dad was talking to Mr Collins, I was stroking the dog. It seemed happy, but all of a sudden he turned his head and bit my right hand so hard, sinking his teeth in deeply.

I was pouring with blood then as well.

Dad looked around and said, "Oh, your dog has bitten John."

Collins looked and said, "Yeah, he gets a bit funny at this time of the morning."

Anytime I go anywhere with Dad, I get injured somehow, but I suppose this wasn't his fault. The work Dad was doing for Collins on this job was to help build the new underpass in Watford. It runs under the roundabout by the town hall on St Albans Road.

After bandaging my hand up to stop me bleeding from what would be another lifetime scar, Dad decided he wanted to go to his bulldozer and do some maintenance on it. The bulldozer was parked near the partly built underpass, but still on the site.

When we arrived, he said, "Let's have some lunch first." He pulled out the sandwiches he had made that morning from his carrier bag, which was literally half a loaf of bread that he had stacked up like a tower and cut all the way down through the middle of it. He got out his flask and said, "Do you want some tea?"

I had one cup, but it tasted funny from his flask. I could taste the plastic.

Then he decided to replace a tooth on the bulldozers bucket. He started hitting it with a hammer and swearing about it. A lady walking past looked over and said, "I'm glad you're not my dentist."

Dad smiled at her and carried on. Eventually, he managed to change the tooth. He then decided he wanted to look at the links on the tracks of the bulldozer. He started the engine and moved it forwards about a foot, so he could see the part of the track that was on the ground as it moved around.

He jumped up and down out of the cab a few times, but then said, "This is taking too long. I can't keep getting in and out of the cab. John, climb up into the cab and I'll show you how to drive the drott."

Excited, I climbed up over the track and quickly realised that it's quite easy. You just push the lever forwards to go forwards and backwards to go backwards. I sat in the cab with the engine running as he walked down to the back of it. He put his head underneath by the track and called out, "Okay, go backwards."

Did he want me to reverse over his head with it? In disbelief, I said, "No, not while you're underneath it."

I couldn't even see him.

"Jesus Christ, John! Do as you are told!" he shouted.

"No," I shouted back. "I won't do it! It will kill you!"

He'd scared the life out of me after what had happened when I ran him over with the car – how could I? He seemed to understand and just said, "Okay, just leave it."

He packed up and we went home. *Thank God for that*, I thought. My dad is a maniac and he expects me to do these things. There are photos of him on his bulldozer in the distance in a book called *The History of Watford* from when the underpass was being built.

One day he came home from work with his head bleeding, because he had been fighting with one of Frankie Piles building workers. They were all Italians and he hated them for some reason, probably because they were as bad tempered as him. The man he was fighting with at work hit him over the head with an iron bar. Irish people and Italians are alike; they don't seem to mind fighting.

Another time, we were all in the car, going to see Granny and Grandad, when a man in a minivan pulled out in front of us. Dad shouted and blew his horn at him, but the man stuck his fingers up at him. Of course, he wouldn't let that go. He chased this man for miles, trying to make him stop, but the man wouldn't stop and they were both driving like maniacs. The man turned down a country lane and Dad chased him down there, driving side-by-side around bends and trying to get in front of him. Eventually, he did get in front of him and cut across, so he could only wait for Dad to get out of the car. Dad got out and started shouting at the man, but the man got his Alsatian out of the back of his van and said he would set the dog on him. Dad got back in the car then and drove off with Mum complaining to him about the whole thing.

Throughout the whole chase, Mum had been screaming. I really thought we were all going to die.

When I was helping Dad build his garage, I was hit so many times by him that I try not to remember. I still have nightmares and I'm still scared of him.

It's the school holidays now, still 1972. It's Saturday night and Mum and Dad have been down to the club. They've just arrived home. Anita, James, and I are in bed. I can hear Dad shouting and swearing. Mum's screaming. There are lots of crashing noises.

This has become a regular thing, almost every weekend. It doesn't make me any less scared. I hope Mum doesn't get hurt, because I'm frozen to my bed in fear and can't help her. Tonight, it seems much worse than usual – that's the loudest crash I've ever heard. Dad's just thrown Mum's record player straight through the living room window, into the front garden and Mum's screaming.

I hear him say, "I'm going to put a light in every room!"

He has crumpled up newspaper and he's lighting it from the gas cooker and placing it in every room to burn the house down with us in our beds. He's put newspaper on the stairs and he's lit that as well.

Mum's screams are horrific. I think we're all going to burn alive in our beds tonight. The smoke's coming up the stairs. I can smell it, and I can hear Mum trying to trample it out. Luckily, she stamps it out, but he's shouting at her:

"I'm going out in the car and I'm going to crash it and kill myself! Whoever else I kill in the process, it'll be your fault!"

I hear Anita run down the stairs, so I have to go down too. I can't leave her to face this on her own. When I get downstairs, through all the smoke, Dad's in the kitchen and Mum's crying in the living room. Anita's standing by the back door, blocking Dad from leaving.

He's saying, "Come on, Anita, get out of the way."

But Anita's screaming and crying, saying, "No, I won't let you go."

I'm standing in the hall, looking at him with Mum now behind me. I wish Anita would let him go. If he could kill himself without hurting anyone else, I'd be happy.

"Look what you're doing to the kids!" Mum says, sobbing.

Eventually, he calms down and Anita won't stop hugging him. He's crying. My father is pitiful. Eventually, we all go back to bed, as if this is normal, and wake up to a new day.

A week or so passes and Dad won't get out of bed. He won't eat or drink either. He's smashed the bedroom up and thrown the wardrobe down on the floor. He's been in that room for days now and he won't come down. Mum doesn't know what to do and so she calls the police. She asks them to come in plainclothes, because she's worried about the neighbours seeing a police car. Two plainclothes police officers come to our house and she lets them in. They talk to him in his bedroom. They make him tidy up the bedroom, then they come downstairs.

On the way out, they look at Mum and say, "It is not the police you need. It's a doctor!"

A week or so later, and Dad's up and around. He's gone back to work. It's a Thursday evening and I've just been watching *Lost in Space*. Mum's still at work and Dad's arrived home early. I hear the iron gates opening. They make a unique squealing sound, so I know it's them. Then the wooden gates behind them are opened and I can hear him reversing his car alongside the house. The next thing I know, he comes charging into the house, using the most frightening words that he always uses when he's going to hit me.

"Where is he?"

He barges straight into the living room and hits me so hard around the head that everything goes black and I see stars. With a *crack* sound, I fall to the ground. He's shouting so loudly at me, but it sounds muffled and I can't even hear what he's saying. After a while, it turns out that my bike was along the wall at the back of the garage, where he told me to put it, but he reversed into it and scratched his car's boot lid. He insisted that I scratched it with my bike, which wasn't even possible. Even if I could have done that, I always kept well away from his car for fear of this happening.

He seems to be getting worse. I'm so used to being hit like this that I don't even care if I die any more. I can't see myself surviving this, anyway. It's going to happen sooner or later, so it may as well be now to get it over with.

Only a few days later, I've been out on my bike and I arrive home to find the milk is still on the doorstep. I put my bike away, carefully, and pick up the milk bottle from the doorstep. The bottle feels good in my hand, like a skittle, so I stand in the hall for a minute, just throwing it in the air and catching it. It's fun. I wonder if I can put a spin on it. I can, and I catch it each time by the neck. I'm good at this. I put a fast spin on it and still catch it by the neck every time. The spins get faster and faster, but then I drop it.

The bottom of the bottle has hit the floor, shot the top off, and there's milk on the carpet. No! I run into the kitchen to get a towel and mop the milk off the carpet, as quickly as I can and it looks okay. Phew! I put the milk away in the fridge and walk down the hallway to go and watch TV. Then I notice something. The wallpaper in the hall: oh my God, it's covered in milk and it's staining it. Dad only finished wallpapering the hall last month. I'm now surely going to die. I run and get a tea towel and frantically rub and rub, hoping it'll come off, but instead of the milk coming off, the wallpaper peels off. I'm staring at it and trembling with fear. I have to run away and never come back.

I get my bike out and ride down to the river, where I always go when I'm traumatised. I sit and stare at the water as it flows, wondering why God made such a beautiful world only to allow so much fear and suffering to go on. I hear people walking past behind me, some talking, some laughing. Are they talking about me? Are they laughing at me? I don't care. I can't even look up to find out. I'm numb and the fear has turned to despair. Whatever happens when Dad gets home tonight, I can't do anything about it. I just have to accept it, and if I die then I die.

It'll be over at least.

Eventually, I drag myself up and get on my lovely bike and start riding slowly home. As soon as I walk through the back door, Mum's in the kitchen and she's very angry.

"How did you do that to the wallpaper, John?" she asks.

With my head bowed, I explain to her what happened and all she says is, "Well, wait till your dad gets home and sees it."

She doesn't have to tell me that. I already know what's going to happen. I go to my room and wait for him to come home. After around an hour of lying on my bed, facing the ceiling, just staring and wondering how bad it's going to be, I hear the iron gates open – that sound again. Then the car reversing in and his voice in the kitchen, talking to Mum. I hear them both talking in the hall and she's telling him what happened.

"Where is he now?" Dad asks.

The fact that he didn't just shout, "*Where is he?*" is really good, because I may not get killed. Mum tells him where I am and he calls me down. He asks me what I did and I tell him, but he just replies, "Don't worry. I can put another strip of wallpaper up at the weekend."

Maybe it was because I'm so broken and numb and he could see how I felt, or maybe he was in a good mood. Whatever the reason, I didn't even get punished.

A week or so passes and Dad comes home from work this evening with a long cane.

I ask him, "What's that for?"

"It's to make sure that everyone behaves themselves," he says.

"Who's going to be the first one to get hit with that?" I ask, as if I don't know.

"You," he replies. Then he puts it in the corner.

I know he means it. I've never seen him hit James, and I've only ever seen him attempt to hit Anita once and Mum went mad at him and stopped him. Why doesn't she stop him from hitting me? What is it about me that he doesn't like, and why does Mum allow it to go on? Within two weeks of him bringing home this cane, I stupidly take a metal box that one of Dad's work friends made for me to play with in the bath. Without me even realising it, it leaves a mark on the bottom of the bath.

Later in the evening, Mum and Dad are down at the club, having a drink, and we have all gone to bed. I'm asleep when they arrive home. In my sleep, I can hear voices and shouting. The nightmare I have is happening again: the loud banging noise of someone walking towards me. Suddenly the bedcovers are pulled off me and I can feel sharp pain across my legs, my arms, and my back. Dad's lashing me over and over, like he's not going to stop. He's shouting and lashing, shouting and lashing, over and over.

I can hear Mum's voice saying, "Stop, Maurice. That's enough! *Stop! Stop! Stop!*"

But this isn't a dream – it's real. He walks out of the room and they go to bed. I'm left with no covers on me, lying on my side, crying with pain all over my body. I don't even know why he did that. I find out the next day that I'd scratched the bath with my metal box. Later in the day, Mum tells me she'd cleaned the mark off the bath and it wasn't scratched; it was just a mark and it had come off, so I don't need to worry.

10

First love feelings

It's the last week in August, 1972. We're going to Ireland again for our holiday. When we arrive, we stay at my uncle Terry's, as always, and they're pleased to see us. They still have no electricity or plumbing. This time, my uncle has geese. James is funny – he has been with the geese, trying to stroke them. I'm sitting in the doorway and he's just gone running past, completely surrounded by geese, and they're running with him, his new geese family. I feel very alone lately and I don't feel safe with my family. I go for a walk next door to the quarry and sit on a rock, throwing stones half-heartedly. Eventually, I go back into Uncle Terry's house and sit listening to the adults talking. My cousin Peggy's funny, too.

She crouches down next to me. "John, will you take a cup of tea?" she asks in her Irish accent.

"No, thank you," I reply.

"You will, you will," she says.

"No, thank you, I'm fine."

"Ah, you will, you will, you will," she says.

She makes me smile and I say, "Okay, thank you."

"And will you take a piece of cake?" she asks.

I just look at her and smile.

"Ah, you will, you will," she says.

Then she cuts a piece for me, puts it onto a nice china plate and hands it to me. I have my tea and cake. Peggy's lovely. I watch Dad talk to Uncle Terry. You would think he's the nicest man in the world.

The next day, we are on our way to visit one of Dad's old school friends; his name is Mickey Harkins and, of course, he lives on a farm, too.

When we arrive, Mickey Harkins and his family are pleased to see Dad. Mickey's a maniac just like him. Maybe that's why they're friends. Dad parks his polished shiny car behind Mickey's old wreck of a car and Mickey gets into Dad's car. He starts the engine and does a wheel spin, throwing mud all over.

Dad's car! But Dad just laughs and says, "Look what you did to my car!"

They both laugh together.

Moira, Mickey's wife, is a very harsh and strong woman. She carries heavy buckets and churns of milk from the cows as though they weigh nothing. Anita and Mum are over by the calves, and Anita's giggling, because a calf is sucking her hand. She tells me to come over and put my hand near its mouth. I do as she says and it feels like it's going to suck my hand off. We stay here quite late and have dinner. As always, it's bacon, cabbage, and potatoes. It's been a warm day and the evening seems to be staying just as warm and humid.

As we are finishing dinner, Moira's farm help girl arrives.

She's coming in and out of the room where we're all sitting. She's about thirteen years old and she's a beautiful girl. Every time she walks into the room to get something, I watch her in awe. Her Irish accent fits perfectly with her looks. She has long brown hair, big brown eyes, and a pretty face. I think Moira's noticed me looking at her. With a smirk on her face, she says, "John, why don't you go out and help her with her work?"

I feel embarrassed, but I quickly reply, "Okay."

As I casually walk towards the door, I think I hear a giggle from Moira.

I walk quietly out to see what she's doing and notice she's in the barn, sweeping a load of hay to one side. I stand at the barn door, watching her, and she looks around at me.

"Do you need any help?" I ask her.

She just tuts and says, "No, I'm all done now. What's your name?"

Trying to look cool, I reply, "I'm John."

"I'm Trisha," she replies. "Wait here, I will be back in a minute!"

I sit down on the hay with my back to the wall, watching the gap in the large barn door, waiting for her to come through it. There's a long ray of light stretching across the floor and over the hay from the moonlight.

She seems to be gone for a long time. It's very warm in the barn, but it's comfy on the hay.

Suddenly, she marches back in and sits opposite me. Looking excited, she starts asking questions about England.

"What's it like in England?" she says.

I start telling her about England, but she interrupts me, saying, "I like the way you talk!"

There's an awkward silence for a minute. I don't know where to look or how to answer that. She's so pretty and I don't know what to do now, except sit there looking at her.

She glances down at her hands, fiddling with a piece of hay, then back up at me, and says, "Aren't you ever going to kiss a girl?"

I'm overwhelmed with embarrassment and out of my depth. I'm only eleven. She's thirteen. I quickly reply, "No!"

"Okay, let's go in then. It's time for me to go home, anyway," she replies.

She looks annoyed with me, but I follow her back into the house, knowing this is the last day of my holiday and I'll never see her again.

In the morning, we head back to Dublin, where we stay in a hotel overnight, so we can catch the early morning ferry back to England. Anita, James, and I share a small hotel room. I'm in a single bed. The mattress is thin, hard, and narrow. Mum opens the door and says goodnight to all of us.

"Sleep well, we have a long journey in the morning," she says.

She turns out the light, then closes the door quietly and goes back to her room. Anita and James are asleep instantly – they must be tired. I'm lying on my bed, with just a line of light shining through the gap in the curtains.

I can't sleep. My mind keeps rewinding back to when I was talking to Trisha in the barn. I want to see her again, but I have no control over my life. I'm leaving this country in the morning, but I don't want to go.

My eyes become watery and I feel very sad. I don't understand this feeling, but eventually I roll onto my side and fall asleep.

It's morning. I'm still half asleep, but before I know it, we're bustled out for breakfast, then straight to the car, and in no time at all we're on the ferry. Once we've boarded, we're allowed to go up on deck. This time, I run to the back of the ferry and stand holding onto the white metal railings. As I watch Ireland slowly disappear into the distance, I'm oblivious to Anita and James shouting and playing in the background. I only feel sadness.

After this long car journey, we'll be back home and I'll have to go back to school, but this time it'll be my secondary school, St Michael's. I'll be starting a week later than all the others.

11

Late to secondary school

Monday morning, mid-September, 1972: my first day at my new school. I have my bus pass and I'm at the bus stop, waiting for the bus. I have to take the 321 now, because it goes up a different road to the 347; it goes along the A405. Mum's taken James to school, so I'm alone now. My new bus is modern and it has opening doors that work off air when the driver presses a button. You have to show your bus pass to the driver, because there's no conductor either. It has an opening door at the front to get on and one in the middle to get off. On the old 347 there's just a platform at the back with a pole to hang onto. I preferred the 347, because I could jump off the platform, swinging on the pole, while the bus was still moving, when it was near the bus stop. The bus conductor had an aluminium ticket machine he hung around his neck with a strap; it had a wind handle he turned to print your ticket. I'm nervous about starting at this big school today. I don't know what'll happen.

The 321 bus arrives. There's a gushing sound and the door opens at the front. I step onto the bus and show the driver my bus pass. It's like a spaceship on here – there are chrome railings to guide you and the windows are massive. I walk down the bus and the stairs are in the middle, instead of at the back. The bus has no bonnet, like the 347 did.

I climb up the stairs and walk to the front of the bus. It's great up here, because you can see so far ahead and it's like being the driver sitting at the front. There are not many people on here, just a few adults, and I'm the only child. As the bus gets near to St Michael's, I stand up and go downstairs to stand at the middle door to get off.

The door flips open. I step off and in front of me is this massive school on the other side of a wire fence.

I hear the bus move off behind me. I'm in my St Michael's school uniform. It's a white shirt, coloured striped tie, navy-blue jumper, and black trousers. It's all brand new. I have a black briefcase in my right hand that has nothing in it but a pen. I take a deep breath and start walking alongside the wire fence, around to the main gate, and into the main entrance of the school. The scale of this building is intimidating. The first person to speak to me is Sister Anthony.

"You, boy!" she calls out. "Follow the others down to assembly!"

Sister Anthony is a nun and she's the headmistress. There's a bell ringing. It's electric, unlike the one in St Catherine's; they just rang a hand-bell there. I do as I'm told and follow the others down to the assembly hall. In the hall, Mr Hayward, the deputy head, is talking on the stage. I'm looking around me to see if I can see anyone from my old school, but I can't. All of these kids are total strangers to me and this place is massive. The way the teachers are with the kids makes me feel like everyone has been sent here to be punished, not to learn.

At the end of assembly, everyone just files out and off. They go to their classrooms, but I haven't got a clue where I'm supposed to go. All this, because I'm starting a week late; all the others seem to have settled in. I wander around the corridors to try to see if I can find a teacher to tell me where to go. Suddenly, behind me I hear a fierce voice with a strong Irish accent, "You, boy, what do you think you are doing? Go back into your class!"

I look around, startled. I see an angry, plump lady, wearing thick black-rimmed glasses and a dinner ladies' uniform standing a few yards behind me, staring at me with her hands on her hips.

"I don't know where my class is," I reply nervously.

"What class are you in?" she snaps.

"I don't know," I reply. "It's my first day."

"What have you been doing for the past week?" she shouts at me.

"I've been on holiday," I reply quickly.

"Holiday? I'll give you a holiday!" she shouts at me. "Go and see Sister Anthony."

"I don't know where Sister Anthony is," I reply.

"No, you don't know anything, do you? Come with me," she mutters.

I think she's my father in a dress. She pulls me by the arm with a tight grip up a narrow corridor and then to a brown wooden door with a name on it, saying, "Sister Anthony". She knocks on the door, still holding my arm with a tight grip, like I've just been arrested. There's an even deeper and fiercer voice on the other side of the door, also with an Irish accent, shouting, "Come in!"

I'm marched in through the door by the dinner lady, still gripping my arm, as though I'll try to escape. She drags me in front of Sister Anthony's desk and says, "This *boy* was walking around the corridors and he says he doesn't know anything!"

Sister Anthony looks at me with a frown, as if she wants to kill me and says, "Okay, Mrs Mulvanity, leave this to me."

Mrs Mulvanity, the plump dinner lady, gives me an angry look and storms off out of the office. Sister Anthony closes the door behind her and says, "Well, now, boy, why don't you know anything?"

I explain that it's my first day and I've got back late from holiday, so I don't know what class I should be in. She mutters, while she looks up on her register.

"What is your name?" she asks.

"John Monaghan," I reply.

"Oh yes, you're in 1B3, Sister Mary's class."

With that, she grabs my arm in exactly the same way as the dinner lady did and marches me through a long corridor, all the way to the back of the school. She bangs on the door and then pushes me into the classroom.

"John Monaghan!" she calls to the teacher. "He's a week late!" She storms out and closes the door behind her.

I stand here, just inside the door, with every head in the classroom turned towards me, and everyone is staring at me.

I have that horrible feeling again. I'm a spectacle in front of everyone. Sister Mary seems to be a bit kinder than the others. She's younger as well. She quietly says, "Sit down next to Jeremy Clifford."

Luckily, Jeremy Clifford went to my old school, otherwise I'd have to ask who Jeremy Clifford is. I walk over to Jeremy and say, "All right, Jed!" quite loudly.

He looks shocked that I spoke so loudly. Everyone seems so subdued here. This place is nothing like my old school and the teachers are so angry all the time. I sit down next to Jed. I call him "Jed" to be friendly with him, but he's not the kind of boy I want to be friends with, because he's a bit dim. He has ginger hair, big lips, and freckles. I fumble my way through the morning lessons and then it's lunchtime. There goes that horrible bell again.

Everyone has dinner tickets, except me. But I have money, so I find out where to get some and I buy them. I go to get my school dinner and queue up in line. I'm on my own again. I can't see my friend, Kevin, anywhere. I sit at a table with my school dinner: two blobs of what looks like it's meant to be mashed potato, with hard lumps inside, runner beans, and liver, yuck. Nobody seems to notice I'm here.

The next thing I know, everyone has started leaving this massive dining hall and I'm the last one.

Oh no! It's that woman again, Mrs Mulvanity.

"You, boy!"

"You! The one who doesn't know anything!"

"Finish your dinner quick now, and come here and stack the chairs."

I do as she says as quickly as I can.

"Now go away!" she says.

She's a strange woman.

I head towards the back of the school to go out into the playground, but she's not finished with me yet.

"You, boy! Come here, take your plate and go away and put your plate back!"

What kind of an instruction is that? I guess she wants me to take my plate back to the kitchen dinner ladies. I take it back.

I make my way down the corridor to go out to the playground and then start walking around the grounds on my own, realising I'm back in that situation again. I'm a fish out of water. Everyone's in their own groups and I'm on my own. There are only three or four boys I recognise, but I never had anything to do with them in my old school, so it would be a bit odd if I were to go over to them, especially as they've seen me and have carried on talking with their group of friends. So that leaves Jeremy Clifford. He's sitting on his own on the ground by the netball courts' wire fence. I suppose it makes sense for me to go and talk to him – maybe he knows why Kevin's not here today. I'll just have to sit next to him and see what he can tell me about the school. I slump down next to him and ask him, "Jed, do you know why Kevin Lee's not here today?"

Jed looks blank.

"Oh yea, he went to another school," he replies.

My heart sinks. He must be wrong. Kevin would have told me.

I ask him some questions about the school, but, of course, he doesn't know anything. After a while, the electric bell goes and everyone has to line up by the door in military fashion, each stream in a separate line. Well, I have to follow the dunce and I end up following him into the wrong queue, thinking he knows something I don't, because there are others in my class standing in the queue next to us. Which, of course, makes me a dunce, too. Oh no, it's Mrs Mulvanity again.

"You, boy! What class are you in?" she shouts.

"1B3," I reply.

She says angrily, *"1B3, Madam!"*

"What are you doing in that queue, then?" she shouts.

"Get into the right queue!"

I quickly join the other queue, leaving Jeremy Clifford in the wrong one. All the girls are looking at me and giggling. Great, the first impression that everyone has of me at this school is that I'm an idiot. My first day and that's the luck I have: Jeremy stupid Clifford. The idiot even followed the line into the wrong classroom and he's been there for a week. Everyone thinks he's my only friend. I'm starting here with a massive disadvantage.

The next lesson we have is music. We all file into the music room, where for the first time I have a lesson with the music teacher, Mr Hogarth.

He looks like a matchstick man, with a massive black afro. As soon as we are all sat down, he hands out instruments to all of us. I'm handed a triangle and a stick to hit it with. How can I play a tune on this when it makes the same sound every time that I hit it? He sits at the piano and starts playing away on it. Every so often he looks around at everyone, smiling. Some people are banging cymbals together, others are shaking maracas, and I'm supposed to sit here, banging this stupid triangle. This sounds nothing like music. It's just a load of horrible noise.

After ten minutes of us all making a racket, he decides to put us into groups of three. He puts me in a group with Roger McCarthy and Martin O'Grady.

Martin seems friendly. He tells me to sit with him, but Roger's not that happy about it. He frowns and says, "Oh no! He's not with us, is he?"

I realise quickly that he was one of the boys who saw me standing in the wrong line, so obviously he thinks I'm an idiot.

Martin jumps to my defence: "What's the matter with you? Give him a chance; it's his first day here."

Roger looks unhappy, but says, "Okay."

After about ten minutes of us all playing in the group, we realise that we're having a great time together and we're all laughing. The funny thing is that Roger is the one who will become my best friend.

After a week or so, Roger asks our teacher if he can sit next to me in class and the teacher says it's okay. Jeremy Clifford ends up sitting on his own, just as he was on my first day, and Martin sits with another boy.

Roger and I have the same sense of humour and gradually become somewhat of a comedy duo. A lot of the other kids gather around us to watch our impersonations of teachers: Jimmy Saville, John Nokes, and many others.

As time rolls on, Roger makes friends with another boy, called Charlie Connolly, and the three of us become good friends. Charlie's quite popular and great fun to be with.

Some weeks later on a rainy day we're kept indoors during lunch break. It's absolutely pouring outside. The three of us are in the dining hall, having finished our stodgy meals. We sit on the table and chairs, talking. Charlie turns to me and asks, "What's your middle name?"

"Maurice," I reply.

Charlie sniggers and says, "Maurice," in a French accent. Then he asks me, "Do you know who the prettiest girl in this school is?"

"Of course!" I reply. "It's Linda Paget. Everyone knows that."

Charlie says, "Yeah, and she told me that she fancies you!"

"Really?" I ask, looking at Roger for confirmation.

Roger replies, "Yea, you should go and ask her out."

Brimming with confidence, I say, "Okay, I will."

I take my feet off the chair back, jump down off the table, and rush off to where the girls always hang around when it's pouring rain outside: the girls' cloakroom. I'm not going to mess this up like I did with Trisha. I walk into the cloakroom, full of confidence, not thinking about where I'm going to take her out to. The cloakroom is full of girls and she's standing in the middle of them, with her back to the wall. They're all talking to her. She's not only the prettiest girl in the school; she's the most popular one, too.

She has very long straight shiny blonde hair, big blue eyes, and tanned skin without a single spot or blemish. I walk straight through the other girls and they move to one side, all looking at me. Linda's just staring at me. She looks stunned that I've walked up to her. I already know the answer's going to be "Yes", because I've been tipped off.

I stand in front of her and all her friends, and say, with a smirk on my face, "Do you want to go out with me?"

She looks confused and replies, "No."

Oh my god. The gears are turning in my head like lighting. They set me up!

All her friends start giggling. She stares at me with her big blue eyes, but doesn't laugh and looks like she feels sorry for me. I'm frozen to the spot and I actually feel like I'm physically shrinking down to the size of a pea.

"Okay," I reply.

Then I turn and run down the corridor, back to Roger and Charlie. I can hear the sniggers behind me as I leave. I will kill those two for doing that to me.

As I arrive back at the dining hall, I see Charlie and Roger, still sitting at the table. As soon as they see me, they're both in stitches laughing. Charlie has a contagious laugh and it's hard to be annoyed with him.

"What did she say?" he asks, trying to hold back his laughter.

"You know what she said!" I reply.

The laughter starts again, and I tell them both I will get them back for doing that to me. I'm interrupted by a loud voice: "You three boys, come here and go away and stack the chairs!"

I'm getting used to this already. The three of us go and stack the chairs, then go outside. Roger and Charlie have smirks on their faces and they both burst into laughter every time they look at me.

It's a new morning, late October, 1972. I'm standing at the bus stop on St Albans Road, waiting for the 321 to get to school. There are only three or four other people here, and I'm at the front of the queue. I've never seen fog as thick as it is this morning. The traffic seems to materialise from the mist. Because of the fog, the 321 has not arrived and it's getting late. Then I see the outline of a bus coming down the line of traffic. I can't make out which bus it is, though.

As it gets closer, I can just about see the old type bus shape with a bonnet, so it's not going to be the 321. As it pulls into the bus stop, the fog-muffled engine gets much louder and the smell of diesel fumes drift into the bus shelter. I see it's the 347. Well, that stops at my old school, so I may as well get on and I can walk up to my new school from there. I jump on the platform, swing around the pole, and up the stairs to sit at the front. After a very slow journey to school, I jump off the platform at my old school bus stop – this brings back memories. I miss my old school, and Kevin. The fog seems to be getting thicker instead of thinning. I make my way up the driveway to my old school, so I can walk across the field up to my new one. I can just about make out where I am as I walk up the driveway, only able to see the kerb stones on either side of me. Then I make my way through my old school grounds, past my old wooden classrooms, and onto the field between the two schools. I walk on for around two to three hundred yards, across the field, but then I realise that I can't see anything in front of me or behind me. Every direction looks the same. I don't even know if I'm heading in the right direction. I stand still for a minute, just looking around me.

This is weird. There's no sound at all. I look up and then all around me again. I'm standing in a perfect dome shape of mist that's all white in colour. The only thing I can see is the green grass beneath my feet. This is a totally new experience for me and my imagination takes over. It's like I'm in my own spaceship, like the Jupiter 2 in *Lost in Space*. I lie down for a minute to look up and take this in. I'm in my own cocoon and I'm the only one in the world. A few minutes later, I get up and start walking. My dome around me follows me. It's fun trying to find my way to school when all I can see is the ground beneath my feet. I don't care about being late, because everyone'll be late today. I keep walking and then I see a wire fence. Is it the perimeter fence, or the netball courts? I can't tell. I walk towards the fence and put my fingers through the dew-soaked wire to look through and see what I can see. The wire's damp and cold. I can just about make out the white lines on the ground on the other side of the fence, about ten feet from me, so it's the netball courts. The only way for me to find my way into the school is to walk around the netball court, brushing my fingers along the fence. I can just about see the entrance to the school now and so I walk in. That was like an adventure, the best trip into to school yet.

It's early November, 1972, a week before my twelfth birthday, and I've just woken up to a new day. I can hear the radio playing downstairs, it's Donny Osmond, singing "Puppy Love". James is already up and the sun has just broken through the clouds, but the wind is blowing things around the garden. I dash to the bathroom, bursting for a wee, and I push down the bathroom door handle, but it's locked. A voice on the other side of the door calls out, "Just a minute!"

It's James. His minutes are long.

I call through the door, "Hurry up!" as I dance around trying to hold it on the landing.

Five long minutes later, I hear the signal. The toilet's being flushed. Thank God! Come on, come on, come on. Another minute passes.

"James! What are you doing in there?" I call out.

Not that I really want to know. The door opens and a sleepy-looking James just squeezes past me.

Phew! What a relief.

A few minutes later, I dash downstairs to have my tea and toast before school. I'm excited about today, because Mum told me that when I'm twelve, I can ride my bike into school each day instead of catching the bus. I'm almost twelve, so I'm sure she'll let me.

Anita's in the kitchen, sitting at the table already with Mum. There's something different about Anita. She looks a bit heavier than before. I notice that she has bumps on her chest. Her boobs have started to grow. Without giving it a second thought, I laugh and say, "I see they've just sprouted, then!"

Anita's face goes red and she doesn't know where to look. As it is my birthday next week, I ask Mum if I can have a tape recorder for my present. I would love to have a spool-type tape recorder, just like the one that Mr Booth brought into school for our lessons.

Mum says, "We'll see."

That means yes. This is the first day I will be riding my new chopper bike into school. From now on, it'll be every day. I won't be going on the bus to school any more. After breakfast, I say bye to everyone and I take my briefcase out to my bike. I try to ride with it in my hand, but it's too difficult. I stop to look and see where I can squeeze it in. I notice a gap between the frame and the long seat. Bingo, it fits perfectly. I squeeze it in the gap and I'm on my way. This is great – freedom from the buses. I have a big smile on my face all the way to school. The world is a great place.

Eventually, I arrive at my school. My face, neck, and hands are freezing, but it was worth it. I love my bike.

A week later, and it's my twelfth birthday. I caught the bus into school today, but just for today, because my friend Roger's coming home with me to stay for a sleepover. When we arrive at my house, Roger says, "I have to give you this," as he hands me 50p.

"Wow! Thanks, Rog," I say as I stare down at this sparkly coin he's put in my hand.

I didn't expect that. It was really nice of him; 50p is a lot of money. As Roger and I stand talking in the kitchen, Mum comes in from the living room. She has a lovely warm smile on her face and she looks excited. She says hello to Roger and asks me, "Did you have a nice day?"

I nod to her because I feel a bit embarrassed. I know Roger will take the mickey out of me tomorrow.

She says, "Happy birthday," then hands me my present.

I thank her and I look at the box. It's not a very big box, so I don't think it's going to be my tape recorder. I don't want to look disappointed, but inside my heart's sinking. I'm grateful, though. I start pulling all the wrapping paper off and I see a picture on the side of the box. It looks like a radio, but it says "Recorder" on the box. It's a cassette recorder, not the big spool recorder that I wanted, but it's an up-to-date recorder, with a microphone. I'm really happy with it, but Mum doesn't realise what I really wanted. The most important part was the spools, because that's what they use in *Lost in Space*, like the one Mr Booth had. It doesn't matter. I probably didn't describe what I wanted well enough.

12

Death and more bullies

It's the last day of school before the Christmas holidays. I brought my ball into school today, because our teacher told us we can have an easy day today. It's a grey day, but at least it's not raining. There's a boy whom I play football with after school, because I can stay later now that I don't have to catch the bus. His name's Michael O'Sullivan. He's not exactly a close friend, but we like to play football together, just the two of us, and he's quite a good footballer. The school day draws to an end and we all file out for the holidays.

Roger and Charlie say goodbye to me and they make their way over to the bus stop and everyone's in high spirits. As always, I go and meet Michael on the school field between the two schools to kick around, and we practise our tackling. It starts to get a bit cold and dark, so I call over to Michael, "I'm going home now!"

Michael calls back, "Come on, it's not that late!"

I call back, "You only live across the road, but I have to ride miles back with a football. It's not easy."

"Okay, I'll take the ball back to my house," he says.

With that, he tackles past me, laughs, and shouts back, "See you after the holidays!"

That's good, because I can ride my bike more easily now and I'll be able to get it back after the school holidays.

A couple of days into the holiday and I'm outside, bouncing a tennis ball against the side of the house with James. Mum calls me in. She looks worried.

"John, look at the newspaper. Did you know this boy?" she asks. She hands yesterday's *Evening Echo* to me. "He went to your school," she adds.

I look at the newspaper and in large bold letters it says,

"BOY DROWNS AT WATFORD SWIMMING BATHS."

Underneath those words, there's a photo of Michael.

I'm frozen to the spot. Surely this is a mistake? But it's not. He's dead.

Every night following this, I lie on my bed, thinking about how Michael would have died, and it takes a long time for me to fall asleep. A few days later, I wonder if I should go and ask for my football back. Would that be wrong? Maybe I should ask Mum to see what she thinks. There hasn't even been a funeral yet, but Mum says, "Of course you should. It's your ball."

I take a carrier bag to put my ball into and ride to Michael's house. When I arrive there, I place my bike on its stand on the pavement. I open the single iron gate and walk along the garden path. I feel nervous. I'm worried about what they'll say to me. I stand at the front door and gently tap the door knocker. There's no answer. I ring the doorbell and very quickly a nice blonde lady opens the front door. As soon as she sees me, she starts to cry, but she's smiling at the same time. I feel terrible now and I don't know what to say, but I have to ask her.

"Hello, sorry to disturb you, but I think Michael has my ball. Can I have it back, please?" I say.

Still crying, his mum, who seems to be such a nice lady, smiles at me as if she wants to tell me to come in and talk to her.

"Are you Michael's friend who he plays football with?" she asks.

"Yes, I'm John," I reply. "Can I have my ball please?"

"Yes, of course you can," she says, smiling through her tears.

She runs upstairs to his room and gets my ball and then she hands it to me and asks me, "Is this the one?"

"Yes, that's it," I reply.

She hands it to me and I thank her, then start bouncing it down the garden path towards my bike. I feel sad for her.

I place my ball into my carrier bag and hang it on my handle bars. I glance back towards her front door and she's still standing there. She looks like she's shaking but, still smiling.

I say, "Goodbye."

She says "Bye" very quietly, then half waves to me and goes back into her house.

I can't know what she's going through. I feel bad for taking my ball.

Every week, for our pocket money, James and I get 10p. It's pocket money day today, as it's Friday, and I'm taking James up to the toy shop, which is on the corner of Bushey Mill Lane and St Albans Road. This shop is great. They sell matchbox cars here and they have them all on display in the window. We normally buy a car each and it's an exciting time choosing which one we want. They sell Jaguars, Rolls-Royces, Cortinas, Capris, Minis, buses, and all sorts. We have quite a big collection between us and whenever we get a new car, we always try to make sure it doesn't get bumped. We play a lot of games with the cars, making up voices for the kind of people who would drive a certain make. Obviously, the man driving the Rolls-Royce would be very posh and a sporty car would be driven by a posh man's son and so on.

The winter evenings draw in and Christmas is upon us: it's Christmas Eve. Mum and Dad have gone down to the social club for the evening. Anita and James are watching TV. I'm so bored. I decide to make some recordings on my new tape recorder. I know I haven't got anything for Christmas, because my tape recorder was for my birthday and Christmas. I spend the whole evening worrying about what'll happen when they arrive home. As soon as I hear them come in, I pretend to be asleep, because James still thinks that Father Christmas comes to him. I might get a stocking full of sweets. That's if they don't argue.

Luckily, they don't. I hear Mum come into our room, rustling presents, and then she goes to bed. Christmas morning, James is opening his presents. I have slippers, socks and a stocking full of chocolate bars. Dad is in the kitchen with Mum, laughing about bathing the turkey in the kitchen sink. That doesn't happen often. It's quite a boring Christmas for me, but I enjoy my dinner and I sit eating my chocolate watching all the Christmas TV. It's over very quickly and this year I'm glad it's over.

It's January, 1973. I feel fed up with never having any money. I wish I could get a paper round, so I can earn some, but Mum says you have to be thirteen, so I'll have to wait until November. That's ages away and all I ever seem to have at the most is 10p. Time moves on and before long the winter is on the way out and I'm now well established in my senior school. Roger and I know just about everybody. Since we have been doing drama lessons, which is my favourite lesson, everyone wants to watch our comedy plays, and they plead with us to put on a show for them during breaktime. Our drama teacher says that she looks forward to seeing what we'll do every week.

We do impersonations of TV celebrities and all our teachers. We also make up our own characters for our plays. We've become celebrities in a small way in our own school. It feels good and I enjoy going to this school now. Sometimes we can't stop laughing at our own plays, so it makes them hard to get through, but somehow we always do. Our teachers sometimes request during lessons that we do impersonations of them, because of the reputation we have. I enjoy English, because we have the prettiest teacher anyone could ask for, Miss Wynn. Maths is okay, but Mr Veal, our maths teacher, is so dumb and all he wants to do is chat the girls up. We do impressions of him a lot. History's ridiculous, because of Mr Lacey, our history teacher; he can't control the class and everyone's throwing things around, talking among themselves, or climbing out of the windows during lessons.

Roger and I do impressions of him trying to control the class. Geography's a subject I really am interested in, but we have a teacher who could make the End of the World sound boring, so I almost fall asleep during each lesson and I don't learn anything. Carpentry's good, but when the teacher, Mr Dunning, comes over to help me, his breath's so bad that I have to hold my breath until I'm blue and then try to remember what he said. As for PE: that's the joke of the century. We all get left to our own devices, while the male PE teachers spend the whole lesson, normally a double lesson, chatting up the female PE teachers. Football at school is the absolute worst. Mr Ridgewell blows the whistle to start play, then immediately walks off to start his chatting-up session. We're all left to play a match which is just a free for all. Nobody passes the ball to anyone and everyone just runs after it like a load of chickens following their mother.

We never win a match against any other school – we always lose. Needless to say, Roger and I just stand on the side lines, practising our comedy acts and kicking mud up.

The ball heads in our direction, like a comet with a tail made of kids. We both let it go straight past. Everyone screams at us, "Why didn't you stop it?"

We make a joke about it and they just accept it. Nobody stays mad at us for long. We've learnt who the bad boys are in this school: there's Chassell, the only black boy in the school. There's Kevin Gilmartin – he acts like he's tough, but he's really just thick. Then there're the Coleman twins: Steve Coleman and Ray Coleman. They go around during break at school bullying all the younger kids. They already got Roger, but I've avoided it so far. During lunch breaks, Roger and I have taken to following the Colemans around to see what they do. I think they're thick, too, as they never notice we're following them and the good thing is, if we're watching them, they can never catch us by surprise. They're two years above us, so they're Anita's year, along with Chassell and Kevin Gilmartin. They're a lot bigger than the kids in my year. One time, we were following the Colemans and as we walked around the back of the science block, we saw Chassell fighting with Mr Veal. Chassell punched him in the face and gave him a black eye. That was the day he got expelled. I think the Colemans were going to meet Chassell there that day and it could have been much worse for Mr Veal.

The day they got Roger, they were laughing at his briefcase and they had some string with them. They tied him up with his briefcase on his back and started rolling him down the hill to St Catherine's. I couldn't do anything to help, because they pointed to me and said, "Don't you try anything!"

They walked away, laughing, when Roger was halfway down the hill. I ran down to untie him.

"Why didn't you do anything to help me?" he asked.

I replied, "I'm sorry, but I forgot my cape and utility belt this morning. What could I do?" as I struggled with the tight knots. "I'm helping you now, aren't I?"

Roger was angry, but he laughed anyway.

I said, "Come on, let's go back up to the school and just forget about it."

Easter comes and goes, and before long it's the school summer holidays. At least eight weeks off school – no more getting up early in the morning for a while. The summer seems very hot this year. James is getting older and he's allowed to go out with me on my bike. It's great, because it's a chopper bike and it has a long seat which is plenty long enough for two people, but the passenger has to dangle their legs, because there's nowhere to put their feet. It's hard on James, but he doesn't seem to mind. The first place we stop is at the shop on the way to get a can of drink each to have on the ride. We stop at the newsagents on Bushey Mill Lane, just over the railway track. James always wants either Coke or lemonade. I've taken a liking to limeade and lager. It's a soft drink but it makes me feel more grown up, because it has lager in it. We carry on with our drinks down Woodmere Avenue, towards the A41. We cross over to the other side of the dual carriageway, where there's a bridleway we can ride along. This is heaven – a really hot day, a ride on my great bike, and a can of ice-cold limeade and lager to keep me cool. The drink tastes so good and being able to share this time with my little brother makes it even better.

As we ride along the bridleway, the latest songs that are always on the radio play in my head. "Candle in the Wind" by Elton John is my favourite. After a while, I stop for a break and put my bike on its stand, then sit on the grass, admiring it. It gives me time to talk to James to ask him how school's going. He talks about the new friends he's made and which teachers he likes. Just big brother and little brother talking about our world. We both enjoy this time together, away from home. It starts to turn a little cooler, so we head back home, not thinking that these will be happy memories that hopefully both of us will keep for the rest of our lives.

Recently, James has been asking if he can have a rabbit. We haven't been buying cars from the corner shop for a while, so I've got some pocket money saved and James has money for his birthday, too.

It's morning. I've just woken up to the sound of Mum shouting, "Bad dog!"

Sooty has raided the larder again. I didn't get to sleep until late last night, because James kept talking about rabbits. He's still asleep, but I always wake up early. Dad is at work, so I rush downstairs, still in my pyjamas, to ask Mum if we can have rabbits. She's picking up eggshells that Sooty has broken all over the floor. I know it's not a good time to ask, but I would like to make James happy.

"Mum, do you mind if James and I have rabbits?" I ask in my most responsible voice.

On one knee with the dustpan in one hand and the brush in the other, she looks around with a red angry face and says, "Rabbits? You can look after them, then."

Wow! That was so easy.

"Yes, of course I will," I reply, trying to contain my excitement.

I close the door calmly, then sprint back up to James to wake him up with the good news.

"James! Wake up! Wake up! It's morning. We're going to the pet shop!" I shout.

I'm about to grab and shake him when he jumps up, rubbing his eyes.

"Are we really?" he asks in a croaky voice.

"Yes, quick! Come on," I say impatiently. "Get dressed. We're going to get you a rabbit!"

"Can he stay in my bedroom?" he asks.

"No, he can stay in Guinea's old hutch," I reply.

For the next couple of weeks, James and I make many trips to the pet shop. Now James has a black rabbit, called Bunty. I have another guinea pig, called Guinea, and I also get two more rabbits, one named Bunion, who's grey – he's just a baby – and the other one is named Snowy. He's older and much bigger. He's an albino, with grey eyes. He gets on well with Guinea, and Bunty gets on well with Bunion.

I decide to make a partition to create two rooms in the hutch, so they're all happy. Guinea quickly establishes himself as the boss of Snowy and occasionally he breaks the door down to enter Bunty and Bunion's room. They both raid the joint once they get in. Guinea uses Snowy as a distraction while chomping away at their food. Snowy is so big and he sits in the way like a bodyguard for Guinea. Carrots are dragged back into their own room. I make sure it gets replaced, though. It's fun taking care of them all and James loves them, too. I'll make sure all of them have plenty of hay this time.

This long summer holiday is drawing to an end and we haven't gone away on holiday anywhere this year, but I've filled it with as many fun things as possible. I've exhausted all the usual games I play with James, like hiding his teddy bears, Biddy and Panda, normally at the top of a ladder or on a roof. Well, I have to entertain myself as well as him, don't I? The thing that I really want to do now is earn some money. I decide to make a trip down to the local newsagent to ask if I can have a paper round, but he asks my age and says the same thing as Mum. I have to be thirteen.

13

Becoming a teenager

It's 9 November 1973, my thirteenth birthday, and at last I'm a teenager.

The greatest thing about being thirteen is getting a paper round. I'm almost a grown up and I'm finally going to have my own money. Last week, I went into the office of *The Evening Echo* local newspaper. They arranged for me to start my new round tomorrow and I can't wait. I'm going to be earning £1.60 a week. I have to deliver the papers every evening and on Thursday I collect the money from all the customers. It's Monday and I'm on my chopper bike, riding home from school. It's a drizzly day and I'm going straight down to collect my bag of papers.

As I arrive, a flustered-looking lady allocates my round to me. I have all the door numbers and road names on a card, with an account of who's paid and who hasn't. I count up how many papers I need and put them in my fluorescent orange *Evening Echo* paper bag. I take the bag out to my bike and tie it across my handlebars. This is a great feeling. I'm working my first job and I feel so important. As I ride along the road, I check my address list and notice there are a few houses in Bushey Mill Lane and then all of Woodmere

Avenue. What a doddle. I have it done in no time and they're going to pay me loads of money for this?

But then comes the day when I have to collect the money. Nobody ever seems to be in, except the old people. I have to keep a record and call back later in the evening to get everyone paying up to date. I always manage it, except for one. He says he paid already, but he hasn't and I have to stop his papers.

After a week or so of getting paid, I start to enjoy earning the money and it's easy enough, so I want to have even more. I ride down to the local newsagents and I ask him for a morning paper round.

He says, "Yes, start tomorrow."

A week later and the newsagent asks me if I can do another paper round as well and I jump at the chance.

Wow! Now I'm earning triple the money.

Each morning, my alarm now goes off at 5:30. I'm up and gone, regardless of the weather, to do both my morning paper rounds and, after school, my evening round, but most of the time I'm home by 6pm. It's amazing how much money I'm accumulating. I have pounds and pounds. I'm rich. I can buy whatever I want.

It's early December, 5.30am, and it's freezing outside. My alarm's just gone off. I grab the clock instantly to stop the metal bells waking everyone else up. It's dark and it seems like it's the middle of the night. I'm warm and cosy in my bed and it's like heaven. Here goes. I drag myself out of bed quickly to get it over with. I have to be quiet, so as not to wake James or anyone else in the house. I don't bother with breakfast; it's far too early. My bike's always on the patio now, so I can't get blamed for any scratches Dad finds on his car. It's completely white with frost. I boil some water and pour it over the seat to get the ice off, then dry it with a tea towel and away I go. The nice thing about this time of morning is nobody else is around and there's not a single car on the road. The patterns made by the ice as people sleep cover all the parked cars and house windows. Frozen cobwebs on garden gates resemble thin white rope. It's so calm and peaceful. I arrive at the newsagents and push the door open with a ding from the bell. Mr Newman, the owner, is there as usual, marking up piles of newspapers with door numbers. It's a small shop and he constantly has a cigarette in his mouth. It's like fog inside the shop with the smoke. As I walk through the door, he says, "Morning, young man," with his grouchy voice, then starts coughing with his cigarette stuck to his lower lip.

"Good morning, Mr Newman," I reply.

"There're a lot of papers," he says as he points to a huge bundle of newspapers with his black felt tip pen.

I reply, "Thank you, Mr Newman," then load them into my bags.

"Can I have four ounces of black jacks and four ounces of fruit salads, please? Oh, and four ounces of Mojos?" I ask him.

"Dear oh dear, you'll have no teeth left, young man!" he shouts over as he starts measuring out my sweets on his scales. He hands me the three white paper bags of sweets. "That'll be 12p, please!"

I hand him my money. "Thanks, Mr Newman," I reply.

I stumble through the shop doorway with a newspaper bag over each shoulder and they're almost as big as me. I lock my bike up outside the shop with my new combination lock that I bought last week – the combination number's 458. Then I start walking along with my papers. This is fun. Early morning has become a special time, just for me.

As I walk from house to house, with the sound of each footstep echoing in the quiet streets, I dip into my sweets and unwrap them. This is my own happy little world; it's so relaxing. But this is the coldest day I've done my paper round so far and I realise near the end my hands are freezing and my fingers are going numb. I finish my round and go back to the newsagent's shop to collect my bike. My bike lock's sticking and I can't use my fingertips to unlock it, but after a struggle I manage to free it. I jump on and start my ride home. I have no handle grips, because they split and came off a long time ago. As I turn into Sandringham Road, I realise my hands are actually sticking to the metal of my handlebars. I never knew that could happen just because of the cold. I wheel my bike in and my hands look blue. Everyone's still in bed. I better warm them up quickly. I have an idea.

I turn on the gas hob and, with a real struggle, strike a match and light the gas. I straight away put both of my hands over the gas hob to try to thaw them out quickly, but then, oh my God, the pain in my fingers. I've never felt such pain in my life. It feels like my fingers are being crushed at the ends: every one of them. I crouch down with my hands between my thighs in agony. What on earth has just happened? I stay crouched down, holding my hands there, and just praying for the pain to stop. Eventually it starts to ease and then goes away. I'll never ever do that again. I'll have to buy some gloves with my money.

Lately, we keep having power cuts, because of the coal miner's strikes, so we never know when the lights will go off. It's a bit scary, as all the street lights go off as well, at exactly the same time. When we're walking around the house, we suddenly can't see at all, so we have to feel our way around. Tonight's one of those nights. Luckily, Mum's prepared for it, and she manages to get some candles lit. It's like being back in Ireland, except at least we have toilets. Even the shops in the city centre don't have power, so they're using candles. It's really weird and quite eerie. I think all these power cuts have spooked a lot of people, especially us kids. Mum, James, and I are all sitting in the living room. Luckily, we've had our dinner because we have a gas cooker. Anita walks in and says to Mum, "Mummy, my friend's been doing the Ouija board each evening. Can we do it?"

Mum says, "Okay, but your dad won't approve, because he hates all that stuff."

Dad's working late, but he'll be home soon. Anita doesn't waste a second; she starts cutting out letters and numbers to make a board, because she doesn't have a real board. She puts all the numbers and letters in a circle on our round table in the living room. She tells Mum, James, and me to all sit around the table and she puts a glass in the middle. We all have to rest one finger on the glass and Anita starts to ask in a spooky voice, "Is there anybody there?"

Just as she starts, Dad walks in and says, "What's that? What are you doing?"

Mum tells him and he says, "I'm not doing it with you!", but he doesn't stop us.

He walks out to have his dinner in the kitchen, then comes back into the living room and puts his feet up. There's only flickering light in the room from the open fire and a couple of candles. All I can see is the table with all the letters and numbers on it, along with the glass with everyone's fingers resting on it. Anita says again, "Is anybody there?"

Something strange happens. I feel the need to guide the glass towards the letter "y" for yes. Somehow it seems easy, like it glides there. Everyone seems a bit worried.

Mum asks, "Who's there?"

Nothing happens. Then Mum asks Dad's mother's name, because he never knew his mum. Somehow, I know her name was Kathleen and I move the glass again, easily, to spell it out carefully.

Then Mum asks, "Is she alive?"

Again, I know she isn't and I spell out the letters, "d-e-a-d".

The scariest part is yet to come.

Mum asks, "Where did she live?"

I know the answer and I spell out the town, but I don't know how.

But then Mum asks, "What did she die of?"

I guide the glass to spell out the word "c-a-n-c-e-r". In years to come, we will discover that all these things are true. There were no voices, no shaking of the glass, and no wind blowing through the room like in a horror movie. I start to feel agitated, and when Mum asks more questions, I spell out, "Leave me alone!"

They carry on asking questions, and I spell out, "What did I tell you? Leave me alone!"

I know I was moving the glass, but it didn't feel like I was – it felt like I was being guided.

Mum stands up. "Stop now … We'd better stop now …" she says quietly.

Anita starts packing it away. The next thing I know, the lights are back on and everyone's sitting in silence, looking stunned. I start thinking about what just happened and I feel spooked.

I don't even know what cancer is. Dad leaves the living room to go to the bathroom and comes back down.

"Come on now!" he says. "Everyone off to bed."

The three of us kiss them both goodnight and we all head off to bed, but then there's a horrific scream from Anita. "There's a ghost at the top of the stairs!" she shouts.

Frozen to the spot, I look up, only to see Dad's hung his white vest on the landing lampshade as a joke.

It's now spring of 1974. Sunday, just after lunch, and Dad's been down to the club for a drink without Mum. On the way back, he crashed his car into the back of somebody else's and I think he was drunk, because he doesn't seem too bothered about it. Later in the evening, he tells Mum he's going to get it repaired and trade it in for a new car, because it's the second accident he's had in it. He says it must be because the car's green and green cars are unlucky. Nothing to do with his being drunk when he was driving it. Within a few weeks, he does exactly that. He comes back with another Cortina. This one has four doors and the registration number is RNK 966J. I always try to remember the car registration numbers. Maybe it's weird, but I do. Anyway, at last I have my own door on our car and hopefully for good this time. The car looks like a gold colour to me, but I can't tell, because I'm colour blind. Dad calls us all out to see our new car.

"What do you think?" he asks with a proud smile.

Anita runs her hand along the paintwork and says, "It's really nice."

I say, "It's a nice colour. I like gold."

"Don't be stupid, John!" he replies. "It's metallic green!"

Embarrassed, I try to brush over my comment and reply, "But I thought green cars are unlucky?", with a cheeky smile.

"You're quick enough that way, aren't you? Go into the house!" he snaps at me.

I do as he says and leave them to it.

A month or so later, it's early evening and he's late home from work. Mum has just had a phone call from the hospital to tell her he's been involved in a car accident while he was driving his van. They say he was turning right at a junction when he ran out of petrol and the side of his van was hit by a concrete mixer lorry. They say it was a bad accident and he will have to stay in hospital. Anita's screaming and crying. Mum looks dazed.

Anita looks at me and says, "John, Daddy's been in a car accident!"

She's looking at me to respond in the same way as she has, but I can't. I don't feel anything. I don't even care. If it were

Mum, I don't think I could cope with that news, but him, after all he's done to me? I'm only worried for Mum's sake and, even then, I think she'd be better off without him.

The next day he's back at home. He has three broken ribs and he's bandaged up. He sits in his armchair, complaining about the pain and almost crying. I still don't feel anything.

14

A broken family

A few more weeks pass. Dad's completely recovered and everything's back to normal. But then one of Dad's work friends keeps coming around to visit when he's not home. His name's Den Adams and we have to call him "Uncle Den". He comes to our house a lot during the day, while Dad's at work. I don't understand why they lock the living room door when they're in there and tell me to go outside to play. I'm thirteen now, so I could stay in there with them. I'm an adult as well.

A couple of months pass. Dad and I are out in the car, dropping rubbish to the dump. As he drives along Bushey Mill Lane, I look over at him and he seems calm and relaxed. I decide to tell him about Uncle Den, because he doesn't seem to know about it.

"Dad, Uncle Den comes to our house a lot, doesn't he?"

"Not that much," he replies.

"Well, he comes a lot when you're not home," I say.

"Does he?" he replies.

"Yeah, why does he lock himself in the living room with Mum and tell me to go outside and play though?" I ask.

Dad looks very angry. Maybe he does care about me after all. Maybe he feels sorry for me being locked out of the living room and told to go out and play at my age.

As soon as we arrive home, he has a big argument with Mum. I don't think he likes Uncle Den.

A week or so later, on a Friday night, Mum tells us that she's going to leave Dad. I think I may have caused all this. Dad's still at work and Uncle Den has arrived in his Triumph Herald car. He knocks at the front door and Mum lets him in.

"Are you all ready?" he asks Mum.

Mum has already packed all our bags.

"Yes!" she replies, looking flustered.

They both start carrying everything out to his car. He has only two doors on his car, so it looks like I'm destined to go around in a two-door car. We all get in and we're on our way, leaving our home. Dad will come home to an empty house this evening.

On the way down the A41, an Alsatian dog runs straight out into the road and stops right in front of Uncle Den's car. He brakes very hard, but in a controlled way, putting his hand out in front of Mum, so that she doesn't hit her head on the windscreen. I can see the dog's eyes staring in shock, but we stop inches from it. I don't think Dad would have done that so calmly. I don't even know where they're taking us, but I'm with Mum and I trust her. We carry on with the journey, down Brockley Hill. I feel panic every time we go down this hill, but Uncle Den stays on our side of the road, where he should be, and doesn't overtake. I feel safe with him driving. Ten minutes later, we turn into Tiverton Road in

Queensberry and we're at Auntie Mary's House. Uncle Den parks the car and Mum rings the doorbell. Uncle Liam answers the door and seems to be expecting us. We all go inside and they're all talking. It starts to get dark and Aunty Mary has a sofa bed already made for James and me in the front room. Anita sleeps in our cousin Eyvonne's room. Mum and Uncle Den sleep upstairs somewhere else.

I fall asleep quickly, because I'm very tired. In the middle of the night, I'm woken by the sound of a car screeching outside the front of the house. I lay still and listen. There's the sound of glass breaking, followed by voices and a knock at the front door. The front door is opened. I can hear Dad and he's brought Uncle Den's wife with him. I hear Uncle Den's voice and his wife shouting. There's a lot of banging and Dad has punched Uncle Den. He really doesn't like him.

Uncle Liam is saying, "You two go outside if you want to fight. You're not doing that in my bloody house!"

Dad's saying sorry to Uncle Liam. The front door has closed and it seems calm. I snuggle into my pillow, but then, *crash*, there's the sound of more glass breaking outside the house. For a while after that I lie in bed, awake, listening to a serious discussion going on through the wall in the dining room between Mum, Dad, Uncle Liam, and Auntie Mary. Mum and Auntie Mary seem to be on the same side against Dad, while Uncle Liam is saying, "Hang on a minute, you two are trying to drive Maurice straight down the bloody dump!"

I start to feel sorry for Dad when he says, "I want to go and see the kids."

"No, you can't. They're asleep!" Auntie Mary replies.

But the door opens anyway and he walks over towards me in my bed. It's not fair – everyone's against him and I've caused all this trouble. He comes close up to me to see if I'm awake, and I put my arms around his head, pulling him closer to me and hugging him tightly. Standing behind him, Auntie Mary tells him off.

"You're not thinking of the kids, waking them up in the middle of the night, are you?"

He replies sharply, "My kids love me! He nearly pulled the head off me to hug me!"

"Of course they love you, but you should think of them!" says Auntie Mary.

He accepts what she says and they both leave the room. Eventually, despite all this madness, I drift off to sleep.

It's morning. I've just woken up and someone's cooking. I can smell sausages and bacon. *Where am I? Oh yeah, Auntie Mary's house.* James is still asleep next to me. Auntie Mary and Mum are talking in the kitchen. I'm getting up, because I'm starving and I'd love a cooked breakfast. I get dressed quickly and open the kitchen door.

"Good morning, young man. Would you like some breakfast?" Auntie Mary asks me in her usual cheerful way, as she throws more sausages on the frying pan.

"Yes, please!" I reply quietly.

Mum, Dad, and Uncle Liam are sitting at the table. I wonder where Uncle Den is. He must have gone with his wife last night and Dad stayed here. Mum's saying to Dad that she's still going to leave him and go with Uncle Den. I don't want that to happen, because Dad's so upset and he's promising Mum he'll change.

I say to Mum, "Mum, if you leave Dad, I'm going home with him. I don't want to live with Uncle Den!"

Mum looks surprised at me, but doesn't say anything.

Only, I know I'm bluffing. If I really do have to choose, I'll go with Mum, but someone has to be on Dad's side. Dad starts crying and calls me over to give him a hug. I go over to him and hug him. I don't want him to feel like none of us love him. After breakfast, he asks me to come with him, because he needs to get his car fixed and I walk to the front door with him. He tells Mum, "Don't worry. I'll be back with him later."

I'm sure Mum won't leave him if she thinks I'll go and live with him. As we walk down the front garden path, there's broken glass all over the place. The windscreen's smashed on Dad's lovely car. Uncle Den must have done that when he left last night and that's what I heard. Dad clears all the broken glass off the seats and tells me to get in. He drives down the road with glass falling into the car as we go and he's crying so hard.

"Everything'll be okay, Dad," I tell him.

He's like a big child, but I'm supposed to be the child. He looks at me, smiling through his tears, and in a crying voice, he says, "Do you really think it'll be all right, John?"

I smile back, nodding, and reply, "Yes, it will be."

We find a windscreen repair shop and drive straight in. The man hoovers out all the broken glass and puts a new windscreen in the car while we wait in the waiting room.

Within an hour, we're back at Auntie Mary's House. As we walk through the front door, Mum's on the phone in the hallway talking to Uncle Den. Dad takes the phone from her and starts shouting at him,

"I just had to pay £18 for a new windscreen!" he growls and then he hangs up.

They all sit in the living room, talking. Eventually, we all head back home and Dad does seem to be better than he was.

A week later, on Saturday, it's a drizzly day and I'm lying on my bed, bored. Dad opens my bedroom door and asks, "John, will you come out for a drive with me?"

He only ever asks me to go somewhere alone with him for work or some chore, but this time he seems different. I agree to go with him in case he needs me. With us both in the car, he drives to Uncle Den's house and around to the garages on the block where Uncle Den's car is parked, which is about 200 yards from his house. There's nobody around and it's very quiet here. He hands me a hammer and says, "John, go and smash his windscreen with this hammer." My mouth falls open in shock. He's joking, surely.

"Really?" I ask.

He looks frustrated. "Yes, John. Do it quickly. Hit it hard!"

I reply, "But he broke your windscreen because you broke his side window!" – which is what Mum told me.

He looks more frustrated. "John, just do it quick!"

I take the hammer and get out of the car. Walking towards Uncle Den's car, alone, I feel upset and scared. I raise the heavy hammer up over my head and close my eyes tightly as I swing it down to hit the windscreen hard, but it just bounces off. I try again. Gripping it tightly with both hands as hard as I can, I swing it down three times, but it bounces even higher. Dad gets out of the car and takes the hammer from me. He hits it harder, but it still will not break.

"It's making too much noise," he says. "Come on, get back in the car."

I get in with him and he starts driving home. There's silence in the car and then he starts crying again, but this time I don't comfort him – he's still doing the same things. Things that I don't understand.

During the school holidays, Mum tells Dad that she wants to go on holiday for a week to Great Yarmouth and stay in a caravan in a caravan park, instead of going to Ireland, like we normally do. Dad doesn't want to go, and so Mum says she will take Anita, James, and me there without him.

He accepts it. So things must be changing, at least towards Mum. Anita gets involved in booking the holiday and somehow gets to arrange for her new boyfriend to come as well. I can't believe who her new boyfriend is. It's Kevin Gilmartin, one of the "problem boys" from our school. Anyway, I'm not bothered, as he'll be with Anita all the time. A few days before we leave to go on this holiday, I'm lying on my bed, staring at the ceiling and thinking about how it'll be to sleep in a caravan, as I've never done it before. I imagine it would be like sleeping in the Jupiter 2 spaceship from *Lost in Space*. I imagine it to be all silver and shiny inside, with no dust, just sparkling clean and modern. I'm so excited, but eventually I doze off anyway with that thought in my head.

Very soon, the day of our holiday is here. It's morning and we're on our way to Watford Junction to catch the train. The journey doesn't take long and we've arrived at the station in Great Yarmouth. We make our way out of the train station, dragging heavy luggage behind us, and Mum's trying to find out how to get to the holiday park. It's pouring rain. She approaches one of the waiting taxis and asks the driver for directions. He looks over at us with all our luggage and I think he feels sorry for us.

He says, "Look, it's pouring rain. I'll take you there."

Mum says, "No, it's okay, I just need to know which bus to catch."

"Just get in the taxi," the driver replies, impatiently, "I'll take you!"

"Well, how much will that be?" Mum asks nervously.

"I'll take you there for 50p," the driver replies.

Mum accepts his offer and we all get in. Thank God for that. It's not long before we arrive at the park. Our clothes are damp from the rain, but at least it's easing now. Anita finds reception, where they give Mum the keys to our caravan.

We walk across a wet field to where our caravan is pitched, and come across rows and rows of caravans – some of them really do look like spaceships. I hope ours does, too. A couple of minutes later, Anita calls out, "This is our one!"

I follow Mum to have a look. I can't believe it: ours looks like it's a hundred years old and it's all dirty and rusty. Anita opens the door for us to go in and we all file inside.

Mum looks worried. "We'll have to sort the beds out," she says.

She stumbles across a bed that folds up into the wall. She opens it up to get it ready and a swarm of moths flies out all over us. There must be hundreds of them. Mum and Anita both scream so loudly that my eardrums hurt while they desperately try to get out, but they can't, because we're standing in the way. The whole musty, mouldy caravan is shaking with the commotion.

Mum marches straight to reception to complain, but they say we have to stay in this one because it's the only one that's available. Mum and Anita start to clean it inside, while James, Kevin Gilmartin, and I play a game of football outside. Whenever I think of Kevin's second name, I always laugh, because Dad always calls him Kevin Go-martin for some reason. Kevin doesn't like that, so I think he's glad Dad's not here with us. During our game, Kevin kicks the ball high into the air towards the caravan. I run to kick it back, watching the ball as it comes down. Then, with a thud, I run straight into the metal towing frame on the front of the caravan.

I whack my shin on the sharp edge and it hurts like hell. I'm lying on the ground, holding it and waiting for the pain to stop. Kevin runs over in a panic. "Are you okay, John?" he asks.

As the pain starts to ease, I answer him, "Yea, I'm okay."

He can't be as bad as people say.

Sleeping in this caravan at night is nothing like I thought it would be – it smells and it's all wooden. It's like sleeping in an old person's house who never cleans.

This holiday is rubbish so far. During the day, there's nothing much to do, except go to the museum in a dilapidated hall. It reminds me of a school hall with a load of dunce kids running around. Night time is even worse: we go to the same place, except the adults get to have a drink there. It's one of those evenings. Mum's talking to a stupid man, who's trying to pretend he's posh. Oh no, she's trying to pretend that she's posh, too. While they try to impress each other, Anita's with Kevin and I'm just standing here with James. The best part of this holiday is when we go to sleep at night and I watch Kevin bang his head against the wall every time he dozes off, which makes him jump and wake up. He keeps doing that for about an hour.

After what seems like a very long week and a long boring journey back, we finally arrive home. Dad's there to greet us. The house is really clean and the fridge is full of lovely food. He's smiling at Mum and he shows her all the food that he's bought. He doesn't even seem to notice us, well, not me anyway. All his attention is on Mum. If things were like this all the time, I'd be happy. I don't care if he doesn't bother with me, so long as he's nice to Mum.

The following week, Dad says to Anita, James, and me that he's going to take us out for a walk and leave Mum to have some time on her own. He says he'll drive us somewhere nice and we'll all walk together. He's never done that before without Mum, so things are changing, maybe. We all get into the car and say goodbye to Mum. It's a warm, sunny day and Dad drives down Woodmere Avenue, where my paper round is. We cross the A41, where he parks by the entrance to the bridleway. This is where James and I always go on my bike. I won't tell him that, though. I don't want to spoil it for him. He thinks he's taken us somewhere new.

He gets out of the car and Anita follows.

"Come on, John and James, get out!" Anita calls out impatiently.

She's like Dad's temporary wife when Mum's not around, and my temporary mum. James and I both get out, then Dad and Anita start to walk ahead, down the bridleway. I follow with James. Am I supposed to look around like I've never seen this place before, when I've seen it a hundred times or more? Do I walk behind Anita and Dad and just be glad he's taken us all here?

I don't feel like he's taking us down here because he wants to. It seems strange to me. I've only felt close to him once in my life so far and that was when he was crying in the car to me when Mum was leaving him. He was like a big lost baby that day – he needed me to make him feel better. After around fifteen minutes of walking with James behind Anita and Dad, bored out of my mind, Anita notices a car parked in the woods. It's a funny place for a car to be parked and it looks damaged. Dad walks over to have a look.

Between him and Anita, they decide the car must have been stolen and then driven down here and dumped. It's a Rover and it's not that old, so they're probably right. Anita acts like a detective and she's coming up with all the possible ways the car could have got here. We have to start walking back quickly to find a phone box and Dad's going to call the police. Anita's all geed up with excitement. Well, I suppose it is a bit exciting, as we've never seen a stolen car before, but at least the police will be on Dad's side this time.

They're walking so fast ahead of us. James has to almost run and I'm getting a stitch. Anita keeps looking around. "Come on!" she keeps calling.

James gets grumpy and then stops. I have to encourage him to keep going. Eventually, we arrive at the phone box. I can hear the operator asking, "Which service, please?"

Dad excitedly shouts "Police!", then goes on to explain.

Very quickly, the police arrive in their blue Wolsey, with a blue flashing light on the roof. They stop by the entrance of the bridleway and ask Dad, "Where did you see the stolen car, sir?"

"I'll show you. Follow me!" he replies.

He gets back into our car, where we're all waiting, and drives like a maniac along the bridleway, quickly followed by the police car. Cars are not even allowed on this bridleway, but suddenly Dad's Jack Regan from *The Sweeney*. We arrive at the stolen car and Dad gets out.

"Wait here!" he says to all of us.

Anita gets out anyway and goes with him, because she's the detective in her eyes. The policeman looks at Dad like he's a maniac and I know why. We could have easily run someone over on the bridleway. Anita and Dad are talking to the policeman by the stolen car. James and I watch from our car. The policeman starts talking on his two-way radio, while they stand watching him. I hear the policeman say, "Thank you for reporting it. The car was stolen."

Dad and Anita get back into our car and we slowly drive down the bridleway to go home. It was exciting, but it was embarrassing as well, seeing how the policeman looked at Dad.

On the way back, Dad's saying to Anita, "Panda one to Panda two."

Anita's laughing, saying, "Come in Panda one."

I wish my dad were normal.

15

School fights and happy days with friends

It's near the end of the school holidays of 1974. I've noticed lately that my chopper bike seems smaller than when I first got it, but it can't be, so I must have grown. I think I need a bigger bike and, with all the money I've made, I might be able to buy one, or at least put a deposit on one and pay the rest on HP. I have a look in Chorlton's book; it's the catalogue that Mum buys things from. I find a racing bike: it has 26-inch wheels; it's red; and it has five derailleur gears. It looks great and it's plenty big enough for me. The price is £37.99 and it's a Royal Enfield. It has blue plastic mudguards and proper racing handlebars with white tape on them. I ask Mum to help me order it and tell her that I'll pay the deposit and pay the rest each week. Mum says, "Yes, of course." I love my mum.

From the day I get my bike ordered, I can't stop reading the advertisement for it over and over. I keep looking at the pictures and dreaming of having it here now. I ask Mum, "How long will it take to arrive?"

"A week to ten days," she replies as she dusts the dining-room table.

Oh no, that's forever. Every day for a week I keep looking through the living-room window hoping to see it arrive. One week goes by, then eight days, then nine days. It must be arriving tomorrow, if this is the ninth day. On the tenth day, I sit waiting by the window all day. A delivery van arrives. *Yes! This must be it.* The man opens the back door of his van and takes out a small parcel, then rings next door's doorbell. The same thing happens the next day and the day after that. Another day passes and I have to go back to school.

The summer holidays are over. It's a grey and damp morning. I wheel my old chopper bike from around the back, then dry the seat off and head to school. It's my first day back and I don't have my new bike.

I'm in the second year now and it's become a drag already. I just want to ride my new bike. On the way home, it's still drizzly and damp. As I ride along the pavement, past the bus station, I start worrying, *What happens if they deliver my bike when nobody's home? Will they take it away and will this have to start all over again?* My chopper bike's looking worn out now. I had to put a new tyre on the front and they didn't have a black one, so I had to put a white one on it. The windscreen has split; it has no handlebar grips; the gears are broken, so it's stuck in third gear, which is really hard to ride uphill; and it's too small for me. I arrive home and put my bike on its stand. Opening the back gate, I glance to my right and, to my surprise, it's here. My new bike is actually here! I'm elated. It's leaning against the wall, with cardboard taped all over it to stop it from getting scratched. I've just risen from the pits to the clouds. Straight away, I start pulling all the tape and cardboard off. Its sparkling spokes and shiny paintwork look fantastic.

Within minutes, I'm on my new bike and testing it out down the road. It's just great – the gears click so smoothly, and boy is it fast. This is the fastest I've ever gone. I can feel my hair being swept back and the wind on my face. It's so great and it's making my eyes water. It's so easy to ride as well, so much lighter than my chopper bike. I ride around for hours before I get hungry and come home for my dinner. Mum must be fed up hearing me go on about my bike this evening, but I'm like a compressed spring with the excitement.

It's Friday morning. I'm about to do my paper round and the back tyre's flat. I can't believe it. I've only had it for a week. I know how to fix it, because I've done loads of puncture repairs on my old bike, but there's no time. Luckily, I still have my chopper bike, so I'll use that today and fix the puncture tomorrow. I go and do my paper round, feeling a bit disheartened, and then it's straight off to school.

For a while at school, I've been noticing John Flanagan and Mick Casey have been acting like bullies. They've been working their way around some of the quiet kids and beating them up. They've been through a lot of the kids in our year, and the first years as well. John Flanagan's not normally a bad boy, but just loud. Mick Casey thinks he's something special, and there's something about him I hate, but I'm not scared of either of them. So far, they've left me alone, but today at four pm, when we all leave to go home, it looks like it's my turn. I unlock my chopper bike and put my briefcase between the frame and the seat, as I always do, and start riding home.

I ride past all the other kids who are walking down the slope of the underpass to get to the other side of the A405.

As I turn to go under the underpass, standing there are Mick Casey and John Flanagan. I think nothing of it and I go to ride through. Suddenly, there's a loud bang with an echo from the walls of the underpass and my bike wobbles. One of them has kicked my briefcase out from under my seat. It's shot out, hit the wall, and flung open. All of my work has fallen out and there's paper everywhere. Mick Casey claps his hands together and shouts out, "Nice one, squirrel!"

A popular saying from the song, "Nice One, Cyril".

I look at him in disbelief, then at my work on the ground that I've worked hard on. His clapping and smug laughing hit me like a bus. They think it's okay to treat people this way and I'm just one in a line to be bullied for their entertainment. I've never felt so angry. I feel like there's a calmness in me but also the determination to teach both of them a lesson.

I calmly get off my bike and put it on its stand. I can still hear the laughter. I pick up all my work and put it back in my briefcase. There's more laughter. I put my briefcase back under my seat. With Mick Casey still ridiculing and laughing, I walk over to him. I'm sure he can see in my eyes what's going to happen. His taunting laughter turns instantly to fear. For the first time in my life, I throw a punch, full-on, straight in his face on his left cheek. He falls backwards and hits his head on the wall of the subway, then falls forwards towards me. I punch him again. Right on his nose and blood spurts out. John Flanagan's shouting, "Stop! Stop!"

SON OF AN ORPHAN FATHER

I can hear girls that have just walked around the corner into the subway and they're screaming. All of it sounds muffled to me. I punch him again in the stomach. John Flanagan's pulling me and shouting, "Look what you've done to him. Stop!"

I start to calm down and his voice becomes clearer. I'd lost control. I wanted to kill him. I become aware of my surroundings again. Then I see how much of his blood is everywhere. It's all over the subway wall, on the ground, on his face, and his clothes are covered in it.

I don't know what came over me, but I can't go through all that again. I get on my bike and ride home, thinking about what happened. I doubt they'll bother me again, that's for sure.

In the morning at school, Sister Anthony talks about what happened, but no names are mentioned and I hear no more about it. A week or so later, John Flanagan wants to be friends with me. He asks if he can come to my house at the weekend.

I say okay and I arrange for Roger, Charlie, and another friend, Dennis, to meet up with us, too.

It's Saturday morning and I'm outside on the patio, fixing the puncture on my new bike. The sun's shining and it's very warm. I've just about finished and Mum calls me. She says, "John, your friend's here!"

John Flanagan walks around the back to meet me.

"What are you doing?" he asks.

"Just finished. I'm pumping my tyre up to test it," I reply.

"Are we going somewhere, then?" he asks.

"Yea, but we'll have to ride to Bushey first to pick Roger up, because he doesn't have a bike."

"I haven't got a bike, either," he says.

"That's okay," I tell him. "My chopper bike has a seat long enough for two, so you can ride that and Roger can go on the back."

He looks happy about that. "Great, let's go!" he says with a grin on his face. Straight away, we head off to meet Charlie and Roger.

"Shall we call for Dennis first?" I ask.

"Yea, okay," John replies.

Dennis is in our class at school and I like him. We call at his house on the way and he comes with us on his bike. We all ride to Charlie's and then straight up to Roger. We pick up Roger and I think it's hilarious watching John struggle to ride my chopper bike with Roger on the back, especially as it's stuck in third gear.

It's not long before John gets tired, so Roger takes over, riding with him on the back. All five of us on four bikes are riding down Little Bushey Lane past the Jewish cemetery towards my house. I'm at the front, then Roger and John, then Charlie with Dennis at the back.

Suddenly, I hear Roger shouting at John: "Take your hands off my eyes! I can't see where I'm going!"

I look behind as they both crash to the ground. I quickly stop my bike to see if they're okay.

"You idiot!" Roger's saying to John. "Why did you do that?"

John finds it hilarious and can't stop laughing.

"You could have killed both of us!" Roger adds.

I pick up my chopper bike and check it over.

"The handlebars are bent!" I tell them, with a shake of my head.

Roger and I try to straighten them, but we can't get them completely straight. We all carry on with the ride. I lead everyone down Imperial Way, where Mum works at Golden Wonder, the crisps depot. It's an industrial area and the road has loads of deep potholes. Some parts are so bad that it floods, but it's great to ride the bikes through. However, John has other ideas. He sees the Golden Wonder crisp lorries parked up and the place is closed.

"Let's get into one of the lorries and nick some crisps!" he says.

"No!" I reply. "My mum works there."

Dennis calls out, "Yeah, I want some crisps. She'll never know!"

Charlie and Roger agree, so I'm outnumbered. The next thing I know, I'm waiting outside Mum's work place, while John climbs the wire fence and onto the back of a lorry that's parked right by the fence. The lorry is not locked. He's in the back, moving boxes of crisps around, as we all watch. Charlie calls up to him, "Get cheese and onion!"

I can't believe I'm standing here while they do this – it's stealing.

John throws a box of crisps over the fence. Charlie catches it and John climbs back over to us. We all get on our bikes and ride towards a field near the park. Roger's riding with John on the back, with a big box of crisps between them. Well, that doesn't look too suspicious, does it. We arrive at the field and all get off our bikes to start eating crisps.

Charlie's complaining to John. "Why did you get salt and vinegar?" he asks with a frown. "I told you to get cheese and onion!"

I hear a man's voice shouting in the distance, "Hey, you lot, wait there!"

We all stuff as many bags of crisps as we can up our jumpers and make a quick getaway. I'm on my new racing bike, so I'm gone like lightning, but the others are not so fast. Right at the back are Roger and John on my old chopper bike. They now have bent handlebars; there're two of them on it; it's a heavy bike; it's stuck in third gear; and, to make matters worse, the only way out of this field is uphill, with a man chasing them. I don't know how they'll get away, but they do and we all ride back to my house. We all go round the back of the house and Mum gives us all orange juice. Roger's taking the mickey out of Mum just after she goes in. He says in a silly voice, "Do you want a cup of squash, John?"

I retaliate by taking the mickey out of his mum. She's a northern lady and when I go to Roger's house, she calls him from the bottom of the stairs, "A war jar."

It doesn't seem to bother him much. Roger and I are always arguing, but we are best friends, so it never lasts long. Last week at school, we started arguing about who lives in the best house during a science lesson. Roger said his house is better than mine; I said it's not and mine's better. Then he said my house was built of mud, so I said his house was built of hay. Then he said my house was built of insects, so I said his house was built of rats. Such a childish argument, but the teacher noticed we were arguing and told us both to get out of class and wait outside the door.

Our heated argument carried on outside the classroom and we started fighting. Needless to say, we both ended up getting "the slipper".

It's starting to get late and everyone heads home. It's been a fun day today and every one of us will remember it hopefully for the rest of our lives. It's not just the end of a great day; it's just about the end of my first summer as a teenager and there've been a lot of happy memories that I'll keep from it. All through the summer this year they've been playing a song on the radio I really like and it's stuck in my head. It's on the radio again as I clean and polish my bike. I think it's number one in the charts. It's called "Seasons in the Sun". I like the music in the song, but it's sad – it's about someone who's about to commit suicide. I think of the fun side of it, not suicide. But I can also relate to the part about being the black sheep of the family. I sometimes wonder if Mum would be okay if I were no longer here.

16

Anxiety and fashion

It's going back to the way it was before Mum left with Uncle Den, at least with me anyway. I still regularly ride my bike down to the river on my own to sit and watch the water flow, while I think about everything. Dad still bullies me most days. I don't think Anita and Mum realise what they're doing, but they seem to support him in what he does. He still hits me for no good reason and puts me down for my existence. I'm still having the same bad nightmares: footsteps getting louder, coming up the stairs towards me, then waking up with a jolt. It's always the day after he's hit me or made me feel bad that I go to the river and think. I don't want to be here any more. I watch the way the water ripples around the rocks, taking different directions, and I go deep into thought. I won't do anything bad, because I couldn't hurt Mum that way. There are two other nightmares I keep having now. One of them is where I walk into my room: it's dark and Anita's in my bed. She sits up and stares straight ahead, with both arms out straight, either side of her. She looks like a vampire in a coffin.

The other one is where I'm standing outside a lift door and, when the door opens, Mum's in the lift. She steps towards me to pull me in with her, but the lift suddenly shoots up with the door still open. I can hear her fading scream. She's screaming, "John!"

But I'm left behind.

If it's not one of these dreams I have, then it's sure to be another. I can remember when I was around five years old. I was sleeping next to Mum in her bed, probably because I was having nightmares even back then. It was very quiet in the house that night and it was late. I was dreaming we were in a rowing boat out at sea and it was pitch black. I could just hear the water splashing. I know now that I was talking in my sleep through this dream. Every so often, I was scared that Mum had fallen overboard, and I kept asking, "Are you in the boat, Mum?"

She was lying next to me and she knew I was dreaming, yet she still kept answering me, dozens of times through the night. "Yea, I'm in the boat," she said.

Maybe I had a fever, but I can't remember. It was only ever the love that I had from Mum that kept me going. I knew I was loved by her then, as only someone who loves you will do something like that.

I think she's scared of Dad, so she doesn't defend me from him. She says that boys need to be smacked. But it always seems to be me.

Time passes quickly, and before I know it November is here and it's my birthday. I'm fourteen years old. I can forget about getting a birthday cake today, because we can't even get any bread. All the bakers are on strike. Dad's gone out to see if he can get some from anywhere. He comes home after an hour and a half, because the queue was so long at the baker's shop.

He tells Mum, "It was the only one that was open!"

Well, at least we have bread now.

I'm getting tired of doing three paper rounds now. I've decided to stop doing the evening one, and one of the morning rounds, too. I told Mr Newman this morning that I only want to do one round from now on. He's not very happy with me, because it's right at the start of winter and he says it's hard to get new paper boys.

It's December, 1974. Roger's come into school with a new Parker pen. It's dark blue, with a silver top. It looks really nice and it sparkles as he writes.

"How much did that pen cost?" I ask him, wondering if I can afford one.

"Thirty-five pence, why do you ask?" he replies.

"I'm going to get one on the way home from school today!" I say, lit up with excitement.

"Well, don't get one the same colour, then!" he says sharply.

"As if, why would I do that?" I reply.

The funny thing is our form teacher, Mr Coutts, has just announced that we have to buy fountain pens, a bottle of ink each, and some blotting paper. Our form class name is 3C. The C is for "Coutts", not the stream.

On the way home, I stop outside Woolworths and go inside to get all my pens and stuff that I need. I see a Parker pen, exactly the same as Roger's, but it's light blue and silver. I prefer light blue anyway, so I'll buy that one. There's a bottle of Quink ink on the shelf and I think, *That's the stuff I need, I'll buy that.* There are lots of different fountain pens, but one stands out: it's black with a chrome lever on the side. I drop that into my basket, too. Oh, he said I might need cartridges, but this pen doesn't need one, because it looks like the lever squeezes a tube that sucks the ink out of the bottle. I can see the blotting paper, so in the basket that goes, too. I take all my new stuff up to the till.

The next morning at school, I show Roger all my stuff. He says he prefers dark his dark blue pen, but it's okay, as they won't get mixed up.

Mr Coutts shouts out, "Quiet, everyone. Can you all get out your fountain pens, as you're going to write an essay."

There are a lot of confused people, trying to figure out how to use the new pens. I get my pen out and take it apart to see how it works. It has like a squeezable bubble in the middle that the lever presses against to make it suck the ink in. I open my ink and reassemble my pen. I put it in the ink and operate the lever. So far so good: it's sucked some ink into it.

After a few minutes, everyone's started writing.

All I can hear around the classroom is, "Oh, God!"

"Oh, damn!"

"Oh, for God's sake!"

I start writing and mine's writing perfectly until I try to put a full stop at the end of a sentence. Every single one of them is the size of a penny. What a stupid pen this is. It keeps letting the ink run through when I'm not writing. Now it's all over my fingers and the middle of what I've just written. I start using my blotting paper, then I notice it's all over the cuff of my white shirt. I grab the pen to stop it leaking any more, but then the ink gets flung down the front of my shirt.

For God's sake! Is this some kind of a joke? What was wrong with the pens we were using? Who would want to use these stupid pens, anyway? Mr Coutts thinks it's funny. All the others are having the same trouble, except Paul Irving, of course, because he's perfect.

Mr Coutts says we have to carry on with them until we get used to them. Eventually I do, but it seems like a lot of trouble for no reason. It's 1974 now, not 1874. Later in the day, I get to use my new blue Parker pen and that's a lovely pen to write with. It's not scratchy like that fountain pen – it's so smooth and no mess.

It's January, 1975, a school day and I've noticed that my friend, Dennis Noonan, is wearing a different pair of trousers to the rest of us. They're still black, but they have a pleated line running from the top of the outside leg all the way down to the bottom. The bell rings for lunch and on the way out to the school grounds, I ask him, "Where did you get them from? I like them."

"Charlie's in the market," he replies.

Saturday morning, I'm straight down to the market, buying a pair, and they look great.

This is the first time I've bothered about what clothes I wear, and it feels good to wear the latest clothes. I need new shoes as well, so I have a look in the shoe shop and there are lots of new styles. They have wedges or platforms and some of them are about three inches high. I buy myself a pair of black wedges. They fit okay, but it feels like I'm standing on a pair of bricks. As soon as I arrive home, I try them on again and ask Mum, "What do you think?"

"Oh, John, they look silly," she replies.

I don't care. I'm going to wear them into school with my new channel trousers. I get used to them quite quickly and when I arrive at school on Monday morning, everyone's asking about them, especially the girls. From this day on, everyone at school seems to be competing on who can get the highest shoes. A couple of months later, high-waist trousers come into fashion: first two buttons, then three buttons, and I'm the first to come into school with four buttons. Everyone says "that's going too far", but within weeks they're all wearing them. Then come the shirts at Charlie's market stall. They have big rounded collars and we're all wearing them, too. *The Sweeney* has become the TV programme that all the boys watch now and I like it, too. It's probably because of the car chases. Jack Regan is the governor and Carter is his assistant. Whenever Regan gives Carter an order, he always says, "Right, Guv!" James and I call him "Right, Guv" now. I think *The Sweeney*'s where the new fashion came from.

I don't think my coat goes with the clothes I wear, though.

Carter has a leather jacket that looks good, so quite quickly I find one like his at Charlie's market stall and buy that, too. This leather jacket has cuffs, so I turn the cuffs back and, boy, do I look cool or what?

Back at school today and it's been a good day. Roger and I have had a lot of fun messing around in class, especially maths. Mr Veal, our maths teacher, is so easy to take the mickey out of and to impersonate. Last lesson today is drama, our favourite. Today we do our best comedy drama of all time: it's about a couple of farm workers in Devon having trouble with a tractor. The whole class, including our teacher, cannot stop laughing. I wish I could do this for a living. I love to hear people laughing. At the end of the drama lesson, our teacher tells us that our performance was so good that she'll be telling the other teachers about it. Just as we are all packing up to leave, the weirdest thing happens. Linda Paget, the girl whom I asked if she wanted to go out with me in the first year, the girl whom my best friends tricked me with, the best-looking, most popular girl in the whole school, comes over to my desk and she's hanging around.

She sits on my desk and says, "You'd be all right if you didn't keep messing around!"

I don't understand what she means: *if I didn't keep messing around*? I don't know what to say to that, so I just shrug. I am who I am and I can't change that. Girls are weird; they confuse me. I pack up my things and go home, and never hear another thing about it.

Anyway, Martin O'Grady, my other friend, is coming to stay at my house tonight. It's winter and very cold outside, so I get my tape recorder out for us to make a comedy audio show on that. It's so funny.

A few days later, as I arrive home from school and put the TV on to watch *Lost in Space*, I hear shouting coming from upstairs. I can hear banging noises and the shouting sounds aggressive. It sounds like a man shouting. It's like when Dad's shouting and it's making me nervous. I can hear Anita screaming and there's only Anita and her boyfriend upstairs.

He sounds like a wild animal up there. I have to go up, in case he hurts her – there's nobody else here.

On autopilot, I run upstairs with my heart pounding and my fists clenched. I get to the bedroom door and it's still going on. I bash the door open and see him fighting with Anita. She's sitting on her bed and he's standing over her. It's Kevin Gilmartin. He stops and looks at me. I stare at him in the eyes, hoping for the best.

"You better go right now!" I say quietly, but with anger in my voice.

I think he can see I mean what I say and, to my relief, without any problem, he just says, "Okay, okay, John. I'm going."

He seems nervous and hasn't noticed that I'm shaking. He has no idea how scared I am. He picks up his coat and walks past me, down the stairs through the front door, and he's gone. Phew! I don't know what I'd have done if I had to fight him.

I guess I would have lost, but he's gone and Anita's okay. Anita says, "Thanks, John."

"That's okay," I reply, still shaking.

I go back downstairs to watch my TV programmes. I suppose they must have broken up today, but I don't understand any of it. What's the point of it? I wonder if it's normal to get as scared as I do in these situations. I always have flashbacks to when Dad's hitting me. I can't tell anyone about it, because they'd think I'm stupid or a coward.

A couple of weeks pass and we're all at school and waiting to go into a double history lesson. The whole lesson is a complete waste of time, because we have Mr Lacey as our history teacher. He's a very gentle man. He's tall and thin, with ginger hair, and he's very well spoken. I feel sorry for him, because he can't control the class. There goes the bell. We all walk into class and sit at our desks. Round one is about to begin: teacher verses kids. As always, Roger and I sit together, near the front of the class, at our double desks. Here we go again, straight away everyone's talking very loudly.

Mr Lacey says, "Okay, can we have quiet please?" in his usual mild voice. "Today we are studying mediaeval Britain!"

He then turns to the blackboard and starts writing on it, while looking at his notes. Nobody takes any notice of him and everyone's still talking very loudly. He carries on writing, regardless, when a paper aeroplane hits him in the back of the head. He turns around and walks towards my desk, moves it very slightly and says, "Stop fooling around!"

It wasn't me who threw the plane. He walks back to the blackboard and I blow a raspberry at him for blaming me. Roger calls him a name, but he carries on writing, when another aeroplane hits him in the back of the head. He ignores it.

Anthony O'Reilly flicks a wet ball of paper from his ruler and that also hits him in the back of the head. He turns around again, with his hair sticking up at the back, caused by the barrage of impacts hitting it, and says, "Okay, this class is in trouble!"

As he speaks, the girls are laughing at him; others are still talking very loudly and Jeremy Clifford is climbing out of the window, while two other boys are having a fight. John Flanagan walks in late with all of this going on in the class.

Mr Lacy turns to John Flanagan and says, "John Flanagan, get out!"

John replies in disbelief, "Why? I've only just got here!"

Mr Lacy, looking very flustered, answers, "You're just about to fool around."

On this occasion, John Flanagan was right and he had only just arrived, but he was late and probably would have started to "fool around", as Mr Lacey put it. The following week, I hear Mr Lacey suffered a breakdown after our lesson.

Mr Coutts takes over our history lesson and tells us it was all our fault and now he'll be hard on us. Mr Coutts is not a proper history teacher, so it's not long before we have our permanent replacement: her name is Mrs Ash. She's an Indian lady and she's very strict.

It's coming up to the school summer holidays and it's a warm day. The sun's shining and we've all queued up outside the history classroom. Roger and I are at the front, waiting at the classroom door, for Mrs Ash to arrive. I think the girls do needlework in this classroom as well, because I notice either a needle for sewing or a long pin on the floor. I pick it up and an idea comes to me.

I say to Roger, "Look, I'm going to put this needle between the beading and the glass window on the classroom door. Maybe we could both come back here in fifty years to see if it's still there?"

Roger replies, "Okay, it's a deal. Good idea."

I push the needle in place, laying it on its side, and that'll be our time capsule. Hopefully we won't forget and we can stick to it. It's not long before Mrs Ash arrives and leads us all into the classroom. She calls out, "Okay, first all of you take off your jumpers. It's too hot to be wearing them."

We all do as she says.

She smiles and says, "That's much better. You all look nice and fresh now!"

Then she calls out, "Today we'll be studying the Egyptians! It's all about ancient Egypt, so get out your textbooks and start reading from page 105."

Again, we do as she says and I start reading, but I'm getting bored already. What's the point of learning about another country's history, when I don't even know much about my own yet?

I stop reading and start doodling with my pencil on a piece of paper. I'm drawing a picture of Mrs Ash with her goofy teeth.

Then, without even looking up, she calls out, "John Monaghan, put your pencil down and read your book. I'll throw the pencil out of the window if you stop reading again, then I'll give you cuts!"

A few times following this threat, she does exactly that. She hits me across the back of my hands and my knuckles with the edge of a ruler until they bleed.

It hurts like hell.

School's not all bad, though. I enjoy a lot of the lessons that we have, and metalwork is my favourite. Today our metalwork teacher is teaching us how to use the milling machine. We all gather around him by the machine. It has a table that you can wind up and down to get to the correct height, so when the cutting tool moves across to cut the metal, it's clamped in place to cut it perfectly.

While the teacher turns away to talk to the other kids, I like to wind up the table a couple of turns, so when he winds the cutting tool across the steel, sparks fly everywhere. Everyone laughs and the teacher can't understand what went wrong.

Woodwork's good, too. We've learnt how to make a dovetail joint, despite Mr Dunning's breath. He's our woodwork teacher. While we do metalwork and woodwork, the girls do needlework or home economics. They're not allowed to do boys' subjects. Today we're doing pottery – girls are allowed to do it, too. I like this subject as well, but it doesn't matter what you make, because, as soon as you look away, someone will have flattened it. It's annoying, because I'm good at it. I've just made a really good pot and Roger's thrown a big lump of clay at it and ruined it. As soon as he looks away, I punch his pot until it's flat and stick a knife through it. Roger looks back and shouts, "John!"

We both start laughing and he throws a ball of clay at me.

I roll a bigger ball of clay and throw it at him.

The balls of clay get bigger and bigger until I roll a ball of clay the size of a cannon ball and throw it straight towards his face. But Roger's cunning. He's lined his smirking face up perfectly in front of the teacher, who's behind him helping a girl with her pot and facing the other way. I throw this cannonball of clay so hard that it goes in a straight line. He ducks and it hits the teacher, Miss Winkworth, straight in the back of her head. It hits her head so hard that her head jolts forwards and her hair is thrown over her face. She turns around and screams out, "Who did that!"

I'm instantly at the table and pretending to make a pot.

Roger's doing the same, but he can't stop sniggering.

"If nobody owns up to hit, the whole class will have detention!" she adds.

Well, this morning in assembly, Mr Dunning announced that he was the temporary deputy head. He said that he's sick and tired of kids being sent to him who've been behaving badly, so if anyone gets sent to see him today, he will kill them and I know she'll send me to him. Roger, being the voice of reason, keeps saying, "Come on, John. Admit it was you. It's not fair that the whole class has detention."

I reply, "No, and it's not fair that you set me up to do it. I never meant for the clay to hit her and you know that."

It's not long before I give way, though. I walk over to Mrs Winkworth's desk and tell her that it was me.

She doesn't answer me. She just writes a note, then puts it in an envelope, writes "Mr Dunning" on it, and hands it to me.

I know what that means. I couldn't see what the note said, but I'm sure it doesn't tell him what a high achiever I am. I nervously take the note, then walk towards the classroom door.

As I open the door, I look back towards Roger. He's silently in hysterics, shaking with laughter. I slowly walk down the corridor, like a lamb to the slaughter, each step getting closer to my fate. I arrive at office door and stare at the sign on it.

HEADMASTER

Here goes. I knock on Mr Dunning's office door. He opens the door and he already looks angry. I hand him the note. He reads it and tells me to put out my hand, then picks up a leather strap and hits me hard three times. It hurts, but to be honest the worst part is his breath. I'm so used to being hit and if that's what he calls killing me, I'm not scared any more. I trust the teachers not to damage me, but I don't trust my father. He still hits me regularly and calls me useless almost every day.

It's the last day of school before the school summer holidays. I like the last day, because it's always an easy day. Today, Mr Coutts has arranged for us to watch a film about how the future will be. It's an American documentary. I find these things interesting, because I want to know how the future will be. The documentary starts by telling us about how robots are already starting to replace humans in the workplace. They're telling us there will be less need for people to do manual jobs; computers will take over most of the work; and robots will do a lot of the hard work. They're also saying working people won't have to work 40 hours a week any more and will probably only have to work half that. We'll also be able to retire when we're 50, instead of 65. They're saying working-class people will have much more leisure time and showing clips of people walking in the park, but I think 50 is old anyway. All this is supposed to happen by the year 2000. Well, the year 2000 is 25 years away and I'll be 40 by then. I can't imagine being 40: that's nearly as old as my dad. Well anyway, it looks like I'm going to have an easy life by the time I'm 40.

The programme's finished, the bell's gone, and everyone rushes to get out of the school gates. Everyone's excited, school summer holidays at last. I'm straight out to the bike shed, taking my bike lock off, I say bye to my friends and I'm gone.

During the school holidays I decide I want to modify my new bike. I want to be able to do jumps with it. I ride down to the bike shop on St Albans Road and buy myself some cow horn handlebars.

I manage to fit them to my bike, then I'm off down to the leisure centre, where they have a field outside that has loads of different levels and sheer drops. It's not long before I get used to it and I'm doing jumps by riding off ledges three feet high. This place is great for this; it's the Watford Leisure Centre on Horseshoe Lane.

Following a few weeks of practising, I call Martin O'Grady to come and have a go, because he's good on a bike, too. He comes and tries it with me and he likes it, but I've had more practice than him, so he thinks I'm a maniac because I jump from the highest ledges.

During the summer break, Dennis and I get into playing tennis at the tennis courts in Watford near where he lives close to the city centre. There are quite a lot of long sunny days and we play for hours and hours. We keep playing every day until the sun goes down and we can't even see the ball any more. The blisters on my feet are so painful, but that doesn't stop me. I can't count the times I've called out to Mum, "I'm just going to play tennis with Dennis." She thinks that's funny.

17

Death and bad behaviour

It's near the end of August, 1975. Dad says he's going to take us all to the seaside, to Southend-on-Sea again. I'm not going to have those jellied eels this time. Early in the morning, we all get ready and head straight out to the car for a maniac journey all the way to Southend. With a journey this long, I think there's a good chance we may all die today. I don't have a choice, though, so I get into the car as I'm told to do. It's not much fun for me to go to Southend. I'd rather be with my friends. Shortly after we arrive, I find the arcades and lose most of my money playing the machines, while the others wander around the beach and the shops.

The day goes quickly and, somehow, we arrive home in one piece. It's late, it's dark, and Dad has just opened the front door. We're all waiting to go in, but Mum's picking up a note from the hallway carpet that's been put through the letterbox.

She opens the note and reads it. I can tell by her face something's wrong. She looks worried and says, "I have to go and phone Mary!"

She turns and barges past us, then runs down the road. All three of us kids run after her. We're all asking what's wrong, but she won't answer. She just keeps running. Dad has got into his car and he's following. Everything with him must involve his car. She runs to the end of Sandringham Road, then onto Balmoral Road, and towards St Albans Road. Then she runs straight across St Albans Road and into the phone box. We're all standing by the phone box. Mum's inside and Anita's holding the door open. She calls Auntie Mary and I can hear Uncle Liam's voice answering. Mum's screaming at Uncle Liam, "Tell me what's wrong, Liam!"

Uncle Liam replies, "Your dad's dead!"

Mum's shrieking, "No, no, no!"

She's almost collapsing, while holding the phone. I can hear Auntie Mary on the phone; she's trying to tell Mum what happened. Grandad was on holiday in Ireland and staying with Uncle Terry, when he had a heart attack and died. Mum just keeps screaming hysterically and then she collapses in tears. A policeman comes over to ask Dad what happened and he tells him. Dad has obviously been drinking, but the policeman says nothing about that. Anita, James, and I all walk home, as Dad helps Mum into his car. She's in a terrible state; I can't bear hearing her scream like that. It reminds me of when Dad's smashing the house up, which he still does, by the way.

We're back at home and Mum's been alone in her bedroom for a while now – she's just come downstairs. Anita, James and I all go to bed. I can hear Mum and Dad packing their suitcases, then Mum having a bath. They're leaving straight away to go to Ireland to be with Granny.

So that means a week with Anita being my stand-in mother: that I really don't need right now. I hope Mum will be okay.

After a week or so, they're back, and Mum tells me exactly what happened. Grandad was in Uncle Terry's house and he had just had a nice steak dinner. He was sitting in an armchair, smoking his pipe. Uncle Terry's cat didn't know him and was sitting on the arm of the chair, watching him. Grandad was blowing smoke into its face and was laughing at how disgusted it looked. Suddenly, he started to make a rattling sound in his throat and his eyes rolled back in his head. Granny was traumatised and went to call Uncle Terry, but was in such shock that she couldn't speak. Uncle Terry saw her and ran into their room, but it was too late as Grandad was already dead. It must have been horrible and a terrible shock for all of them.

It's November, 1975, about two days before fireworks night. Roger, Dennis, and I have gone out for the evening and we're walking around the town. I've just been in a shop and bought some fireworks, well, just bangers., really. We're trying to find somewhere to let them off to see how loud they are. The town centre is not the best place. It's hard to find anywhere. Just round the corner from the Empire cinema, I find a garage in a back entrance to a row of terraced houses and both of its doors are wide open. I call to Roger and Dennis, "Let's see how loud they are when they explode inside this garage!"

They both agree, so I light a couple of them and throw them in there.

Wow! What a bang! They sounded like bombs. Immediately, a man comes running out of the house. We see him and we all run in different directions. Well, I get clean away, but I don't know if the others have been caught. What if they have been caught? I can't see them anywhere. I decide to go back to look for them.

I start walking back towards the Empire to see if they're there, but a man grabs my arm from behind me and says, "You were throwing fireworks!"

Shocked, I reply, "No, that wasn't me. I'm just going to meet my friends!"

He looks at me sternly and says, "No, I saw you."

Okay, so now I'm really in trouble. He takes me into the newsagents and tells the newsagent not to let me go until the police arrive.

Oh my God, the police? Am I a criminal? Will I go to jail? In no time at all, a policeman walks in and tells me to get in the police car. He takes down my name and address. I can't believe this is happening. I never thought this would happen. And where are the others? Obviously, they didn't get caught and they've gone home. I should never have gone back to look for them. On the way home with me in the front passenger seat of the police car, the policeman talks on his radio, saying, "I've got one of them. Shall I take him back to his parents and tell him off in front of them?"

I ask the policeman, "Can you please just let me out near my house? I'll never do it again."

He looks smug. Then he replies, "No!"

I try to appeal to his sense of fairness and tell him what happened with my friends. Then I say to him, "You don't know what my dad's like and what he'll do to me. He'll probably kill me!"

He just stares at the road ahead and, without even a glance my way, he replies, "That's what they all say."

I realise it's hopeless trying to talk him out of it. He won't understand. When I said my dad might kill me, I meant it.

He seems to know exactly where I live. He switches his indicator on to turn right into Balmoral Road and my heart sinks. Then he indicates left to turn into Sandringham Road, *my* road. I place my hand onto the door handle. I want to jump out and run, but he looks over at my hand.

I realise I can't. I feel sick. Is this really happening? It's like a bad dream. With his head ducked down to read the door numbers in my road, he pulls over directly opposite my house.

He gets out and opens the door my side. "Come on, then, come with me," he says quietly.

It's dark in my road, dimly lit, and it's very cold. Everything seems magnified to me right now. It all feels like slow motion, like I'm heading into a car crash. He knocks on the front door with me standing beside him and Mum opens the front door.

Straight away she starts screaming, "Oh, God, what's happened?"

The policeman starts to explain, but Mum won't stop screaming and crying. It's weird, but Dad's very calm. He invites the policeman in to sit down in the dining room and we all follow him in. Everyone's sitting at the dining-room table to discuss what I've done. I wish I could just disappear. The policeman looks worried. I don't think he expected this kind of a reaction. He looks concerned at Mum and says, "Your son was caught throwing fireworks into the queue at the Empire cinema!"

"That's not true!" I jump in. "I didn't do that!"

"Well, you threw one into a man's garage!" he replies sharply.

"Yea, I did that," I reply with guilt on my face.

Mum starts screaming and crying again. She looks over to me, her face red from crying and says, "John, once the police know you, they'll never leave you alone!"

The policeman replies, "No! It's not that bad. I can assure you I did things like this when I was a kid."

Eventually, Mum calms down and the policeman leaves. Now I think Dad will kill me, but instead he just laughs and says, "That was a stupid thing to do."

Well, that's me, "stupid" – no change there then.

I reply, "My bike's still at Dennis's house and I need it for school in the morning. Is it okay if I go and get it now?"

He seems relaxed and says, "No, I'll take you to get it in the car."

Off we go in Dad's car to Dennis's house. I really don't want to go with him, because he'll talk to Dennis's Dad and the whole thing seems to be getting worse. I don't understand why he's not annoyed with me. It's almost as though he's glad I've been up to mischief. I give him directions to Dennis's house and we've arrived. Dennis lives near the town centre. It's a street with terraced houses all along both sides of the road.

"Which house is it?" he asks me.

I point to the house. "It's that one," I say.

He parks the car outside, then gets out and walks to the front door and I follow him, feeling sick with worry. As he knocks on the door, I notice the living-room curtains move.

Oh God, what's going to happen now?

Dennis's dad opens the door. Dad starts to explain what happened in his fake posh accent. He seems like such a gentleman. He tells Dennis's dad we've come to collect my bike.

I'm going to try to keep Dennis out of trouble and not mention that he was involved. There's no point in him getting in trouble as well. But then Dennis comes out and creates a drama.

"What happened, John?" he asks me very loudly.

I start to explain to him, knowing he already knows what happened, as he was there.

I say, "I was out with some boys and fireworks were being thrown."

Unbelievably, Dennis replies, "Who were these boys, John?" still on full volume.

I reply quietly, "Just boys, Dennis."

Can he not see I'm trying to get him off the hook?

But then he asks, "Did you throw any fireworks?"

He knows I did, because he was there and he threw some, too.

I reply sharply, "Yes, Dennis, and that's why I was caught!"

Then, to my disbelief, he starts shouting louder in the street and his voice echoes, "How could you be so stupid? Oh, you really are so stupid! So stupid!"

I've had enough, so I reply, also with a raised voice, "You were stupid, too, then, Dennis, because you were one of the boys and you were throwing fireworks as well!"

His dad looks over at him and his mouth drops open.

Dennis looks shocked as well and squeals, "Who, me?", pointing at himself. "I would never do that!"

I reply, "Yes, you did, Dennis, so stop lecturing me!"

Dennis is bustled inside by his dad.

My dad's calm and just puts my bike in the boot of his car and drives me home.

"You won't do that again, will you?" he says.

I feel like I'm in *The Twilight Zone*. He doesn't even seem bothered and I thought he'd kill me.

It's spring of 1976. My friends, Charlie and Roger, and the Duggen brothers, Mick and Chris, are all with me. We're on our way to a fair that Chris tells us is at Kings Langley. It's around 7:30pm and it's getting dark. We've walked from my house in Sandringham Road, along St Albans Road, through Garston and we've just gone past the bus station. I don't feel like doing this tonight. It's cold. It's been a long walk so far, but Mick and Chris Duggan are so excited, especially Chris. We have to go up Horseshoe Lane. We could go under the subway, but we cross the A405 and climb over the railings on the central reservation. I'm at the back, following tonight, because I don't know where we're going.

As we cross the dual carriageway, we all climb over the railings and Chris is chatting away to Charlie. Nobody notices there's a girl crossing the carriageway and also climbing over the railings a few hundred yards to our left.

There's a loud, screeching sound, as a Ford Escort that's heading fast towards us skids. Then there's a thud. I look down the road to my left and see the car stopped diagonally across both lanes of the carriageway, with a broken windscreen. The girl has stepped out in front of it. Her head's hit the windscreen and she's been thrown along the road. I think she may have looked in our direction and not noticed the car coming. She's lying on the road, motionless, and the driver's still sitting in the car. Somebody must have called the police and ambulance, as they arrive very quickly. Charlie's the first to say, "Let's just go home!"

He's right, nobody would go to a fair after something like this. The next day, in the *Evening Echo*, I read that the girl died from head injuries.

It's May, 1976. John Flanagan and I have been talking today at school about our futures and what we'll do when we leave school. He wants to join the army.

I've been thinking about joining the army, too, as they have a lot of different careers: military police, mechanic, or just infantry are the choices I've been looking at. I saw an advert in a motorcycle magazine that I bought, *MCN*. It shows a photo of a soldier and all the equipment he would have to do his job. I've spoken to my uncle, Eddie, who was in the army, about it and he recommends it. But, surprisingly, John tells me he's in the army cadets and he asks if I'll go with him tonight to join up. I agree to go, because it'll give me an idea of how it would really be.

It's Thursday evening, and the two of us take a long walk to central Watford, where the cadet hall is, and John gets me joined up there. Every Thursday after school, I walk there with him, and within two weeks I have my army uniform. A month or so later, the sergeant major books a trip for our regiment. We're staying at the barracks in Letchworth.

On this weekend at Letchworth, we all climb into the back of a Bedford army truck. We're dumped in the middle of a field with nothing but a compass and a mediaeval map, then told to find our way back. We're all in groups of four and we manage it with no problem. I like using maps, so I navigate, but we arrive back second. Well, second out of six groups is not too bad, I suppose.

Sleeping in the barracks is a nightmare. Everyone's throwing things and having pillow fights, but all I want to do is sleep.

Then the sergeant major bursts through the door and anyone who has a pillow in their hand has to stand on parade outside for the rest of the night. In the morning, we all walk across the courtyard to go and have breakfast. The boys on parade look exhausted. We all file into a wooden building and queue up with a tin mug and plate. We all plunge our tin mugs into a pail of stewed tea, then a sloppy egg is thrown onto our plates. I'm going off this quickly. The man with the sloppy eggs looks at my face and says, "Eat it all. It'll put hair on your chest!"

The way I woke up this morning was not good either. The sergeant came into the barracks, pulled my pillow from under my head, and hit me over the head with it, shouting, "Get up, you horrible lot!"

I like to wake up slowly, not like that. All the marching, standing on parade and running is not really for me either. I enjoy shooting and, even if do say so myself, I'm good at it. The first time I went onto the rifle range, I was told to lie flat on my belly behind some sacks of sand, then to aim at the target, which was a piece of paper with a picture of a man's face on it. I was told to shoot five rounds grouping. I did exactly that, but I was looking through the wrong part of the sights and missed the target completely. The corporal told me I have to try again and he put a bigger target at the end of the range. It was a much bigger target and everyone was laughing. I realised straight away what I'd done wrong, so I wasn't going to make the same mistake. He told me to shoot again, five more rounds. I made sure my aim was perfect. After I had fired my last shot, the corporal walked down the range and picked up the massive target. Every bullet hole was linked and they were all through the bullseye. He held it up for everyone to see and there was a gasp from all of them; they didn't expect that. Every time after that, my shots were all just as accurate. The sergeant major called me into his office and told me he was going to put me forward to train as a marksman for the army.

The field training that we do is also really good and the camaraderie is something I've never experienced before. On field training today, I've made another new friend, Mark O'Malley, and he goes to my school, too. We're all split into pairs and we learn to put ourselves in danger for the sake of whomever we're with. It's a good feeling and I find it comes naturally to me. Mark's very similar to me, and although we can't get killed on field training, we've learnt self-sacrifice. He's in the year below me, and I've learnt more about him in a couple of weeks than I've learnt about others in years of knowing them. I'm talking about the depths of their character and what they'd do in "life or death" situations. Mark genuinely would sacrifice his life to protect mine. Sadly, a month after knowing him, he died of an unknown illness.

I'm starting to realise death is always all around us and we should never take anyone for granted. Every time we say goodbye to someone, it could be the last time, so we should value one another.

18

Motorbike mad and good times with Mum

At last, it's the school summer holidays of 1976. Next year will be my last year at school. It's not long since I modified my bike with cow-horn handlebars. I've been doing jumps and all kinds of different stunts, but now I feel like that's just for kids. I want to move on to motorbikes, but I have to wait until I'm sixteen to even have a moped and that's not until November. For the time being, I'm reading magazines and trying to decide which moped I should get. I've been looking in the *Evening Echo* at the free adds and I've found a Honda PC50. If I buy that one now, I can at least ride it on our driveway and work on it. But there's also a BSA Bantam for sale in central Watford, so I'll look at that one first. I make the call to the owner of the BSA and ride over to look at it. The owner's name is Abdul Aziz. It's a funny name and it's not until I arrive at his house to meet him that I realise he's foreign, but he didn't sound like he was on the phone.

The bike's blue, with chrome on the tank, and it's a proper British motorbike, but it doesn't have pedals and I realise that I would have to be seventeen to ride it. Definitely not that one, then. I drop my bike off at home and walk up to see the

Honda PC50, in case I buy it. It's much closer to my house, on a road called The Harebreaks in Watford. This one looks a bit like an old man's moped, but it has an engine and that's great.

I buy the Honda, thank the owner, and push it home. I paid fifteen pounds for it, so now I'm broke. It has its own card log book and a tax disc: all really grown-up stuff to me.

Now that Mum and Dad's friends know I'm into motorbikes, one of them, Billy Goldfinch, gives me a scooter. It's a red Triumph T10. And then, shortly after that, Dad's friend, Joe Sheridan, gives me his old scooter: it's a white Lambretta TV 175, with bronze side panels. Neither of the scooters runs, but it's not long before I learn a bit about them and have both of them running again. Maybe I should learn to be a mechanic. This has got me interested in motorbikes, and a friend tells me I should go and meet a friend of his, called Mick Beck. He lives on The Meriden council estate and he's really into motorbikes, as well.

It's the weekend, and it's a hot and sunny day. I ride down to The Meriden to see him on my pedal bike. I ring the doorbell and a mild, blond-haired, trendy-looking boy around 17 years old appears from the side of the house.

"Yeah!" he says.

"Oh, are you Mick?" I say.

"Yeah, why?" he asks, looking worried.

"I've come to see your bikes. A friend said you wouldn't mind," I reply.

"Okay, come through," he says, looking a bit more relaxed.

He leads me around to the back garden and I can't believe my eyes. He has loads of scooters and trials bikes. His back garden is like a motorbike storage place. He tells me he hires them out at 50p a go to ride in the woods opposite his house. He's so cool. He seems very laid back and knows a lot about motorbikes. He's stripped loads of them down and even built different bikes.

Mick and I become friends, but I still have to pay 50p to hire a bike. I take them over to the woods regularly. It's great fun until the police come along one day and stop the whole thing.

From all the times I had in the woods, I learnt a lot of skills and I've become great at stunts now. I can do anything on a motorbike, including jumps. In the weeks to come and through the summer holidays, James and I are going to Moore's of Watford every week to look at all the new motorbikes. I'm amazed at the size of some of them and the speed they can do. Going by the speedos, some can do 160mph.

The biggest bike there is the Honda Goldwing 1000cc. Then there's the Honda CB400 and the CB250. I really like the Kawasaki KH400, because it has triple exhausts. It looks so stylish. There's also the Yamaha RD400 and the RD250 as well; coming soon is the RD125. Suzuki has a cool bike, too: the GT750. It has a radiator, just like cars do to cool the engine. But even when I'm sixteen, I'll still only be allowed to ride a 50cc, so it's between the Suzuki AP50 and the Yamaha FS1E for me.

It's the second week of August, 1976. I've gone down to Mick Beck's house and I'm looking at some of the bikes he has in his garden.

"Do you want to sell any of your bikes, Mick?" I ask him.

"Depends how much money you have," he says with a smirk.

"I've got ten pounds," I reply.

Hiding my excitement, I wander around his garden, looking at all the bikes and running my hands across them. It's such a hot day, even touching the metal on the fuel tanks almost burns my fingers.

"Well," he says, looking thoughtful, "you can have that one for ten pounds," as he points towards a BSA trials bike.

I look over at the BSA and notice it has a chrome petrol tank and big chunky tyres on it. It's a proper trials bike for off-road, with no lamps on it, and the frame's black. Mick can see I'm interested and goes straight into sales talk. "I think the carb's a bit iffy, so it's hard to start," he says.

"Can I see it running?" I ask.

"I'll give it a go," he says.

He tries to start it with the kickstart, but it won't start. He then puts it in gear and runs down the garden with it, holding the clutch in, then jumps on it, riding side saddle, as he lets the clutch up and it starts.

Wow, it sounds so beefy and this is so cool. He stands there, revving the engine and it's loud.

"It's a deal!" I tell him.

I hand him the ten pounds and he stuffs it into the pocket of his jeans, then leans the bike towards me.

"It's all yours!" he shouts out over the sound of the engine.

I can't stop grinning, but I'm trying not to show too much emotion.

"Great, but the only trouble now is I have to push it all the way home," I shout as he turns the engine off.

Well, that's exactly what I do, and it's a heavy bike and I'm sweating all the way home. I don't care, though, because I've got a real trials bike and I'm only fifteen. Am I the coolest kid or what?

The next day I get straight to work on it to find out why it's so hard to start. Bump starting it like he did on our short driveway is difficult, so I'd like to get it running properly.

Later the same evening, Mum tells me we're going on holiday to Ireland. Oh no, not again. I don't want to go to Ireland again, right in the middle of all my bike projects.

The following week we are packing and getting ready to go. But this time's different, because we're going without Dad. I don't think things are very good between Mum and Dad, unless she's just trying to be more independent. It's the morning of the holiday and Dad drives us to Luton Airport. This'll be the first time I've ever been on a plane, so at least that part will be fun. We're flying with Aer Lingus, because they're the Irish airline and they have cheaper flights. They have green aeroplanes, with shamrock logos on their wings. I'm quite excited, but I don't show it, because I'm not a kid any more. It's not long before we're all on the plane: Mum, Anita, James, and myself.

We've entered the runway and we're waiting to take off. This is strange. I don't know what to expect. Suddenly, there's a roar from the engines and our Boeing 737 starts moving down the runway. I can feel the pressure of the seat's back pushing me forwards. Wow! This is great. But then it's almost as though we're on a bus, driving up a hill. I look through the window and I can see the fields and buildings getting smaller as we climb. Within what seems like minutes, we've climbed up through the clouds and all around I can see white clouds beneath us. This is out of this world. The sun on the clouds makes the whole place look like how I always imagined heaven to be. It's only about an hour and we seem to be on our way back down again. The entire trip seems to consist of going uphill and straight back down again.

Then there's an announcement from the pilot. He says, in his Irish accent, "Good afternoon, this is your captain speaking. We're having a bit of trouble finding Dublin Airport, because the fog is so thick, but don't worry, we'll find it in the end."

Now I'm getting nervous. Was he joking, or is he drinking Guinness? Is he a trained pilot, or just a drunk Irishman? My father hasn't given me any confidence in Irishmen. Well, eventually we land anyway and I think he was just joking, but it did scare me bit.

We all get off the plane. Uncle Terry's there, waiting to drive us to his house. It's nice to see him. He's so easy going and a real pleasure to be with. He drives us to his house, chatting to Mum on the way, and it's nice to be in his car. He's a good driver – the exact opposite of Dad. He's talking about his new car: a white Ford Escort Mark 1. He says he likes it, but he should have bought a new tractor and instead he bought a dear car, as he put it. As we pull into his driveway, everyone comes out of the house to greet us. It's so nice. it reminds me of the Walton Family. There's Auntie Maggie, PJ, Peggy, and Thomas, who's Peggy's boyfriend.

After the first day of settling in, Uncle Terry tells us that today he's going to take us to Bundoran.

Bundoran is on the north west of Ireland. It has beautiful sandy beaches and rugged rocky parts, but the sea's so blue. Straight after our customary cooked breakfast, we all squeeze into Uncle Terry's car. There's not much room, because there are six of us: Uncle Terry, Mum, Anita, James, Thomas, Peggy and, of course, me. Auntie Maggie's not coming. She's too busy and I don't know where she would sit, anyway.

After a short drive, we arrive at the Northern Ireland border.

There's a strange tower at the roadside. I ask Uncle Terry, "What's that tower for, Uncle Terry?"

"It's a watchtower," he replies.

Then I notice British soldiers with guns. They stop us to check our documents. I know that he hates all this. He speaks about it a lot and tells me how much he hates what the protestants do to Catholic people. He doesn't recognise the Northern Ireland border.

He wants a united Ireland and says the British have no right to be in his country. I've only just started to learn a bit about the history of Ireland. We hear on the news at home about how bad the IRA are for bombing London and killing innocent people, but I can see now first-hand the intimidation that Britain uses over Ireland. I don't think innocent people should ever be used or killed under any circumstances, but I have learned that when cornered and rebelling against oppression, people always end up going underground and terrorism takes place. Britain would do the same if the tables were turned.

What if Ireland had invaded Britain and had borders where the Irish checked the documents of British people. The answer seems simple to my young mind. Britain should just hand back the stolen land to the Irish. Anyway, enough about that, we go through border control and arrive at Bundoran.

We all go for a walk along the beautiful beach. It's warm and sunny, which is rare in Ireland, but in England at the moment it is over 32 degrees.

We're all trying to navigate some very slippery rocks. Mum looks at me and says, "John, fold the cuffs down on your leather jacket. It looks aggressive!"

I just do as she says, but I don't know why it looks "aggressive". To me, it's just cool.

After a couple of hours of walking around on the seaweed-covered rocks and slipping over a few times, Mum calls me and says, "It's time to go back to the car!"

James, Anita, and I all make our way back to the car. It's a beautiful place, but, to be honest, I'm bored. Thomas and my cousin Peggy are way behind us and they are very much in love, so this is a nice day for them. Every time I look around at them, they're hugging and kissing. Thomas is very quiet and doesn't say much at all. He has long hair and he's quite fashion conscious. He looks like someone from a boy band.

We're back at Uncle Terry's quite quickly and on the way back into the house I notice a Honda C90. It's on its stand by the front door. I ask Uncle Terry about it, and he says it belongs to Auntie Maggie. He says I can sit on it if I like. It's a bit of an old person's bike, but it's a bike, so I like it. After a while, I go in with the rest of them and Auntie Maggie has made us all dinner: boiled bacon, cabbage, and potatoes.

They seem to have this every day. It's a good dinner, though, and I'm starving, so I eat the whole lot. After dinner, Uncle Terry takes us all down to the pub: it's called The Tank. I've heard them talking about "The Tank" and I imagine it to be a massive tank where everyone drinks beer with long straws. It turns out to be just a normal pub with lots of drunk people in it.

Uncle Terry turns to me and asks, "What would you like to drink?"

Well, I've had a can of Long Life beer at home, so I think I'm allowed to have beer in a pub in Ireland.

I reply, with my head held high, "Can I have a Long Life, please?"

Uncle Terry laughs and says, "Tell the barman what you want!"

I'm suspecting they're going to make a joke out of me, but I ask the barman anyway, "Can I have a long life please?"

He looks at me, laughs, and says, "Ah now, I can't give you a Long Life, that's up to the man himself."

I look at Uncle Terry, confused.

"Give him a Guinness!" he tells the barman. Then he turns to me and says, "They don't sell Long Life beer here."

After a couple of beers, I'm starting to feel drunk. I'm only fifteen, but I'm allowed to drink as much beer as I like in this pub.

Uncle Terry asks, "Do you want another one, or are you drunk already?"

"Yes, I'll have another one, please. I could drink all night and not get drunk," I reply, slurring my words.

"Ah now, listen to the young fella talking!" Uncle Terry calls out.

He orders another pint and hands it to me. Everything looks blurred and it's a nice feeling. I feel so relaxed and I'm enjoying this evening. There are people dancing, a band playing Irish music, and a man singing. It's a really warm atmosphere. Everyone's enjoying themselves. PJ is on the dance floor, dancing with a few different women, and Uncle Terry's been dancing, too. By the end of the night, I feel quite ill, but I really did enjoy it.

It's the next morning and the sun's shining through the window straight into my eyes. I can barely open them and I have no idea what time it is. There's nobody else in the room. I can hear talking coming from the living room. It sounds like Uncle Terry's telling Mum I had better get up. But as I sit up my head is aching and the light from the sun so bright. I don't know why my head is aching so much. I get dressed and mosey to the range to get some cold water from the bucket to wash in. There's not much left. Uncle Terry calls out, "Ah now, here's your man!"

Auntie Maggie asks, "Will you take some breakfast?" in her harsh Irish accent.

"No, thank you, Auntie Maggie," I mumble.

"Ah, you will, you will," she replies.

Out comes the frying pan and lard, then she starts cooking breakfast for me. Sausage, egg, bacon, and fried bread. I don't really want all that, but I eat it all and thank her for doing it. I sit down and listen to Uncle Terry. He's talking about the trouble in Northern Ireland. I'm wondering when's the right moment to ask if I can go for a ride on Auntie Maggie's

Honda? After a while, there's silence so I ask him, "Uncle Terry, do you mind if I have a go on the Honda?"

He looks at Mum, then back at me, and says, "I suppose, but there is not much petrol in it."

I'm over the moon. I rush straight out to the bike and I'm on it like a shot.

"Hold on!" he calls out. "I'll have to tell you about the gears. It has three gears: one up and two down."

I reply, impatiently, "It's okay, I've ridden loads of motorbikes."

"Okay then, away you go," he says.

With no helmet or anything, I'm riding the Honda down the driveway and out onto the open road. This is brilliant. I'm riding a real motorbike on the road. I was drinking in a pub last night as well. Everything's allowed in Ireland. There don't seem to be any laws here; it's not like England at all. I ride and ride for ages through all the windy lanes, till I have to stop for petrol. It's a funny petrol station: just two old-fashioned petrol pumps, with a Shell sign on top of each one. I put the bike on the stand and a man comes out of his scruffy shelter and puts the petrol straight into the tank for me. He doesn't even ask how much petrol I want. He has a funny smirk on his face.

Maybe he can see I'm too young to be riding a motorbike, but he doesn't say anything. I pay him the money and I'm on the road again. I don't know why he was smirking, but I'm not bothered about him anyway. I'm enjoying myself way too much. These windy lanes are great fun. Eventually, I start to feel hungry. I'd better go back, as they may be worried.

I start to retrace my tracks, by looking out for landmarks I saw on the way out, and in no time at all I'm turning into the driveway of Uncle Terry's house.

I stop by the front door and put the bike on its stand. Mum rushes out in a panic and looks angry.

She says, "John, where have you been all this time? We were worried you'd fallen off!"

I burst into laughter, saying, "I wouldn't fall off."

It's nearing the end of this holiday and I can't ask to ride the Honda every day, so I'm just sitting outside on the grass, wishing I was back home. I want to work on my bikes and get them fixed up.

Suddenly, a car turns into the driveway: a shiny metallic green Cortina Mark II, with Irish heather tied to the front grill. It's sparkling clean and it rolls along the gravel driveway in almost silence, with just the sound of the stones under its tyres. It looks like our car and the driver looks like Dad.

Oh God! It *is* Dad. I feel instantly excited seeing him, but then immediately my heart sinks again. I suppose it's normal to feel excited, because he is my dad, but he doesn't care how I feel. He stops outside the house, gets out of the car, and I walk over to see him. He has a beaming smile on his face, like he expects me to be over the moon because he's surprised us. I pretend I'm happy to see him, because I don't want to hurt his feelings. Mum tells me the following day that he'd been in Ireland for a day or so before he'd driven here to join us. She tells me he'd gone to visit an old girlfriend, but he said he was just visiting an old friend. I believe Mum. She wouldn't lie to me.

After a couple more uneventful days, we all head back to England in Dad's car on the ferry. Arriving home is a shock to the system. There's a heat wave here and it's 32 degrees every single day. It's just blazing sun from morning till night, but I like it like this.

There's about one week left of the school summer holidays. I'm outside in the driveway, working on my BSA trials bike.

James is bored, so he comes out to see what I'm doing.

"Do you want to play something?" he asks.

I try to think of something that we can play out here.

"I know, how about you sit on my scooter, the Triumph T10, and I'll push you on it towards the big wooden gates? You press the brake pedal at the last minute and see how close to the gates you can stop?" But you mustn't crash into them!" I add. James is always up for any games I make up, so of course he agrees. He sits on the scooter and I show him where the brake pedal is.

And so, the game begins.

I start pushing him from one end of the driveway towards the closed wooden gates. I start to pick up speed, but James brakes way too early.

Frustrated, I tell him, "James, no, you have to get closer to the gates than that!"

So, we try it again and again, until he gets closer each time. Eventually, he starts braking perfectly and stopping an inch before the gates. Okay, well now I have to really put him to the test. I take the full 30-feet length of the driveway, pushing him as fast as I can, and James crashes straight into the gates. Luckily, there's no damage, or Dad would kill me for sure.

19

A voice from the dead

The school summer holiday of 1976 has drawn to a close. It's Sunday night. It's still hot and we have to go back to school in the morning. James and I have just gone to bed and I've invented a saying for Monday mornings. I always tell him on a Sunday night, if we have school in the morning, "Tomorrow morning, it's off the edge of the cliff we go!"

I must hate school to compare it to falling off the edge of a cliff.

Mum calls up to us, "Go to sleep, you have schoolie woollies in the morning!"

God, I hate it when she says that, but James doesn't seem to mind.

It's morning and I've just woken up. It was hard to get to sleep last night, because I was thinking too much about school today and James was asking his usual list of questions. I've only just opened my eyes and Mum's calling up the stairs, "Time to get up, John and James!"

This is the most horrible time, getting up Monday morning after seven weeks off school. Well, this is the last time I'll be going to school after the summer holidays, so I may as well get it over with. I slide out of bed and Mum shouts up the stairs, "Don't forget to wash your hands, face, and teeth!"

Do I really need to be told that? I have to wash my hands, face and teeth? Just the parts that can be seen? After a quick wash, I reluctantly make my way down to the kitchen, already in my school uniform, and James follows. Mum has the radio playing on Radio One. "Dancing Queen", by Abba is on, followed by "Don't Go Breaking My Heart".

Mum asks us the usual question: "Do you want some toast?"

"Yes, please," I say.

Then we sit, quietly drinking our tea, until Mum hands our toast to us straight off the grill. We butter it from the block of Kerrygold butter that's in the middle of the kitchen table. I love this butter, but it's always solid when I want to make a sandwich and I end up with lumps of it on torn bread. Mum takes it out of the fridge as soon as she gets up, ready for the toast, though.

Within minutes, I'm saying goodbye and I'm on my bike and gone.

We still have Mr Coutts as our form teacher and he's his usual laid-back self when I arrive at school. But during our first lesson, he tells us we have double history this afternoon and our new history teacher is Mr Tia. Mr Tia is an old-fashioned, Scottish man. He's tall and thin, with grey dark hair. He seems to hate teenagers. He's the strictest teacher and I think he's a complete maniac.

Our double history lesson has just started. Roger and I are sitting near the front of the group. There's silence in the class. Mr Tia introduces himself to the class by taking a large leather strap out of his desk drawer and slamming it down on his desk. Then he just stares around the whole class, as if he's memorising all of our faces. He's a scary man, but I don't think anything bad will happen, so long as we concentrate on our work and don't give him any problems. I'm not scared. I'm used to being hit anyway. He walks over to the first line of desks and asks the names of the kids in that row. He progresses around the whole class in an intimidating manner. Each person politely tells him their name, including Roger and me, until he gets to Anthony O'Reilly. He asks him, "What's your name, boy?"

Anthony O'Reilly replies, without even looking up at him, "Tony O'Reilly!", in a cocky manner.

Mr Tia's face turns red. He shouts, "Tony O'Reilly, lump it or like it?" With that, he goes up to Anthony's face and says in growling voice, "You will never speak to me like that again, boy!"

As the weeks pass, we're all starting to get used to Mr Tia. He always asks questions on what he's just been talking about. Most of us make sure we listen to him. Today, he's been talking about the Spanish Armada and just when I'm not expecting it, he calls out, "The boy Monacan, how many ships in the Spanish Armada?"

He always calls me "the boy Monacan", because of his Scottish accent. Luckily, I've been listening and I reply, "One hundred and thirty ships, sir."

"Correct," he says abruptly.

Then, without looking up, he calls out, "Prendergast, how many men in the Spanish Armada?"

Prendergast looks blank. He must not have been listening, because he replies, "Two hundred and fifty, sir."

Mr Tia's face looks like it's turning purple. He screams as though he's possessed, "Two hundred and fifty men, sailing in 130 ships? Two men to each ship? Some ships just with one man?"

He appears to be having a fit. His face is going blue and his neck has veins that are bulging, as he lets out a scream, like a wild animal, "*Prendergast, get out!*"

With that he throws the board rubber straight towards his face. I will be glad to go home after this lesson.

It's October, 1976, just two more weeks until my sixteenth birthday. I've chosen my moped; it's a yellow-and-black Yamaha FS1E DX. It's a top of the range bike, with disc front brakes. It's Friday evening and I'm going to see Roger and Charlie to celebrate. I ride my pedal bike to Charlie's house first, then Charlie and I walk up Bournehall Avenue to Roger's. He lives at 57 High Street Bushey. We all start walking towards Bushey Heath, because Roger's been told we can have a drink in the Royal Oak pub, as they don't ask how old you are in there. We arrive at the pub and all three of us walk in, trying to look more grown up than usual. Charlie walks straight to the bar first, because he looks the oldest. He orders us a pint of lager each and we sit at a table. The pub's empty, apart from us, and I think that's why they let us have drinks. It's a small pub, with just two tables by each window on both sides of the entrance door. The landlady's friendly and she can see we're not eighteen, but we don't realise that. We just think we look old enough.

After a couple of drinks, we decide to make our way home. Charlie and I stop at Roger's house on the way back and say goodbye. I walk with Charlie back to his house and we have a cup of tea and a chat before I get on my bike to ride home. It's a mild evening; there's no wind at all and it's quiet on the roads. I cycle down Little Bushey Lane, feeling relaxed and content. Halfway down the lane, I need to go for a wee. I stop and lean my bike against a tree right by the Jewish cemetery.

Just as I finish, I hear a whispering voice: "Listen to me."

Was that really a voice?

Is there someone messing around in the graveyard?

I don't believe in ghosts at all and I'm not afraid of anything like that. I look around for a second to see if I can see anyone, but there's nobody anywhere.

But then the voice whispers louder, "Listen to me!"

It seems to be coming from inside the cemetery. Now I'm looking over the fence and into the cemetery. This must be a joke. But then the voice gets louder still, "Listen to me!"

It doesn't sound human. It sounds like something I've never heard before. I'm looking deep into the cemetery to see what's going on, but it starts to sound unearthly and louder.

"Listen to me!" it says, much more clearly.

It's definitely a voice and it's clear what it's saying. I need to get away from this place, because it sounds evil. I grab my bike from against the tree and jump on it, but the voice seems to be getting louder – it's deep and groaning: "Listen to me!"

This is real and now I'm very scared. I start riding my bike as fast as I can down Little Bushey Lane, towards Bushey Mill Lane, to get home. The voice groans even deeper and louder. It's as though the ground vibrates with the sound, whatever it is. It sounds evil.

I can feel its presence right behind me as I ride as fast as I can, and then out of nowhere the treetops on one side of the road start to curve from a strong wind that's coming from behind me. The leaves are blown from the trees in front of me and I can still hear the deep groaning right behind me. I arrive at the crossroads to Bushey Mill Lane and I'm supposed to stop, but I don't. I would rather be hit by a car than stop. I keep riding as fast as I can. I don't even look out for cars; I just go straight across the road and up Bushey Mill Lane. I keep riding all the way home, as fast as I can, to Sandringham Road.

When I arrive home it's late, so I go straight to bed. I know I had a couple of drinks, but it's not the first time, and I've drunk more than that before. I lie on my bed, thinking about what just happened. I'm sure it was real. I don't know what it was or what it wanted to tell me, but it was a form of energy that I don't believe had my welfare in mind, if it even had a mind. I'll never forget this night and I know people will joke about it or say I was drunk, but I know the truth and I'm glad I got away from whatever it was.

The next morning, Mum and Dad are sitting in the living room. I have to tell someone about what happened, so I start to tell Mum, but Dad just laughs and says, "You should have listened to it. If it was a Jew from the cemetery, they might have told you where there was some money hidden!"

20

A dream come true

The day I've been waiting for, for what seems like all of my life, has finally arrived. A couple of weeks ago, I went into Moores of Watford and ordered my new Yamaha FS1E DX. It's in the showroom, waiting for me to collect. Mum has to come with me, to sign the HP agreement, because I'm under eighteen. We're on our way to collect it. I've ordered a few extras, like crash bars, a rack, and also a top box to put my matching yellow crash helmet in. Hopefully, they'll be fitted and it'll be all ready to go. We arrive at the showroom and I find it hard to contain my excitement. There it is on its stand and it looks really great – everything's been fitted. It's been polished and is waiting with its tax disc in place and the registration plate fitted: PKX998R.

Mum asks, "Does it all look okay, John?"

"It's definitely all okay!" I say, trying to contain myself.

The salesman talks me through all the controls and gears.

Then, he says to Mum, "Okay, now we can sort out the finance."

I can't take my eyes off it as we sit at his showroom desk. It's a shame it's two days until my birthday, so it's not legal for me to ride it until then. I'll have to push it home.

After pushing this beautiful machine all the way home, which is only half a mile, I open the driveway gate and wheel it down the side of our house. To my surprise, Mum tells me to open the French doors to the garden and push it into the dining room. I don't think she likes the idea of something so expensive being left out all night and I'm glad I can bring it in as well. I put some newspaper under the stand and it has pride of place, right in the middle of the dining room. Everyone comes in to look at it, including Anita's boyfriend, Dave, who comments, "It'll soon get dirty!"

I know for sure that, as soon as it does get dirty, I'll be cleaning and polishing it straight away, because that's how I was with my chopper bike. Well, for the first year of owning it anyway.

The next two days of waiting to ride it are going to seem like forever. I can't wait. I can't walk past the dining room without going in there, just to sit on it and admire it. That smell of polish and the sparkling chrome, it's like a jewel.

It's Sunday morning and I've just got up. I go straight into the dining room and check my bike. I'm sixteen years old tomorrow, so I'll be out on the open road. Mum has just made tea and toast. She calls me in to have tea with her. She's sitting at the table, with a cup in her hand, and she's smiling.

"You may as well ride it today!" she tells me.

"Really?" I ask, completely stunned.

"Yes, well, you're sixteen tomorrow, so it's only one day. Nobody would give you a problem for that," she adds.

"I'll be careful!" I tell her.

I rush to the dining room and open the French doors. Reaching for my bike to wheel it out, I almost drop it on the way out of the dining room. I'm just too excited. Okay, here goes: helmet on; I turn on the fuel tap; then the ignition; the green neutral light comes on; I give it some choke; push down the kick-start; and the engine's running. I smoothly open the throttle with it in gear, let out the clutch, and I'm away down Sandringham Road. This is the happiest day of my life so far. I have to run the engine in so I'd better stay below 30mph. I'm so happy that I'm laughing to myself as I ride. I really love my life.

It's 9 November 1976 today: my sixteenth birthday. What a great feeling it is to be sixteen. Finally, I'm an adult. I'm old enough to ride a motorbike on the road. I can get married if I want to. I can smoke. I can do most things. But today I have to go to school.

School is definitely not the right place for someone like me. I need to be out in the real world getting a job and earning real money, so I can pay for the kind of life that I want. But at least I get to ride my fantastic Yamaha into school, so I'm down the stairs early having my breakfast. Mum looks worried. She says, "Be careful and don't go too fast!"

I reassure her, "I'm fine, don't worry."

Away I go. As I arrive at the school gates, I wonder where I should leave my bike, because it's not really right to put it in the bike sheds and I don't want the other kids getting at it while I'm not there. I decide to park it up in the teacher's car park. I take my school things out of the top box and walk into school, looking back at it to admire it. I'm the only one in the whole school to have a motorbike, and as soon as everyone finds out that I have it with me, they all want to see it. By breaktime, everyone's out in the carpark, surrounding me and trying to have a look. Some are asking questions and admiring it. Others are jealous – they start trying to take parts off it and make annoying comments. After the break, I get told off by Sister Anthony for "causing such a commotion", as she put it. She says that it's a teacher's car park and I must put my bike in the bike shed with all the pedal bikes.

As the weeks go by, I start to realise the cost of running this bike is high, so I find a job just cleaning for a contractor as a morning job before I start school.

Looks like I'm back to getting up very early again. I have to clean a supermarket every morning with a few others. It's boring, but at least I get a lot of money for it. After a couple of weeks into this job, the weather starts to turn cold. This morning, on my way in, everything was completely white with ice everywhere. I managed to get to work safely, but it's as though it's getting even colder as the morning goes on. It's still dark and it's even cold inside the supermarket.

Anyway, the supermarket is all clean now and I'm out by my bike and leaving to go straight to school. As I leave, I realise just how much ice there is on the roads. I get to the town hall roundabout and, as I enter the roundabout, *crash*, I'm straight down to the ground. The whole roundabout is a sheet of ice.

Now I'm lying on the road, with my bike across my right leg, and I can't move to get up. The traffic is very busy. Luckily, the man behind me in his Austin Maxi has stopped and he's positioned his car to protect me from getting run over. Thank God I have a good driver behind me.

He gets out of his car and comes over to check I'm okay. Then someone behind his car starts blowing their horn. He turns and swears at them. A couple of seconds later, there's a policeman standing over me. He asks me, "Can you get up?"

What does he think I'm doing down here, sunbathing?

"No, I can't get up, because the bike is on my leg and my foot's trapped!"

He picks up my bike and asks, "Do you need an ambulance?"

I clamber to my feet, trying not to slip on the ice, and say, "No, thanks, I'm fine."

He seems more interested in my bike than if I'm okay anyway. He starts pushing the kick-start down and trying to start it up. Then he says, "I thought these things were supposed to have some compression?"

He tries to start it again and I tell him, "The ignition's not on!"

Looking embarrassed, he replies, "Okay, I'll leave you to it!"

He gets into his car and sits there with the blue lights flashing, waiting to see me get back on. I jump on, putting my hand up to thank him, and then I make my way to school. That was so embarrassing.

I've realised that ice and motorbikes don't mix. There are a couple of scratches on my crash bars, but apart from that, luckily, my bike's okay.

After a month or so of saving, I buy some good clothes for riding my bike, especially in the winter. I've bought a really good brown leather bomber jacket; a Honda Gold Wing badge that I've glued onto the right arm, as I can't find a Yamaha one anywhere; bike gloves; some boots; and a couple of pairs of Levi's 501 jeans.

All this gear makes me feel like I really look the part now and I'm pretty good on the bike, too, so long as it's not icy.

21

Creepy teachers

It's January, 1977, back at school and all the teachers seem to keep saying is that we must work hard for our CSC exams. I'm so bored of cosines, sines, stupid tangents, cross-country running, and PE.

Roger and I have started messing around a bit more recently. I think he feels the same, but he still works harder than I do. Mr Veale, our maths teacher, has to be the prime target. He's such a useless teacher and all he wants to do is chat the girls up.

Mr Heywood, our creepy French teacher, is just as bad, but he's much older. He's bald, with thick black-rimmed glasses. He arranges some desks around his desk, then tells all the girls to sit on them cross-legged. He spends the whole lesson talking to them, while looking up their skirts, then complains that they're too long and how he much prefers shorter skirts. "You look like a load of old grannies in those long skirts!" he tells them. We boys sit in our usual seats by our desks. He's a dirty old man.

I'm sure Mr Armstrong, our PE teacher is gay, because of the comments he makes and the things he gets the boys to do. That we're not allowed to wear any underwear under our tiny, loose-fitting gym shorts is one example.

It's the start of another gymnastics lesson. We've all been told by Mr Armstrong in the changing rooms that if we don't have a jockstrap, then we must leave our underwear off and just wear our shorts. He says it's for health reasons. He shouts out to everyone, "*From now on, no underpants!*"

I don't think anyone has a jockstrap, so we all have to leave them off. We all make our way down to the gym, where we're told to sit on the floor cross-legged, with Mr Ridgwell and Mr Armstrong standing in front of us. They're both scanning with their eyes up everyone's shorts. I look to my left at Micky Duggan and there's something terrible hanging out of the leg of his shorts. Oh my God. I really didn't want to see that. It looks like a dead plucked chicken with a broken neck.

Mr Ridgewell calls out some boys' names and sends them back to the changing rooms to take off their underwear.

This so-called lesson comes to an end and it makes me sick.

Along with all this, I've had Mr Armstrong with me, telling me to use a different gym mat, because the one that I'm using, as he says, is "scratching your lovely back", as he runs his hand up and down it in a creepy way.

I really want to get out of here and start working full time.

Straight after, we all get changed back into our uniforms and the school day is over. The girls have just come out of their changing rooms, so I ask them, "Are you allowed to wear your knickers under your gym skirts?"

They all start giggling and say, "Yes, why do you ask?"

I think they thought I was asking for a different reason. I tell them, "Because we're not allowed to wear our underpants!"

They start going red-faced and giggling again. I'm glad they're entertained, but it's not very nice for us. I think it was Mr Armstrong's idea and Mr Ridgewell went along with it.

22

The rebellion and freedom

It's March, 1977. The weather's still very cold, and I'm starting to get tired of this cleaning job in the mornings, mainly because I have to be up at five every morning and then go straight to school afterwards. This morning I've gone to the utility room to collect the usual ten gallons of water to wash the supermarket floor. The utility room is on the next floor up and the water bucket is so big that it's on wheels. It has four caster wheels, so that it's easy to move around, but when it's full I have to be careful.

This morning, I don't feel much like being careful, and the bosses are being quite annoying anyway. I fill up the bucket in the utility room, put the soap in, then wheel it into the lift. The lift stops at the supermarket floor and the doors open. I push the bucket out of the lift carelessly, and one wheel has just got stuck on the joined part of the floor by the lift door. The bucket tips and it's so heavy that I can't pull it back up. It empties the whole ten gallons of water and soap right across the supermarket floor, just as my boss is walking past.

It's like a tidal wave and there's a display of Omo soap powder stacked 20 boxes high from the floor. It's right in the path of the tidal wave of soapy water. The bottom row of soap powder boxes is soaked. They're stacked so high that the display instantly collapses into the water and all I can do is stand here in disbelief.

My boss stares at me with a very red face and says just three words to me: "You're sacked!"

I didn't want that to happen, but I'm not bothered about losing this rubbish job.

A week or so later, I decide I really am going to leave school as soon as I can and get a real full-time job to earn some good money. I find out I'm legally allowed to leave school at Easter, which is before my exam date, but who needs school exams anyway. For the time being, though, I'm going to make school as much fun as possible.

This morning we have double maths and that's really boring, especially with Mr Veale. The bell has just gone and we all file into the maths class, but he's not here yet. What can I do to annoy him? I open his desk drawer and find some drawing pins. I place a whole load of them on his chair and put the rest back into his drawer. Everyone's seen me do it, but I don't care any more. Rogers asks me, "Are you really going to leave them on his chair?"

"Yep, I certainly am!" I reply.

Immediately, Mr Veale walks into the class, carrying his briefcase, and gives his usual side smirk to all the girls as he passes them. The girls all start giggling. He smirks even more and raises one eyebrow, as if to say, *Yes, I know you all fancy me.*

He stands at his desk and I think he might see the drawing pins, but he's so distracted by the girls that he sits straight down on them.

He bounces straight back up like he's been shot in the backside. His face looks furious.

He shouts, "*Who did that?!*" as he pulls the pins from his rear end.

A couple of girls call out, "It was John Monaghan, sir!"

He mutters, "Go and wait outside the classroom door." I do as he says, but I'm laughing as I leave.

After a few minutes, the door opens. He comes out of the classroom and says, "Follow me down to the staff room!"

I follow him, wondering what he's going to do. I don't have any respect for him as a teacher, because of the way he acts. He walks into the Head Master's office and tells me to come in with him. He doesn't talk to me about it, or ask why I did it; he just stands facing me, looking up to me, because he's so short.

He says, "Okay, are you going to accept the slipper?"

They call it "the slipper" when you have to bend over in front of a teacher for them to whack you on the backside with a big plimsoll or trainer. I'm tired of being hit. This creepy little man in front of me wants to treat me like a child and humiliate me.

I quietly reply, "No!"

He looks angry and says sternly, "Well then, you are no longer in my maths class. I'll set your work and you'll have to do it alone in the dining area."

I say, "Okay, that's fine by me."

In the coming weeks, I sit alone in the dining hall, doing my maths work up until we take our mock CSCs just before Easter. This has only reinforced my decision to leave school at Easter and get a job.

The weeks roll on and it's time to take our mock CSCs. I go through the process with virtually no enthusiasm, because I know that I won't be taking the real exams. The results arrive quickly and I have made grade one in English; grade two in Maths; grade one in Metalwork; grade three in RE, and about the same in all the other subjects. I know I'd do well in all of my CSCs, but I don't want to go to school for one minute more than I legally have to.

The day has finally arrived, the school Easter holidays, but for me, it's my last day at school, not just for the term, but forever. I gather all my things, I walk out of the school buildings main entrance, then I throw my arms in the air and shout out loud, "*I'm free!*"

It's Easter weekend, 1977. My school days are over and now my real adult life is about to begin. Mum's very annoyed with me, because I won't go back to school to take my proper CSCs and she knows how well I did in my mock exams. But for me it's the end. I've finished for good, but I do feel a little bit guilty. It's time for me to get a job, so first thing on Tuesday morning after the Easter holidays, I'll go out and I'll get one. This Easter weekend brings a great feeling of liberty for me and I can't explain the feeling well enough. I feel like I've walked away from an institution that has been trying to make me into something that I'm not and has been trying to crush who I really am. They haven't succeeded in doing what they wanted to do to me. I refuse to go back and take the exams, because I don't want them to know what I know. I'm not an object that belongs to them to test and examine. I'm a free spirit. I belong to me and only me. I'll make my way in the world without their stupid exams.

23

Out into the world

It's Tuesday morning, and it's mild and cloudy outside. I've just had some tea and toast, and I'm on my way out to get a job. Away down St Albans Road I go on my Yamaha. The first place I stop at is the big petrol station on the Odhams roundabout.

I walk in and luckily there's not the usual queue. I ask the cashier politely, "Hello, do you have any vacancies?"

She says, smiling, "You'll need to ask my boss, but he's not here at the moment. If you call back later, though, he'll be back."

She's a young girl, so I'm not surprised she said that. Oh well.

I thank her and leave, but I'm not fazed. I get on my bike and ride on along St Albans Road, then up Horseshoe Lane until I come across a small village petrol station with a repair garage. It's on the right-hand side of the road in Abbots Langley. I turn in and put my bike on its stand on the forecourt and walk in to see them. There's an old man in a grey overall coat, rushing in and out, putting petrol in the cars, and a middle-aged man standing behind the counter.

I walk straight up to the counter and ask, "Hello, do you have any vacancies?"

He looks quite happy I've asked and replies, "Actually, we do have a vacancy for a forecourt attendant!"

"That would be great!" I say excitedly.

Within minutes, I'm filling out a form. He talks to me for a while and says, "The job's yours. When can you start?"

"I can start today!" I tell him.

He chuckles and says, "Well, that's a bit quick. You can start tomorrow, though." Then he runs through my hours and pay: "The hours are eight am to three pm one week, and noon to seven pm the next, changing from week to week, and your wages will be £18.50, per week."

I shake his hand with a beaming smile and he smiles, too.

"See you tomorrow at eight am," I say.

Then I'm on my bike and gone. Riding down Horseshoe Lane. I'm elated, £18.50 per week, and for me to get that job was a walk in the park. Life outside school is great. I'm going to have more money than ever before. As soon as I arrive home, I rush in and tell Mum, but she seems disappointed.

She says, "You'll have to pay me ten pounds per week for your keep!"

"What, ten pounds per week?" I say.

"Well, it costs money for you to live, you know!" she replies.

"Okay," I say, downhearted.

Then I walk out and clean my bike. It's getting late and I decide to go to bed a bit earlier, because I want to be up with plenty of time before I start my new job. I'm lying on my bed with my hands behind my head, dreaming about how great it'll be to be working.

It's morning and time to leave for work. This is what I've been so looking forward to. I arrive at the petrol station and lock my bike up. It's 7:45am, so I'm a bit early. The middle-aged man, Derek, who seems to be the boss because he interviewed me, says, "Good morning, John. Would you like a coffee?"

"Yes, please," I reply.

His brother, Doug, goes off to make it. It's a family business, called Flowers, because Derek and Doug's surname is Flowers. I didn't realise that they were brothers; they look nothing like each other and they're complete opposites in character.

Derek tells me I'll be working with Bob, who'll be showing me what I have to do. Bob's the old man whom I saw putting petrol in the cars when I first came here looking for the job. I think this is a retirement job for him. He's quite tall and bald, with strands of grey hair combed over the top of his head. He has a hangdog, weathered face. Throughout my first day here, I start to get the impression he resents my starting work here.

I notice that he behaves in a creepy way to all the women customers, because he always comes up behind them when they're at the counter. He leans against them, with his hands on their shoulders and then whispers into their ears.

I can see they don't like it, but that doesn't faze him. When he stands at the counter, he always fiddles around in his pockets and lifts up his bits to rest them on the counter. With his baggy trousers, everyone can see what he's doing.

Derek hands me an overall coat. It's grey and drab, but at least people know that I work here. I've learnt how to do this job in just one day and it's easy, even with Bob seeming reluctant to teach me anything. Maybe he thinks I plan to steal his job or make it look as though he's not needed.

It's three pm on my first day and I've enjoyed working here. It's way easier than school and more interesting. I'm going home now and everyone else is still at school. Life is great for me. I have a job that I enjoy, a bike that I love, and now I'll have my own money, lots of money. When I arrive home, Mum still looks disappointed with me, and in the evening, Dad takes the mickey out of me, saying, "Bob's your mother now, boy!"

It's my second day at work in my new job. I'm very busy today, because tomorrow morning petrol is going up in price to 91p per gallon for four-star and 89p for three-star. Today I'm working with Doug and he turns out to be a nice man. He commends me on how well I do and always has a friendly smile. He likes to chat when we get a chance and doesn't have a bad word to say about anything or anyone. Although the business is a partnership between the brothers, Derek seems to be the big boss and Doug seems to manage the repair garage behind the shop mostly.

There are three mechanics who work in the garage and they're all nice people. The petrol station, which is now my job, is very much based on service to the customer. We go out and put petrol in their tanks for them, clean their windscreens, and ask them if they would like us to check their engine oil. If their oil's low, then we top it up for them, too.

My second day seems to fly by, as do the next couple of weeks, and I'm so glad I left school. I'm starting to get to know the customers and that helps.

Most people pay with cash, except for a snobby lady, who has to pay by cheque every single time. She talks in a posh accent and drives a brand-new white Morris Marina. There's also a rich man who comes in with his great big Bentley and, to my amazement, he has ten pounds worth of four-star every time. It's funny how I see the same people over and over again. One man comes in with his motorbike. He doesn't get off the bike. He just sits on the seat and opens his tank cap, then says, "Gallon of four-star!", in a cockney accent.

After I've been doing this job for a few weeks, Derek decides that he wants me to start working the parts counter as well. Doug teaches me and I enjoy learning all about it.

Just down the road from the petrol station is Leavesden Hospital. It's a hospital for people with mental illness, which I didn't know about. Every Thursday, the hospital lets the harmless patients out to wander around Abbots Langley and please themselves. Today's Thursday. I'm working the parts counter and Bob's on the petrol pumps. It's not very busy on the pumps and he's doing his usual thing, chatting to the female customers and keeping them there as long as possible. I'm serving a man who wants brake shoes for his Morris Minor, which I've looked up and I've put them on the counter. He's a dithering man, and there's another customer standing in the queue behind him, who's obviously getting fed up waiting. I thought I'd finished serving him, but then he decides he wants points, condenser, and plugs, too. I start looking them up for him, when two more people join the queue behind the next man. I'm trying to get a move on now, because it looks like I'm too slow.

I've put the parts on the counter and now he's asked me for some bulbs and a rocker cover gasket. Then, suddenly, three more people join the queue. I can't believe it. That makes a total of six people in the queue behind this man. I hope Derek doesn't see this, or he's going to think I'm useless. I have to think quickly, so I say, "Sorry, we don't have the gasket in stock!"

He looks at me and says, "What's that hanging up behind you, then?"

Just as he says that, two more people join the queue. Now I'm really under pressure, and this customer has just caught me out saying we don't have something when we do.

"Oh, sorry, yes we do have one!" I say and I put it on the counter. "Will that be all?" I ask him, politely.

"I think so," he says, oblivious to all the people queuing up behind him. "So, where's Derek then?" he asks.

I can't believe he actually wants to start chatting.

"He's out the back. That's £5.20, please!" I say quickly.

He starts rummaging through his pockets for the money and then counts it out slowly, penny by penny, while I'm starting to panic. If anyone else joins the queue while he's searching for pennies, I don't know what I'll do.

Finally, he pays for his parts, takes them, and leaves. The next customer only wants oil, so at least that's quick, but I can see why he was getting impatient. The next customer after him, a short middle-aged bald man, with black thick-rimmed glasses, asks for a carburettor for his Mark II Cortina.

"I'm sorry, but we don't stock carburettors. But I can order one for you. Do you know the year of the car?" I ask him.

"No!" he says.

Why is everyone being so difficult?

Maybe I can go by his registration number, so I ask, "Do you have the car with you?"

He replies, "Yeah, just a minute." He starts rummaging through his pockets. I just can't believe this. Another one with all the time in the world. He must be trying to find his keys. But then, to my disbelief, he pulls out a toy matchbox Mark II Cortina and places it on the counter. "There it is!" he says, looking proud of himself.

He raises his eyebrows as he stares at this toy car on my counter. I just stare back at him. I don't know what to say. I haven't got time for someone making a joke out of me. He looks back up at me, raises his eyebrows again, and sighs.

I'm getting annoyed now and I tell him, "Sorry, we don't sell parts for toy cars!"

He picks up his car and storms out, muttering to himself.

Now I have about nine more people to get through. The next man steps forwards. I ask, "What can I do for you?"

He hands 50p to me and says, "Got any change?"

My God, has he been waiting for ages just for change? That's weird.

I hand him five ten-pence pieces and he walks out, whistling.

The next man steps forwards and I ask, "What can I do for you?"

He just stands there, staring at me.

I ask again, "Can I help you?"

He still just stares at me.

Just at that moment, Bob comes back into the shop. He looks at the queue of people and shouts at them, "What the hell's going on in here? Get out, the lot of you!"

I'm so shocked that I stand there with my mouth open. He starts pushing them one by one out through the door. He almost slaps one of them on the back of the head. They're all putting their hands out to protect their heads. He looks like he really is going to slap them with his hand raised to them.

Then they all leave and I'm wondering what just happened.

Is that what he does to all the customers when it gets busy?

Then he shouts at me, "They're a pain in the arse. Don't let them hang around in here again!"

What? He doesn't want customers?

"They're from that bloody hospital. They let them out every Thursday!" he adds.

Well, I don't know what I'm supposed to do now, because how am I supposed to know who's who? Does he want me to treat all the customers like that?

Why does he have to treat them like that, anyway? And how does he know they were all from Leavesden Hospital? The first two bought parts from me.

When I arrive home in the evening, I tell Mum about it and she feels sorry for them.

24

Wild times

It's May, 1977. I'm so glad the weather's warming up now, because it makes it much easier to go to work in the mornings. I prefer doing eight am to three pm, because I'm finished earlier. Doing noon to seven pm is nice, because I get a lay in, but I prefer to finish early. Lately, I've been meeting up with a boy who goes to my old school, Shaun Sinclair, because he lives in Abbots Langley, near the petrol station. He came in to see me and we've arranged to meet up after work. He's a blond, curly-haired boy, who acts a bit cool, and he smokes. I've been thinking about smoking lately, but I'm a bit put off since I smoked three massive Castella cigars in the bathroom at home, one after the other. I was so sick afterwards and couldn't get the horrible taste out of my mouth for ages.

We're meeting up this evening, because I'm on the late shift. Maybe we can smoke together at the bus stop. On the way into work today, I bought a packet of Consulate cigarettes, because they're menthol flavour and I like the minty taste. They have white filters, instead of the usual brown ones that most cigarettes have.

My work shift is over and I can see Shaun standing outside, waiting for me. He rode here on his Garelli moped. I finish up at work and go out to my bike. He comes over and says, "All right, mate!"

"Yeah, all right," I reply, as I start my bike up.

He follows me to the bus stop and we both put our bikes on their stands. Straight away, he pulls out his packet of Number 6 cigarettes from the top pocket of his denim jacket.

"Want a fag?" he asks, pushing the open packet towards me with just two in the box of ten.

"Cheers, mate," I reply as I take one.

Then I light his and mine. He takes a puff and starts looking around my bike.

"Cool bike, innit?" he says.

"Yeah, thanks," I reply.

I can't say the same about his pile of junk. We chat for a while and I can see it's time for me to offer him a cigarette.

"Another fag?" I ask.

"Yeah, cheers, mate," he says.

I open my packet of Consulate and offer him one.

He pulls one out of the packet and says, "What's this?"

"A fag!" I reply.

He looks at it again and says, "This isn't a proper fag. These are mint-flavour fags for kids!"

I reply, "They don't make fags for kids!"

He smokes it anyway and moans about it for a while.

"I have to go now, because I'm starving," I tell him.

"See you tomorrow night?" he asks.

"Yeah, okay," I reply, putting my crash helmet on.

"Same time?" he asks.

"Yeah, same time," I say.

"Bring some proper fags tomorrow!" he shouts as I start my bike up.

With that, I open up the throttle and I'm racing down the road towards home.

The following day is very busy and so the hours seem to just disappear. I bought some Number 6 cigarettes this morning, ready for this evening. It's nearly seven pm and, sure enough, Shaun's just pulled up on his bike and he's waiting outside for me. I get washed up, put on my leather jacket, crash helmet, and bike gloves, then I'm outside on my bike. Shaun's sitting on his bike, watching.

"All right, mate!" he says.

"Yeah, I'm okay and you?" I reply.

"Yeah, I'm okay, but sick of school, though," he says.

I start up my bike, laughing, then race off the forecourt, and he follows. I get to the bus stop and put my bike on the stand. Shaun pulls in behind me.

"Have you got some real fags tonight?" he asks.

"Yeah, I've got some," I reply as I undo the packet.

I hang my crash helmet over my handlebars and offer him one. It's a clear and cool evening, but that's perfect for bike riding. We chat for a while about school and why Shaun's sick of it. Then we talk about the bikes. Shaun would like a Yamaha, but can't afford one while he's still at school. After the first cigarette, he tells me he doesn't have any to offer me, because he's broke.

"Don't worry about it," I tell him.

"Do you think I could have a go riding your bike?" he asks. "You can have a go on mine!" he adds, looking sad and hopeless.

"Thanks!" I reply sarcastically.

"Oh, go on. I won't wreck it, you know. I'm a good rider," he says.

"Okay, but not on the road!" I reply with authority.

"Where then?" he asks.

"Let's go down to the school. We can ride all around the school," I reply.

"Great, let's go," he says, looking so excited but trying to hold it back.

He jumps straight onto his bike, pumps down the kick start, and revs it up, thinking it sounds cool, but really it sounds like a bee in a jam-jar.

Away we race, riding through the night, flat out, all the way to the school. Shaun's having trouble keeping up. His Garelli's not as fast as my Yamaha. I pull into the school grounds and put my bike on its stand. Shaun drifts in, followed by a cloud of blue smoke. He puts his bike on the stand and climbs onto mine with a beaming smile.

"Be careful!" I tell him.

I get onto his wreck of a bike and it feels like rubbish. He rides off around the school on my bike and I follow him on his. Then he zooms down between two classroom blocks towards a dead end and a brick wall that's the height of the building. He stops at the end and watches me follow. I race down behind him, flat out, but as I slow down to stop, I pull the front brake lever and nothing happens. My God, it has no front brakes and I'm heading towards a brick wall. I can't turn away from the wall, because there are buildings either side of me. I don't panic. I go for the back brake, which is the foot pedal, but it's not where it should be. It's bent underneath the engine. I can't reach it. How the hell does he ride this thing? I'm changing down fast through the gears to slow the bike down, but it's not slowing much and I'm getting closer to the brick wall. I'm down to second gear and the engine's screaming as it tries to hold the bike back. It's no good; I'm going to hit the wall. I have to brace myself. Somehow, instinctively, I stand up on the footrests heading fast towards the wall; I put my hands up in front of me, slightly apart to try to cushion the impact. Then, *crash*, I've hit it square on. The front forks are bent right down to the engine, but I'm okay. I haven't been hurt at all. I get off the bike and just drop it in shock and anger. I look over at Shaun. He's still sitting on my bike, looking shocked too.

I shout at him, "Why the hell didn't you tell me it has no brakes?"

"It has got brakes!" he replies.

I look at his bike and shout, "Where? You show me where it has brakes!"

He replies, "You have to push the pedal around under the bike."

"You're the only one who knows that. It's not how it should be and there're no front brakes, either!" I tell him.

"Jesus Christ, you idiot!" I shout.

He gets off my bike and walks over to pick his bike up.

"My forks are bent," he says, looking sorry for himself.

"I know, but that's your fault," I reply.

"If I damaged your bike, I'd pay for it!" he says.

I feel sorry for him; I shouldn't as he nearly killed me, but I do.

"Find out how much the forks will cost and I'll pay for new ones," I tell him.

We have a smoke together and then we both go home. It's a shame the day had to end this way, but it's done now, so I'll have to sort it out for him, as he has no money.

The following day at around five pm, while I'm still working, Shaun turns up and he's hanging around outside. As soon as I get the chance, I go over to him and ask, "Why are you so early?"

"I just came to get the money for the repair to my bike," he replies.

"How much is it going to cost?" I ask.

"It's going to cost eighteen pounds," he replies.

"That's my whole week's wages!" I reply.

He looks at me and shrugs his shoulders.

"Okay, well I don't get paid until tomorrow, so you'll have to come back then," I tell him abruptly.

He just says, "Okay."

The next day, he's back at the same time. I've been paid, so I go out and give him the money. He looks happy. He thanks me and stuffs the money into his pocket, then walks off.

He didn't ask how I was going to manage for the week. He doesn't seem like much of a friend, so I won't bother meeting up with him after work any more. Later in the week, just by chance, I see another old school friend who also lives in Abbots Langley. He came into the petrol station with his dad for petrol and tells me Shaun managed to get his front forks on his wreck of a bike straightened out and it didn't cost him a penny.

I haven't seen Shaun since and he kept my money, so I was right about him. It seems to me some people value money more than friends. I really struggled for money that week and had to borrow money from Mum for petrol to get to work.

A few weeks later and it's now June, 1977. The Sacred Heart Social Club in Bushey opposite the Red Lion in the High Street has a disco on tonight.

We call it "McGinty's", because so many Irish people drink there and Charlie's dad runs it. Sometimes Charlie works behind the bar. It's Friday, so it's payday and I have plenty of money in my pocket.

The sun's been shining all day and it's been warm. I've been on the late shift today and I've just finished. I'm rushing home to have my dinner, get washed, and get to the club disco as soon as possible, because everyone'll be there already.

I race my bike from work, weaving in and out of the traffic, and I'm home in no time. I'll have to meet them all there. I'm wearing my black cap-sleeved T-shirt, my 501 Levi's, my real leather bomber jacket, and my Dr Marten boots. I've combed my hair back, using my new steel comb that's now tucked into my back pocket. I had to use some of Dad's Brylcreem and left a couple of strands of hair to hang down on my forehead, just like Elvis does. I'll have to do it again when I arrive, because my crash helmet flattens it. It's eight pm, and I'm just pulling into the carpark outside the disco.

This is a great feeling. It's a buzz. I can feel the energy from the building as I walk towards the door with the rock music playing loud. As I walk in, I try to look as cool as I can. I hope I got my hair right, because it was hard to see in the car park, looking in my rear-view mirror.

Straight away I can see everyone at the bar. There's Charlie, Roger, Shaun, Ted, the Duggan Brothers, Chris and Mick, Anthony, and also Mark. Charlie's buying a round of drinks, but he's still the first to see me.

"All right, Maurice, do you want a drink?" he shouts, almost getting drowned out by the sound of "Jailhouse Rock" being played by the DJ.

"Thanks, Charlie, pint of lager please," I say.

None of us are old enough to drink, but Charlie's dad lets us anyway.

There's a lot of quite girly music playing at the moment, like "Yes sir, I can boogie", so we all stay at the bar, buying rounds of drinks and we're all getting a bit drunk, but it feels great.

The DJ has started to play some more rock music, so we all go out towards the dance floor. Kevin McDonough starts doing the "Hop". He's really good at it, so I join him. I don't know where our energy comes from, but there are so many great rock songs being played that we just keep dancing. I'm not thinking about who's watching – it's just great fun. At the end of the disco, everyone starts to leave and Kevin notices I have my bike with me.

"Come on, show us a wheelie then?" he shouts out.

Wheelies are easy for me to do, so I reply, "Okay, no problem!"

There're around five or six people standing outside and I start up my bike and ride down the road. I turn around, rev up, and go past them doing a really long wheelie.

"Go on, again!" he calls out.

I ride up and down a few times, doing stunts, and then I look around and see I have quite a big audience. Now I'm starting to really show off my skills on a bike. It comes naturally to me and it's easy. I ride even faster and closer to them pulling wheelies, but then Charlie's dad comes out and tells me to stop.

I have to do as he says, because it's Charlie's dad. I turn the engine off and take off my crash helmet. I'm sitting on the bike, just talking for a while. The evening's warm and more people are starting to leave the disco.

Everyone seems happy and it's been fun. The music's still playing from inside the building, "Be My Baby" by The Ronettes. The atmosphere is great and it's alive. I'm realising that life really is good. It just gets better and better. The night must end, though, and so I say goodbye, start up my bike, and head off home. As soon as I arrive home, I realise it's 12:30am so I must have been talking for ages.

It was the best night of my life so far and I'm smiling thinking about how much fun it was. I'll go to bed happy tonight. I had better creep in quietly, though, because I don't want to wake up Mum and Dad. Quietly as I can, I put my key into the front door, opening it in almost silence and then I close it just as quietly. But as I look up the stairs, I see Dad standing at the top.

"What do you think you're doing, coming home this late?" he says in an angry voice.

For God's sake, he has to ruin any bit of fun I ever have. I look up at him and reply, "I can come home any time I like now that I'm sixteen!"

He instantly runs down the stairs and in a split second all I can see is stars and blackness. After a few seconds, or possibly minutes, I don't know how long for sure, I realise that he's gone and I pick myself up off the ground. He's hit me so hard around the head that he's knocked me unconscious. I stagger up to my room, with my head pounding, and quietly get into bed. Although I haven't mentioned much about the bullying and hitting from Dad recently, it still goes on and on. He still makes me feel as though I have no right to be in this world and reminds me of how useless I am every day.

I don't think I can live like this any more, and I wonder if they would be bothered if I weren't here any more. My pillow's getting damp from tears. I rub my eyes dry and tell myself to stop acting like a girl. Then I fall asleep.

It's morning and I've woken up quite late. The sun's shining brightly into my room.

James is already downstairs and he must have opened the curtains. It's hard to open my eyes and my head is aching. I start to remember what happened last night and my heart sinks. I have to go down and face them now. I get up, dressed, and washed, then slowly walk down the stairs. Dad's not around, and James and Mum are in the living room. Mum looks annoyed with me.

"Where were you last night?" she asks.

"I was just talking to my friends," I mutter.

"Well, you shouldn't come home that late," she replies.

I walk out of the room and check to see how much money I have left. Damn! Just £5.50, and I haven't even paid my keep yet. I walk back in, hand what I have to her, and tell her I will pay more next week.

"Where's Dad?" I ask.

"He's gone to the club!" she replies abruptly.

I don't know why he hates me as much as he does. I know Anita and James are just like him. They even look like him.

I'm more like Mum and my uncles from her side of the family. I don't feel anything for him. He's never done anything with me. He's never even kicked a ball to me or talked to me about anything other than fixing his cars.

Oh, yes, there was that one time, when I was being bullied at school a few years ago? He talked to me about that, but even then, it was just to show me how tough he was by telling me he threw a brick at someone. He adores Anita; she's his princess and he is her idol.

James is his little man – the one he always smiles and winks at. Mum has always shown me so much love and bought me anything I ever asked for. In fact, she buys me more things than the others have ever had. I'm spoiled by her, but I feel deep down that she's ashamed of me and doesn't defend me from Dad. Mum says that boys need to be hit, but he doesn't hit James. It's always me. Am I really that bad? I think I've always shown respect to him, until last night, anyway. There must be something about me. Why does he think I'm stupid? I don't know. I know I'm nothing like him, though.

25

The struggling teenager

It's Monday morning and I'm back at work on the early shift. I think there's something wrong with Bob. I'm beginning to think he's gay or something. It's bad enough that he goes up behind all the female customers and leans against them while he talks into their ears, but he's has started doing it to me now. I've just checked the oil on a car for a customer and I'm leaning over the front of the car as I'm pouring the oil into the engine. He's come up behind me, pushed himself against me, and he's holding my shoulders as he talks in my ear. I've put the oil can down, twisted around, and pushed him away.

What the hell's wrong with him? I don't say anything; I just look at him as if to say "weirdo", then pick up the oil can and close the bonnet. Hopefully, by the way I responded, he won't do that again. It's getting very busy in this small petrol station and Derek has been talking about taking on another pump attendant. He says he wants to train me up to manage the whole site. I'm not sure if that's what I want to do, but I'll think about it.

A couple of weeks on and Derek has taken on another attendant. His name's Mark and he's very much a goody-two-shoes. Bob's hardly spoken to me since the incident. Anyway, he has a new target now: Mark, the new boy. It's not long before Bob starts doing to Mark what he did to me. Mark is putting oil in an engine and there Bob is, leaning up behind him, talking in his ear. Mark's not stopping him, though; he's just letting him do it. It's making me feel sick and then he walks in with his arm around Mark.

A week or so passes, and whenever Bob speaks to me it's just to put me down. He stands with Mark and says, "John thinks he could be a mechanic!", adding, "Here's my mechanic," as he squeezes Mark more tightly around the waist. "You haven't got it up here to be a mechanic!" he finishes as he points to his head.

That's exactly what my father tells me. Maybe they're both right. I must have mentioned to Bob that I'd like to train as a mechanic, but I don't remember. Is he saying that because I pushed him away, or because he really believes it? Anyway, if Mark's okay with a gay old man pushing himself up against him for brownie points, he can carry on, because I'm not doing that.

I've spoken to Derek and told him I'm in two minds whether to accept his offer to train as a manager or a mechanic. I'm thinking more favourably about training as a mechanic now, since Bob told me I don't have the brain for it. I want to prove him wrong. Derek's not sure if he wants to train another mechanic, though. He tells me he'll think about it.

Back home, in the evening, and I've just had dinner. I mention Derek's offer to Mum, saying that I'm thinking about it, but I want to train to be a mechanic. Mum replies, "Well, you don't want to train in a backstreet garage, or you'll never get anywhere!"

So that looks like both my options are rubbish. I'll just have to make my mind up alone. Mum seems to be backing Dad even more lately. I wanted to talk to her about the problem that I have with Bob as well this evening, but I don't feel like I can now. I wish I had some support from my family instead of being put down all the time.

Even when I'm working the parts counter, I still have to work with Bob, because the parts counter is right next to the forecourt till and the shop.

The following day at work, it's around midday and I decide I will talk to Derek and take him up on his offer to train me to run the site. I can't get away from the forecourt at the moment, because it's too busy. I'll just have to wait for him to come here. The right moment finally happens – the forecourt's empty and Derek has just walked in.

As I walk over to see him, a big man walks in and starts shouting at him. He says, "Aye, mate, I put my car in this place for an MOT and it failed on a suspension bush yesterday!"

Derek turns around to the man and says, "So, what's the problem?"

The big man responds, "It shouldn't have failed because I checked that car over beforehand and I've been a mechanic for over 20 years. You're ripping people off!"

Derek looks angry. He immediately snaps at the man, "Don't you dare enter my premises with that attitude. Get out!"

But the man has no intention of leaving and carries on shouting. Derek tries to usher him through the door, but the man pushes him over straight through my oil display and the air fresheners. Derek's now on the floor, with oil cans leaking all over him and air fresheners on his head. Perhaps now is not the time to ask him about training.

Later in the day, Mark and I are talking about bikes. He tells me he has a Puch Maxi: that's basically an old man's moped. It's nothing like my bike. In fact, it's the opposite. He asks if we can go for a ride together in the evening and I half-heartedly agree, because he's a goody-two-shoes with a rubbish bike.

Anyway, I promised I'll go for a ride with him and I shouldn't let him down, so after work I go home, have dinner, and then come back to meet him at the petrol station. When I arrive, he's already there, waiting on his bike. I pull in and park next to him. He watches my bike as I stop with an expression of admiration. I take off my crash helmet and hang it over my handlebars.

"All right?" I ask him.

"Yeah, I was just looking at your bike. It looks so cool!" he says with a grin. "You wear all that cool gear, too! I wish I could be more like you," he adds.

He's the complete opposite of me. He's well spoken, obviously has two good parents who teach him words that I've never even heard before, but he wants to be more like me?

If only he knew I'm just a boy who feels lost and alone. I have no confidence and my stomach churns every time I go home, because I don't know what my father will do or say. I'm just putting on a front with this image to try to convince everyone around me that I'm not scared and I'm in control of my life.

Anyway, Mark turns out to be not so bad and it sounds like he comes from a good family. They support him with whatever he decides to do with his life. He says his mum never worked, so she taught him a lot. My mum always worked, mostly to pay for the expensive cars that my dad always bought for himself.

I decide not to mention Bob to him, because this doesn't feel like the right time. After chatting for a while, I want to go home and, just for fun, I say, "Let's race to the traffic lights and back?"

He replies, "Okay, but you'll obviously win."

I laugh and give him a head start of about a minute, then very quickly catch him up. He's just come into sight and I can see that stupid old man's crash helmet with the old man's moped just around the next bend. I'm going to ride by close to him as fast as I can. I'm not slowing down much for the bend. It's a right-hand bend and I'm taking it at 50mph. Suddenly, I see oil on the road in my path, but it's too late.

At the sharpest part of the bend, my back wheel slips out from underneath me. I'm still on the bike, but all I can see is the speedo, the handlebars, and the sky. A split second later, I've come off and I'm rolling over and over. I keep my arms tucked in to protect them.

The rolling seems to go on and on. I'm expecting to hit something any time now, but I don't. I just roll to a stop. I'm lying on the road near the kerb. I move my arms and legs and, thank God, I'm okay. Then I stand up and look for my bike – it's about 100 yards away from me.

Mark has turned around and come back. "Bloody hell, are you okay?" he asks with panic in his voice.

"Yeah, I'm okay!" I say.

"That looked so cool!" he adds.

"Well, I didn't plan it!" I reply.

Straight away, people start coming out of their houses. An old couple comes over to me. The lady asks, "Do you need an ambulance, darling?"

"No, I'm okay, but thank you."

I manage to undo my crash helmet with my hands shaking, and then I take it off. I know my head hit the kerb, so I take a good look at the helmet and that's when I see the three grooves that have been cut deeply into it right the way along one side. Instantly, I realise I would have died today had it not been for that helmet. I feel a bit sick with shock. To distract myself, I walk along the road to pick up my bike. My crash bars have deep grooves, too, and they're ground flat on the right-hand side.

Mark says, "There were sparks coming off your crash bars when they were being scraped along the road."

"Were there?" I ask.

"Yeah, I've never seen anything like that," he says with excitement.

Thank God for the crash bars, because that would have been my knee. After realising the two or even three bad injuries that I've just escaped, I feel very shaky. I sit on my bike and smoke a cigarette for a minute before we carry on. That's the worst accident I've had on my bike so far. Maybe I should slow down a bit. I finish my cigarette and we ride on back to Mark's house, then I tell him I'm going home. As soon as I arrive home, I walk into the living room to see Mum and tell her what happened. She's shocked. She says, "I had a feeling something had happened," then turns to Dad and says, "He's come off his bike, Maurice. Thanks God he's okay!"

My dad doesn't seem bothered. He just shrugs and carries on watching TV.

It's Sunday, just coming up to dinner time. I'm not doing anything like going out today, because I don't have any money left. I've just finished polishing my bike, so I've gone into the living room for a rest. Dad has just arrived home from the club after having a drink. He's sat down in his armchair, and within a couple of minutes he's started putting me down. He starts to talk about my job, telling me how useless I am and making sure I know that he thinks I'm rubbish. This is why I go out as soon as I get home, because I know he'll start on me. There seems to be nothing I can do to get him to leave me alone. In the end, I answer back to him, because I can't do anything else. Right at that moment, Mum brings our dinners into the living room, as we often eat our dinners off our laps in the living room on Sunday.

As she leaves the room, Dad turns to me with fury in his eyes and says, "You know what you want!"

That always means he wants to hit me.

Looking at his aggressive expression and the hatred in his eyes makes me angry, too. I mumble under my breath, "Yea, I know what I want – I want you to leave me alone."

With that, he hurls his plate, still with his dinner on it, straight at me. The plate hits me in the chest and his dinner and gravy are running down my front.

For the first time in my life, I feel anger instead of fear towards him. I've hurled my dinner straight at him. He has cabbage and gravy all down the side of his face. My plate and the rest of my dinner is in his lap.

With perfect timing, Anita walks into the living room with her dinner. She laughs and walks straight back out again.

He actually starts laughing, too. I thought he'd kill me. I still don't think it's funny, and so I walk out and go to my room. Neither Anita nor Dad gives a second thought to how Mum took the time to make us all a Sunday roast dinner just to throw it like it's worth nothing and they think it's funny. I know I threw mine at him, but it was a shock reaction to him throwing his at me.

I'm in my room, lying on my bed, and I can hear Anita laughing as she tells Mum what happened. I can't hear Mum saying anything. She's so downtrodden. I hate living like this. I'm hungry now, and I have no dinner. I'm not like them. I'm not aggressive, and I care about other people's feelings. I don't like hurting anyone, but I'm sick of being walked over.

So far in my life, I've experienced bullies at school, paedophile teachers, and a gay predator at work, but by far, the worst and most consistent of all is the mental and physical abuse that I receive from my father on almost a daily basis. Why the hell is my world like this? I only want people to treat me how I treat them. I hate him!

I will never be like him, and no matter what he does to me, I will not let him make me be like him.

One day, I'll get married and I'll have children of my own. My role model is John Robinson, from *Lost in Space*. I know that sounds childish, but he's how a father should be.

I'll show my children the right way to be by my example.

I'll give them security and they'll feel safe.

I'll guide them and protect them.

I'll praise them when they deserve praise.

I'll play with them, spend time with them, teach them, and, above all, I'll love them like a father should.

I'll catch them when they fall, not just when they are children, but until I take my last breath.

I will break this chain of abuse, so that it will never be passed down to my grandchildren.

I wish I could get out of this place and go somewhere where I can live a normal life.

26

Life and emotions

A week or so passes and Mum tells me that Granny's coming to live with us for a while. A few days later Granny arrives with her suitcase. She's lovely, and I'm happy she's staying with us. She's been staying at Auntie Mary's house, but she's getting fed up there and she hasn't wanted to live on her own since Grandad died.

It's the weekend, and Mum and Dad have gone down to the club together. Anita's out so it's just Granny, James and me watching TV. *Rich Man, Poor Man* has just come on and it's James's favourite programme. The first scene is a couple lying in bed together in daylight having a conversation. The man is in his pyjamas and the woman is well covered, wearing a heavy night dress.

Granny jumps out of the armchair and says, "That's disgusting, you can't watch this!" She turns it over and adds, "Kayleigh's Band is on, so you can watch this instead."

James shouts out, "No!" and turns it back over to *Rich Man, Poor Man*.

With that, Granny picks James up and throws him straight at the settee, then turns the TV back to watch Kayleigh's Band. I have to say that Kayleigh's Band is pretty boring, but it was funny how Granny threw James.

Now that Granny's living with us for a while, Dad will hopefully start acting more normal. It doesn't seem that long ago since he went to his bedroom, pushed the wardrobes over across his bed, and smashed the whole bedroom up. He stayed in bed then and wouldn't go to work or come down and eat anything for a whole week. In the end, Mum had to call the police. She asked them to come in plain clothes and an unmarked car, as she didn't want the neighbours to know what was going on. They did as she asked and when they arrived, they made him clear up the mess and put everything back. They then came downstairs and, as they were leaving, they told Mum that it's not the police she needs; it's a doctor.

Yet he makes me feel like *I'm* not normal.

Anyway, back to this evening. After an evening of watching Kayleigh's Band and James sulking, we all go to bed. Granny's sleeping in James and my room, but I didn't realise she snores so loud.

She also has a lot of wind. She burps a lot, but she doesn't just burp, she actually says "a-burp" very loudly. She does this every minute throughout the night. It's hard to sleep with it, but James seems to get more annoyed by it than I do.

I can hear him seething, "Oh, for God's sake!"

Then he covers his head with his pillow. He gets very frustrated and fidgets, complaining under his breath. Poor Granny, it's not her fault.

It's morning. It was a long night last night, but I did sleep in the end. I don't know if James did or not, but he's still in bed now.

Granny, Mum and I are all sitting at the kitchen table having breakfast – sausage, egg and bacon. During breakfast,

I tell Mum I'm going to Brighton tomorrow with Sean, Roger's brother, on our motorbikes, as we arranged it together last week.

Granny looks at me and asks, "Which way will you be going to Brighton?"

I say, "I'll go through London, then take the main road to Brighton."

Granny looks flabbergasted. "Oh no! You can't go through London!" she says.

Surprised by her response, I ask, "Why not, Granny?"

"Well, you're underage – you can't go through London if you're underage!" she says.

"I'm not underage, Granny. I have a licence."

"It doesn't matter – you still can't go through London," she replies, looking very concerned.

I guess she doesn't like the idea of my riding through London, because it's dangerous with all the traffic. But she must think I'm so gullible if she thinks I believe that I'm underage. I really do love her to bits.

Mum has had a gas fire installed and a phone just for Granny. The phone's a cream colour, and it's so cool having a phone. We also got a colour television recently and it's great to watch things in colour. It seems so real – you can see the colour of the clothes that people are wearing instead of everything just being grey, black, or white.

Anyway, Granny comes over to me and puts her hand onto mine. She uses her old Irish saying in a consoling manner, "You'll be time enough going through London."

But the next morning I pack all my things anyway, load up my top box on my bike, and ride up to Sean's house so we can hit the road to Brighton together. It's early, around seven am, but Sean's expecting me so hopefully he should be ready. When I arrive at his house, I'm really excited – this is an adventure. I put my bike on the stand and ring the doorbell. There's no answer so I ring again. After what seems like ages, Sean opens the front door with his eyes screwed up and still in his dressing gown.

He squints at me and says, "John, I'm so tired. I'm not going."

He's joking … He must be.

I reply in disbelief, "Really?"

He half-turns to go back in and starts to push the front door closed, then says, "Sorry, but I'm going back to bed", and closes the front door.

I'm standing on his doorstep wondering what to do now. I was so looking forward to this and there was only the two of us going, so I'll either have to go home or go on my own. He's missing out on a great trip, but I decide I'm not going to. I get on my bike and off I head to Brighton alone.

It's a long ride, but I finally arrive near the seafront, where I look for a B&B to stay at. I eventually find an old Victorian house with three storeys. I walk up to the massive front door and press the doorbell. I can see the seafront, smell the fresh sea air, and hear the seagulls.

The B&B owner opens the door. She's a middle-aged cockney woman, quite short with grey curly hair.

"Can I help you?" she says.

"Do you have a single room available?" I ask.

"Here on your own, are you, darling?" she says.

"Yeah, a friend of mine let me down," I reply.

She smiles at me and says, "You don't need friends like that, darling!"

I smile back at her and she shows me to my room. It's a small room with just a steel-framed bed and a 1920s wardrobe, but the ceiling is much higher than my room at home. I put my suitcase down on the floor and open the sash window, then lie down on the bed and put my hands behind my head. I'm in Brighton, totally alone, and this is my own room that I got with my own money. I'm lying here for a while thinking about the journey down here, trying to get a feel for what it's like to be alone in the world. There's a warm breeze blowing in through the window. Sean has really let me down today. I start to unpack my bag after a while and then I go for a walk along the stony beach where there are old people sitting in deck chairs and families playing in the sea. I sit down on a wall for a while to watch the waves drifting in towards the beach and the way some kids play, throwing a beach ball to their father. There's laughter and happy screams from kids as they run in and out of the cold sea water. All these things we take for granted are sounds of families making happy memories. It brings a smile to my face as I watch a little boy wrestling with his father. The dad pretends the little boy is winning the match. I wish I could have memories like that.

After some time of just watching, I find a fish and chip shop and buy myself sausage and chips, then slowly walk back to the B&B, where I stay for just one night. I have a great breakfast alone at my table, then pay the lady and say goodbye. "Have a safe journey, darling!" she says. I smile, then leave.

It's a long journey home. When I get as far as London, the traffic is crazy and I get lost at Hyde Park Corner. It's hard to read the signposts as well as watching cars either side of me, but I find my way and eventually I arrive home.

It's Monday morning and I'm back at work. Doug's son, Allen, has come into the petrol station on his Honda 400/4. It's a big bike and it's much faster than mine. He talks to Doug for a while, telling him he's going to Brands Hatch on Saturday with a few other biker friends. Doug says to him, "Why don't you ask John if he would like to go with you?"

"Want to come mate?" Allen shouts across to me.

"Yeah, great – what time are we leaving?" I say.

"Nine o'clock in the morning. We're all meeting here," he says with a smile.

"I'll be here," I reply.

"Great, see you then," he says as he walks out onto the forecourt and straddles his bike.

Doug follows him out to say goodbye as Allen starts his bike and revs it like crazy. Two seconds later, Allen rides off the forecourt with his bike screaming down the road.

Bob laughs and says, "He's a maniac!"

I'm worried now. How am I going to keep up with him on my bike? Its top speed is only 55mph.

All week I'm excited about this trip to Brands Hatch. The days seem so slow.

Finally, it's the day I've been waiting for. I've arrived at the petrol station early and I'm waiting for the others to arrive. One by one, all of these big bikes start to roll onto the forecourt.

Allen is first, followed by a Honda Gold Wing 1000cc, a massive bike; a Kawasaki KH600; a Honda CB750 and two more Honda CB400s. That's a total of six bikes, with me on my Yamaha 50cc. I feel ridiculous.

Allen says, "Come on, John, jump on the back of my bike – you'll never keep up with us on that!"

Reluctantly – and feeling a bit sad that I have to leave my bike at the garage – I lock it up, then jump onto the back of his Honda. They all start up their bikes and rev them up. The sound of all those engines gives me a rush; my adrenaline's pumping. Then one after another we all leave the forecourt and the power of the engine pulls me right back as we accelerate down the road through Abbots Langley. In no time at all we're on the M1 heading south. At first, we're cruising at around 70mph but then the CB750 thunders past us, followed by the Gold Wing and the Kawasaki KH600. Allen opens up our Honda and I can feel myself being pulled right up to 120mph along the white lines between the cars. There are bikes behind us and bikes in front of us. This is out of this world for me – it's a great feeling being part of the group, with the people in their cars watching the bikes as we pass them.

We arrive at Brands Hatch to watch the motorbike racing and that's a thrilling experience, too. There are hundreds, if not thousands, of bikes here. Watching the bike racing on TV can never compare to actually being here. The atmosphere is electric. The journey home is just as fast and just as exciting – if I die today, at least I'll die enjoying myself.

It's 16 August 1977. Charlie and Roger have told me they want to go for a drink in the Royal Oak in Bushey Heath. I don't know if we will actually get a drink or not, as it depends on whether the same landlady is still there.

I'm on my way up to Charlie's house first and we'll stop at Roger's house on the way, before all walking to the Royal Oak. Luckily, it's the same landlady and Charlie gets us a pint of lager each.

Three pints later and we're all starting to get a little drunk.

The landlady notices and says, "I think you should slow down a bit with your drinks, because you're all young lads and you're getting a bit drunk now!"

Just as she says that, Roger comes out of the toilet and says, "I'm not drunk – I just couldn't find the flush in the toilet!"

Oh well, that kind of confirms what she's saying. Did she really need to know that?

She lets that go over her head and brings three more drinks to the table. We carry on having a great laugh at what Roger just said.

A few minutes later, the landlady comes back over to the table. She looks distraught as she says, "Hey, lads, do any of you like Elvis?"

Well, that's a funny question – we all love Elvis and Elvis is Roger's idol. He's always singing his songs and doing impersonations of him.

We all reply "yes" and Roger says, "Why do you ask?"

She says tearfully, "I've just heard on the radio that he's dead!", and starts wiping the tears from her eyes.

Roger looks stunned. We're all shocked and don't know what to say. That's changed the mood of the night and we all sober up a bit.

The following day, I go up to see Roger and when I knock on the door of his house, his mum opens the door. She calls up the stairs, "Roger, Roger!", but there's no answer.

"He must be around the back, John – go around and see," she says.

"Okay, thanks," I say.

There's a long driveway that curves around the back of the garden that leads to his garage. To the right of the driveway, the house backs onto a farm. As I walk down the driveway, I hear a voice call out, "Maurice!"

I look around only to see Charlie and Roger in the barn.

I walk over to the them and ask, "What are you doing?"

"Smoking!" Roger says.

Roger likes giving one-word answers.

"Smoking?" I say, confused. "Why are you doing that?"

"It's something to do," Roger says.

I'm surprised they're both sitting in the hay smoking – they could burn the place down if they're not careful.

I ask them, "Do you want to go and do something?"

"Nah!" says Roger.

"We just want to sit here and smoke," Charlie adds.

It sounds boring to me, but I sit with them and Charlie hands me a cigarette.

"Do you want one, Maurice?" he says.

"Okay, I may as well," I say.

I stay with them smoking but I haven't smoked for a while and it makes me feel light-headed straight away. Pretty soon

I get bored of it, so I say goodbye and leave to go home. The following evening, I speak to Charlie on the phone and he tells me they managed to burn the whole barn down. I don't think anyone else knows they were there smoking when it happened. I'm glad I wasn't there.

Dad's giving me a hard time at the moment for being out all the time. I go out as much as I can to be with my friends, because they make me feel better about myself. I could understand his going on at me if I didn't have a job and was always around the house. My job and my friends are what keep me going.

Last year, he wanted us to move to Milton Keynes, because they're building a new city there and he was working on the building sites levelling the ground with his bulldozer in a place called Eaglestone. We went to look at a detached house there – 11 Buckingham Gate. The house was brand new. It looked nice inside and he wanted to buy it. Mum said she didn't like it because all the private houses were too close to the council houses. There's nothing but houses and a few roads in Milton Keynes; it doesn't even have a town centre. Who would want to live there? Just my dad. Thank God we didn't move there because now I would have no job, no bike, no friends, a smaller room to share with James, loads of mud everywhere, and Dad going on at me every single day. That shows how much he thinks about his family – Mum's right to say no to moving.

It's September, 1977. I've just got home from work. I was on the late shift today and it's 7:30pm. Mum says she wants to talk to me as soon as I've finished my dinner. I start to wonder what I've done wrong while eating my dinner. I finish quickly to get it over with, then sit down in the living room to talk to her.

Mum turns to me and says sternly, "My boss has a good friend, his name's Charlie Greenfield and he's the managing director of the Ford dealership in St Albans. The company's name is Godfrey Davis. I want you to go for an interview with him – an appointment's already been made for you.

"As long as your interview goes okay, you'll get the job. You're wasting your time in that back-street garage doing a menial job. You should take this job because you need a trade and they can give you a proper career." Well, I'm shocked.

That's a lot to take in. It sounds like good news and I don't have much choice but to accept it. It's a Ford dealer with a proper apprenticeship and I've been saying I would like to learn to be a mechanic, so how can I let her down after she's gone to so much trouble.

Mum continues, "You're very lucky that they'll even entertain you because you never took your school exams!"

Very soon the day of my interview comes around. I'm at Godfrey Davis London Road, sitting outside the office waiting to be seen with butterflies in my stomach. My interview is with Mr Clarke. He's around 35 years old, going bald, he wears a grey pinstriped suit. The place looks busy and there are brand-new Mark III Cortinas and Mark II Escorts everywhere. It looks like these will be the cars I'll be working on. Mr Clarke calls me into the office.

"Okay, take a seat," he says in a complacent manor.

He asks me a few mechanical questions about my bike, which I answer quite easily because of all the work I've done.

"How much are you earning in your present job?"

"Eighteen pounds fifty per week," I reply.

"You'll have to take a drop in pay to £16.25 per week!" he says with a sigh.

I give him the reply I know he wants to hear because I don't want to let Mum down: "That's fine because it'll be worth it in the end!"

He looks at me with a smug expression and says, "Yes, exactly!"

I'm not feeling right about this but I have to go along with it, don't I? He makes a phone call to Charlie Greenfield and I can hear him saying, "Yeah, he's all right."

Charlie Greenfield must have asked about me.

He hangs up the phone and says, "Go down to Ashley Road and ask to see Charlie Greenfield at our truck department."

"Okay, thanks for seeing me," I say.

I leave and make my way straight to Ashley Road. I ask to see Charlie Greenfield at reception and they send me up to his office. A tall ginger-haired man with big ears opens the door and I go through a second interview with him.

At the end he asks, "How much notice do you have to give at your current job?"

"One week, I guess," I reply, not even knowing really.

"Okay, you can start a week on Monday – go and hand your notice in today!" he says in commanding manner.

"Where will I be working?" I ask, feeling a bit nervous.

"Well, here of course!" he says.

"So, I'll be working on trucks then?"

"Yes, you'll be working on the Ford D series."

"Okay, thank you, Mr Greenfield," I say as I leave.

He just mutters under his breath and says, "Close the door on your way out."

On the way home, I'm churning all this over in my mind and trying to process it. I don't want to work on trucks.

I was thinking about learning to be a car mechanic, but lorries are completely different. I can't let Mum down now, though, can I? She's already disappointed that I left school early and she'll be over the moon that I got the job here today.

I arrive home and Mum's in the kitchen. The first thing she says to me is, "Well, how did it go?" She seems annoyed with me.

I say, "I'll be starting a week on Monday because I have to give notice to the job I have now."

"We're not bothered about them!" she says.

"I am!" I reply sharply.

She looks angrily at me and says, "My boss had to call in a favour for me to get you this job, so you had better not let me down!"

This has set me right back and I feel totally worthless again.

I only got the job because of someone who my mum knows and the job I got for myself is as worthless as I am. I love my job and I'm happy there. Now I've been put back in that cage again, the one I spent my whole childhood in, because I'm useless and should just do as I'm told. Anyone would say I'm a fool not to take the job, so I have no choice; I just have to do it.

Over the weekend, I write up my notice to Flowers.

Dear Derek and Doug,

Thank you for employing me at your service station. I've enjoyed working here very much. I'm very grateful for all the training and experience I've gained, but I'm sorry to say I'm giving you notice of one week as from today. I have to further my career and have had a position offered to me at a main dealership. I wish you all the best for the future.

Yours sincerely,

John

As I was writing my notice, I could feel a lump in my throat. My gut was telling me not to do it, but I felt like I was writing it with a gun to my head. Derek had already said he wanted to train me to run the whole service centre and I know he meant it. There's a great atmosphere there, apart from Bob, but then there's always one, isn't there? I don't want to work on lorries and the atmosphere doesn't seem good at the new place. I feel I want to rebel against this. How can I? I just can't, so I put the letter into an envelope, then into the top box of my bike, ready for Monday morning so I don't forget it.

On Monday morning, it's dry and sunny outside. I'm on the early shift and it's seven am. I've just had some tea and toast and I'm ready to go to work, sitting in the kitchen, thinking about how they'll respond when I hand my notice in. Deep down I know I'm doing something not for me but for Mum and Dad to get their approval.

No matter what I do, somebody's going to be disappointed in me – Derek and Doug, or Mum and Dad. I get my things together, start up my bike, and make my way to work. I keep telling myself all the way there: *I have to do this, it's for the best.*

As I approach the petrol station, I'm following a single-decked green bus. I'm still thinking about what I have to do and I'm not concentrating. I'm quite close behind the bus when it's time for me to turn right onto the forecourt. I notice Doug filling a car up with petrol and, without even thinking, I just turn from behind the bus, but there's a car coming in the opposite direction. I've gone straight across the road in front of the car and I can hear it skidding as it approaches the side of my bike.

I can hear a woman screaming – she's a passenger in the car. The driver can't stop in time; he's going to hit me. I open up the throttle to get across the road more quickly, but then I feel my bike wobble and I hear a crash. But my bike is still upright. I see my rear number plate flying across the forecourt before it lands on the ground right in front of Doug, of all places. Doug just looks down at it as if he's reading it, then looks up at me and continues to fill the car with petrol.

I get off my bike and put it on the stand. Damn, this accident is my fault ... The man jumps out of his car and I expect him to go mad at me, but he doesn't. He just runs over to me, asking, "Are you okay?", with a panicked expression.

"Yeah, I'm okay ... Is your car damaged?" I ask him.

"Forget the car, I'm not worried about that, so long as you're okay!" he says, looking surprised that I even asked him that.

"I'm okay, really, but thank you!" I reply, embarrassed.

"Okay," he says as he walks back over to his wife to console her.

I walk over to my number plate and pick it up.

Doug asks, "Are you okay?"

"I'm okay, thanks," I say, wishing everyone would stop asking me if I'm okay.

Doug says, "Don't worry about your bike – just pop it round the back and someone'll fix it for you."

As I wheel my bike around the back, I feel even worse about handing my notice in. I'll leave it until around lunchtime, but I feel I have to tell Doug first.

"Doug, there's something I have to tell you," I say.

"Oh, what's that?" he says with his usual warm smile.

"I have to give in my notice!" I say quickly, feeling sick to my stomach.

Doug looks down at the ground, pauses and says, "Oh dear, that's a shame. It's best you give the letter to Derek."

Now I have to wait for Derek to come into the shop, which he does every so often to check the till at around two pm.

A few minutes later, Derek walks in and he looks flustered.

I have to do it now. I take a deep breath and walk over to him. "Derek, I have to give you this!"

"What is it?" he asks.

"It's my notice. I have another job!" I say quickly.

He opens it in front of me, reads it, and looks very angry. He says nothing at all, just storms off back to his office. Well, that's it done now. Derek hates me and Doug's looking very disappointed. At least I can go home in an hour.

The last week goes by very slowly. Derek has barely spoken to me at all. Doug still speaks to me, and he asks about my new job, but he keeps asking if I'm sure that's what I want to do. I keep telling him I'm sure, but the truth is I'm not and I think he knows that.

It's three pm on Friday and I'm leaving for the last time. Derek hands my wages to me and I open the envelope in front of him. I count £74 in there.

"Why so much?" I ask him.

"That's your holiday money and a little bonus!" he says smiling.

"But I don't get a bonus!" I say.

He winks at me and says, "Good luck in your new job!"

I normally only get £18.50 and that's all I was expecting, plus my holiday money, of course. I'm over the moon – I've never had so much money. I look around at Doug.

He seems to just fake a smile, then shakes my hand and says, "Good luck, John!"

"Thank you! Thanks for everything!" I say.

Unable to hide my excitement I shake Derek's hand and then Doug's again. They're such great people and I think they know I'll miss them. I walk out to the forecourt, get on my bike and start it up. I hear a voice muffled by the sound of my bike's engine calling me and I look around. It's Doug.

"Don't forget to pop in and see us once in a while, will you!" he's shouting.

"I won't!" I say.

Then I ride off the forecourt for the last time. I feel very sad, deep in the pit of my stomach, but boy am I excited about all this money. They've been so good to me and I'll never forget them – especially Doug.

27

Losing control of my life

I've been excited about this day, but also dreading it – my first day at Godfrey Davies Truck Department in Ashley Road, St Albans. The day I start my apprenticeship. It's miserable and foggy, the opposite of how it was when I left my last job. I've arrived at the big workshop reception. I don't know where to put my bike, so I leave it around the back and lock it up. I walk into reception and the phones are ringing. Everyone's busy doing different jobs. Eventually I get to speak to a thin middle-aged man with ginger hair whose name badge says "Pat". He's the head receptionist.

"Can I help you?" he says in a cockney accent.

"I'm starting work here today," I reply.

He looks at me, then calls out twice over a Tannoy to the workshop, "John Duddridge, reception, please."

A tall bald man in white overalls comes through a door at the back of reception behind the counter.

"What is it?" he asks Pat the receptionist.

Pat points his pen at me and says, "He says he's starting work here today!"

"What's your name?" John Duddgridge asks me.

"John Monaghan," I reply.

"Okay, come with me," he says.

He lifts up the counter door and I follow him through to the workshop. It's very noisy, so I find it difficult to hear him speak as he asks, "Have you got any work boots?"

"No, I haven't," I say.

"Get some by the end of the week," is all he says.

He shows me into a dirty smelly changing room with grey beaten-up lockers and plastic chairs all around the walls. The old Victorian bare brick walls have been painted with dark blue gloss on the lower half and white on the upper half. The windows are steel framed with frosted glass so you can't see out, and they're filthy. The floor is greasy and black – there's dust everywhere and it's around a quarter of an inch thick where it's been trampled into the ground. He rummages through a bag of old overalls and throws me a pair of screwed-up dirty ones, saying, "Put them on!"

I hold them up to look at them and they're miles too big for me, not too big in height but in width. They must have been made for an elephant. Or maybe my dad. I put the overalls on and they have a stale damp smell. They're so big, they're hanging off me.

John says, "They'll have to do for now. Come on, follow me out to the workshop and I'll hand you over to Stan. You'll be working with him from today onwards."

I follow John through the workshop and I can hear people singing along to the radio which is blaring "Knowing Me, Knowing You" by Abba. There are lorries starting up with clouds of black smoke and there's soot everywhere from the exhausts. Each mechanic has his own work bay, and as I follow John through, they all look at me but nobody says anything. I feel like such an idiot in these overalls – like a spectacle being paraded.

Finally, we arrive at Stan's bay and John introduces me. "Stan, this your new old boy!" he says.

So, I'm an "old boy"? I thought I was going to be an apprentice.

John walks off and leaves me with Stan, an old man of around 60 years or more with glasses, grey hair, and a corduroy flat cap. He's quite stocky, probably from lifting heavy things when he's working on the big trucks. He looks at me in these massive overalls, then tuts and carries on with his work as if I'm not here. Eventually, when John's out of sight, Stan starts speaking to me. I realise he's Polish and his English is poor.

He says in pidgin English, "Last old boy was no good so sacked like anything nun it!"

He's working on a Ford D series truck and has the cab tilted. "Okay, taking exhaust off!" he says.

I think he means he wants me to take the exhaust off, so I get under the truck and start taking it off.

"You know what you do nun you?" he says.

"Yeah, I know what to do," I reply.

But the exhaust is very rusty, and it takes me quite a while to free the rusty bolts.

"You not using air tools nun you!" he says.

I don't know what he's talking about, so I reply, "Pardon?"

"You not using at all nun you, for that I say nun it!" he replies.

This is crazy – what the hell is he saying? I just look at him. He hands me an air ratchet and socket.

"Thank you," I reply.

This is going to be difficult.

As the week goes on, I start to understand his mixture of Polish and English, but it's hard. It's also hard work and I've cut my hands a lot.

On Thursday evening, Mum asks, "How are you getting on in the job?"

I tell her about Stan, and Dad takes the mickey out of me and says, "Stan's your mother now." Followed by, "You'll never be a mechanic working on an old Ford D!"

Even after leaving my old job and doing what Mum wanted me to do, I'm still being put down. I'm nobody, and it seems to me I'll always be nobody in my family.

I wish I'd never left my job now.

The next day at work during tea break, one of the other mechanics is asking Stan, "What's your boy like then, Stan?

Stan finishes his sandwich and says, "He's too slow!"

My heart sinks. I can't feel any more worthless than I do right now – what's the point of my even being here? Now in front of everyone in my new job I've been labelled "too slow". My dad would be glad to hear he has support here in breaking me.

It's Friday evening and I've just got back from work. It's still damp and drizzly outside, and I feel miserable. I've finished my dinner of egg and chips that Mum made for me.

When I go into the living room, Mum says, "Our friend Ralph Prince is scrapping his Ford Anglia and says you can have it if you want it to practise your mechanical work."

"Wow, really?" I ask.

This day has gone from miserable to great in just one second. Mum always manages to put a smile back on my face.

"Where will I put it?" I ask.

"You'll have to rent a garage or something because you can't bring it back here," she says.

"Okay, I will," I reply.

Straight away I start looking in the *Evening Echo* and find one almost immediately. I'm very excited now – this will be my first car. I call the owners of the garage and go down to see it the same evening. It's on Woodmere Avenue, so it's close to home.

They show me the garage and straight away I say, "It's great, I'll take it!"

I pay the deposit and the next morning I go with Dad to look at the car. It doesn't really matter what condition it's in because I'll only be working on it. When we arrive at Ralph's house, he comes out to show me the car. It's dark blue with a white stripe down each side and it's an Anglia Super, just like the spruce green one Dad bought new back in 1966. Ralph's a scruffy middle-aged bald man and he's always smoking. He seems to be playing the part of a used car salesman in the way that he's talking about the car. It looks to be in good condition, except it has massive rusty holes in both of the front wings. I start looking at the holes, but Ralph calls me over and says, "Yes, the front wings are a bit rusty, but the back of the car's perfect, my son!"

I'm really not worried about the holes in the wings; I was just looking.

Ralph says to me, "Would you like me to drive the car down to your garage?"

"That would be great, if you don't mind," I say.

We follow him to my garage in Dad's car and he reverses the Anglia into my garage for me. Today's a great day, and I thank Dad for helping me do this. He seems happy to see me this excited.

Every evening and weekend from this day on, I'm down at my garage working on my car. I take the engine out, strip it down, and rebuild it. It's great fun. I get it running again and invite my friends down to practise driving it all around the garage block. I know how lucky I am and my friends can't believe I have my own car.

Back at work on Monday morning, it's tea break. There are four other apprentices here and one of them, Graham Lazenby, has just got himself a Garelli moped. Paul Graves, also an apprentice, has said he wants to set up a race at lunchtime between Graham and me. I go along with it, knowing my bike is faster than a Garelli, but Graham insists he'll win. So, Paul sets out the rules for the race. We have to start from the gates of the workshop, go down Ashley Road to the end, then turn around and come back to the gates.

Lunchtime's here and the race is on!

I'll stay with Graham during the race, but then I'll open mine up flat out near the end. During the race, I notice Graham's bike's faster than mine on acceleration but mine has a higher top speed. Around 500 yards away from the finish line, we are side by side, but then I move ahead, and I'm winning.

I'm close to the gates. I'm nearly there. Yes! I beat him.

I slow down past the gates, then turn around and ride up next to Paul just as Graham rides in through the gates.

Graham calls out, "I won!"

"How do you make that out?" Paul says to him.

"Because I was the first to come back through the gates," he says.

"Shut up, Graham. Obviously John won and he was going too fast to come through the gates, unlike you on your spaghetti machine."

I think Graham's just a sore loser and for the rest of the week all the others keep ribbing him about it. I don't think they like him very much, but I don't know why because he's okay, just a bit big-headed.

On Friday evening, I decide I'm not going to go out tonight because I feel very tired. Working on lorries is hard enough, but with the noise of that rattling compressor, the sound of lorry engines starting up, the hammering and shouting, the black dust in the air and then trying to work fast enough for Stan's approval all makes it like hell on earth. My hands are cut to pieces – I have chunks out of my knuckles and a burn on my wrist from the hot exhaust of a truck. The grease is stained into my skin and it will not come off, no matter how much I scrub it. I'm sitting on the sofa just staring at the TV; *Coronation Street* is on. I'm watching it, but I'm not taking it in. I'm daydreaming. I'm actually starting to miss going to school and my last job was nowhere near as hard as this one.

At the end of September, 1977, I start going to college in Welwyn Garden City, which is part of my apprenticeship and paid for by Godfrey Davies. College is much better than work because I'll actually learn something from people who speak English. We still work in a workshop, but it's clean and it's all cars, too, so no trucks. After my first day here, which I really enjoy, I head off home. It's starting to rain a lot, and my bike engine cuts out.

I coast it over to the side of the road and check to see what happened. I can see the spark plug is full of water. They've designed the bike badly where the water comes straight off the bottom of the front mudguard and streams into the spark plug. I dry it all out with my overalls because that's all I have with me and continue on my way, but it happens again. Well, this is no good. I have to do something to stop this happening. I tie my overalls around the crash bars and across the front of the engine to stop the water spraying in. Away I go again down all the lanes through the pouring rain and it keeps going fine. The bonus of it is that my feet feel lovely and warm too, which must be due to the overalls wrapping around my feet.

As I go through St Albans, a lot of people seem to be waving to me so I wave back. They seem very friendly here today, but I'm more concerned about my feet … They seem to be getting a bit too warm, so I look down and I can't believe what's happened. My overalls have wrapped around the exhaust and they're on fire. Not just on fire, but there's a blaze halfway up the bike. That's why everyone's waving – I'm riding a fireball. I quickly pull over and put the bike straight on the stand. My instinct is to get away from it and let it burn or explode, but I don't want to lose my bike, and the flames are up to the petrol tank now. I grab the burning overalls and pull them away from the bike, burning my hand in the process. What a stupid thing to do – I should have known better than to wrap the overalls around the bike. At least I got the fire out.

The following day, the weather's just as bad, pouring rain on the way home. I've managed to go down the long lane from Welwyn Garden City and have arrived outside my work at Godfrey Davis, but the bike has cut out twice and now the engine is soaked. I walk into reception and ask if I can use the phone to call home. Pat tells me to go ahead.

Mum answers the phone and I explain everything to her. I ask if she can pick me up and I'll leave my bike here till tomorrow.

Mum says, "Your dad wants to tow you home with his car."

"I've never done that before," I say, feeling a bit confused.

"He says you'll be fine – wait there and we'll be with you soon," she adds.

Within half an hour, Mum and Dad arrive outside the front.

Dad gets his tow rope out of his boot. I ask him, "What do I do if I need to stop for any reason?"

"Don't worry, you'll be fine," he says.

He ties his rope to his car and then around the frame of my bike. I really don't feel safe doing this, especially with this maniac driving.

Just at that moment, an old man comes over and says,

"The only safe way to tow a motorbike is to wrap the rope through the handlebars and hold it with your hand, so if you need to unhitch you can just let go of the rope!"

Phew! I agree that's a safer way, so I go ahead and feed the rope through the handlebars.

Okay, here goes … Dad's in his car and he's taking up the slack of the rope. I'm gently resting my foot on the rear brake so that the bike doesn't jolt.

Away we go out onto Ashley Road and down to the traffic lights. So far, so good, but I'm not sure if this is legal. Also, it's getting dark and it's still raining. The roundabout goes well, but as we move out onto the A405 dual carriageway, Dad starts to accelerate past 50mph, then 60mph. This is the fastest I've ever been on my bike and I'm being towed. Now my speedo is reading 70mph; the bike doesn't feel stable and it was only designed to do 50mph.

Oh my God! He's still accelerating … I have to let go because he's trying to kill me.

I'm rolling to a stop, slowing to 70mph, 65mph, 60mph, 55mph, and still rolling at my bike's top speed. I drift to a stop. That was scary. Now Dad has pulled over.

"What did you let go for?" he says with a frown.

"Because you were going too fast!"

"That's not too fast for a motorbike. What's the matter with you?"

Here we go again … Thank God that man came over and said don't tie the rope to the bike or I'd be getting dragged on my side at 80mph at this very moment. The same thing happens again twice before we arrive home. It's a battle of wills. I have a choice between him shouting at me and telling me how useless I am, or dying. I choose the first one. By the time we get home, Mum's a nervous wreck – she thought I was surely going to die. I really wonder what goes through my father's head sometimes.

By the weekend, I work out a way to cure the problem. I buy myself a mud flap from Moores of Watford and fit it to the bottom of the front mudguard. The water doesn't spray up to the spark plug any more, so it's cured. No more breaking down in the rain. Yay!

28

Becoming an adult

My seventeenth birthday is here – 9 November 1977. I've applied for my car licence so I can take driving lessons. I really want a car now so I can be warm and dry going to work in the winter. I'm scrapping my Anglia, as it was really just something to mess around with and I need the rent money that I pay for the garage to use for driving lessons.

At the end of November, I start taking driving lessons with Cobb's School of Motoring. Mr Cobb is my driving instructor. He's an elderly gentleman who's very well spoken, and his car is a Ford Escort Mk3. I enjoy the lessons with him, but he does keep going on at me to slow down. I have six driving lessons over six weeks with him, and in the middle of January, 1978 I take my driving test.

It's the morning of my test and I've caught the flu. It's pouring rain outside. Mr Cobb has just arrived outside our house and he's waiting for me to come out. I feel ill and I think there's no way I'll pass, but I may as well go through with it because I've paid for it.

He gets me to drive to the testing centre. I'm bumping up kerbs and stalling the car. He tells me to pull over to the side of the road right outside the centre and says, "I don't think you'll pass today because you're not having a very good day, are you?"

"No, I don't feel very good," I say.

"Well, just do your best," he says in his usual reassuring way.

I walk into the waiting room and sit down on an old wooden chair, my head aching and spinning. There are three others in the room and they all look nervous. A man walks out of the office holding a clipboard. He's wearing thick-rimmed glasses and a pinstriped suit with a raincoat. He looks like a 1950s detective.

"John Monaghan, please!" he calls out.

I stand up and say, "Yes, that's me!"

"I'm your Ministry of Transport driving examiner today. Follow me," he says in a BBC accent.

We both walk out to the car park and stand under a shelter.

"Can you read the number plate on that white car to me, please?" he asks, pointing his pen at a Morris 1000.

That's easy enough. I read it to him and he makes a note on his clipboard.

We both get into Mr Cobb's car and Mr Cobb leaves us to it. I follow all of the examiner's instructions. We drive past Watford Junction and so far I think I'm doing okay, but the rain is pelting down.

We turn onto Leavesden Road, which is a long, narrow road. There are cars parked all the way along this road on my side. I have to drive quite close to the parked cars to leave room for the oncoming traffic. I can see the examiner watching the door handles of the parked cars go by on our left. At the end of the test, he asks me to name a few signs from the highway code and I do that quite easily, but I must have done a few things wrong because I've been a bit careless. I don't expect to pass today.

But after making a few notes on his clipboard, he turns to me and says, "Well, Mr Monaghan, I'm pleased to say you've passed your test!"

"What, really?" I ask in disbelief.

"Well, don't sound so surprised – you drove very well indeed," he says.

I've done it, and on a day like this. It's over! No more lessons and I can get a car. This is too much for me to take in; it'll change my life. I'm grinning like a Cheshire cat.

"Thank you!" I say to him.

"That's okay, just drive carefully," he says as he gets out of the car.

Mr Cobb walks over and says, "Okay?"

"Yes, I've passed!"

"Well, that surprises me after the way you drove on the lesson before your test," he says.

"I drove a lot better on the test," I tell him. "Thanks for all your help," I add.

"You're welcome – now you can go and really learn how to drive," he tells me. "Keep your speed down and be careful."

He drops me home in his car and congratulates me. I'm drained and elated at the same time. There's nobody else at home and I have to go back to bed, but it's hard to stay in bed to recover when you're as excited as I am right now.

The rain is pounding against the window pane as I lie on my bed. I'm finding it hard to control my temperature. I'm either sweating from being too hot or shivering from being too cold. At least I'm in the dry now and away from that cold wind and rain. When I should be out celebrating, I curl up in my bed and start to daydream about what'll happen in the future. I'll get my own car, then my own place, and all the things I ever dreamed of when I was a boy. This day is a turning point in my life, a very important day for me.

I think about all of the things that have happened over the past year. I've left a job that I really enjoyed. It was the Queen's Silver Jubilee and I can't think of how many of those Jubilee coins I gave to customers either with a gallon of oil or with their petrol. It was good to see the faces of the people's kids when I gave them the coins. I've started a job that I hate – it's dirty, heavy, and I can't understand a word Stan says, so I can't learn anything from him. Every morning when I wake up, my heart sinks at the thought of going in to work. In the mornings, all of the mechanics are putting barrier cream on their hands and arms, and the smell of that stuff makes me feel sick. As I started there late in the year, just like at my secondary school, everyone had already selected their friends and I was the new apprentice. I don't feel like I fit in there and I spend all my days with Stan. I don't have much to do with the other apprentices and, to be honest, I don't really want to try.

They all seem to be more into the job than I am, and I feel as though I'm in the wrong place all the time I'm there. I was making my way in the world the way I wanted to and Mum should have left me to do that. Now that I'm living the life that they wanted me to live, both Mum and Dad still seem as though they're ashamed of me. I should have stood firm and said no to Mum and carried on with my life the way I'd started it. But then, how could I when I was living in their house under their roof? Is this apprenticeship really worth sacrificing my happiness for? When I left my job, I felt like I'd left part of myself behind. I can never get that back now that I'm following someone else's road and they're ashamed of me because they felt like they had to intervene. My sacrifice was made only to find I still don't have their approval. Will I ever get it?

Now that I can buy myself a car, I'll be able to drive away somewhere. Somewhere far away from everyone – everyone who puts me down. But I'll have to come back; I'll have to go to work and I'll have to accept being put down again. I wonder what Mum, Dad, Anita, and James will say when I tell them I've passed my test today? I think I already know. Mum will say, "Oh good." Dad will say nothing or, if not, it will be a sarcastic comment or some joke. Anita and James, well, they're not really bothered. No, this driving test pass is for me and not for them. I'll do this stupid apprenticeship and I'll see it through. When I have all my qualifications, I can work on my own; I'll start my own business and I'll do it all my own way.

Nobody will tell me what to do; nobody will talk down to me; nobody will bully me; and nobody will be ashamed of me. That's it! I'll make them proud of me because they'll have to be. How could they not be proud of me if I have my own business? Now that I can drive, I'll be able to buy my own van and sign write it with my name. Instead of "Godfrey Davies", it'll say "John Monaghan". Yes! Just imagine me in a van with my own name on the side. My own business advertising my own name. That's exactly what I'll do as soon as I can – then I can be in control of my own life and everyone'll see what I'm really made of. Let's see if they all call me stupid then. Let's see how useless I really am. It's not the life I want, but at least I can end this feeling of not being good enough. I want to know how it feels to be respected, worth something, and not laughed at. But most of all, I want Dad to be proud of me, love me, and respect me. I'll try and I will succeed with my business, but if it fails, I have nothing to lose.

29

A car, a girlfriend, and a looming wedding

It's February, 1978, and being able to drive anywhere is the ultimate freedom. Mum's so good to me. She lets me use her car whenever I ask. I use it more than she does to practise driving and drive my friends around. With all the practice I've had, it's not surprising I'm quite good at driving now. Mum's car isn't fast, but as it's only a Mini 850cc, it's pretty good, and it can do 80mph with four of us in it.

This evening I'm out driving again. I've picked Charlie up and now we're on our way to Roger and Sean's house to pick them up. Charlie is impressed with the wheelspins I've done so far, and also the handbrake turns I've done in a gravel car park. It's dark, it's raining, and it's a Friday evening, so after a drive around town, we're all going for a drink at the Three Crowns in Bushey Heath. I've stopped outside Roger's house and Charlie has just rung the doorbell. Roger and Sean have both darted out of the front door straight away. I think they're looking forward to this, as I'm the first one to be driving a car. The passenger door opens and Sean's first in. He flips the seat up and clambers straight into the back, closely followed by Roger.

"All right, Maurice!" Sean says.

"I'm all right – you?" I ask him.

"Where are we going?" Roger asks.

"I don't know yet, just a drive around," I say.

Charlie jumps in and off we go with a screech of the front wheels. It's full throttle everywhere, as I love to drive fast.

I show my friends the driving skills that I've learned all around Bushey until we arrive at a junction. There's a blue Ford Capri turning right into the road that we're turning out of. I accelerate to pull out, but the Capri cuts the corner short and then, *crash*, I hit the Capri in the side.

Sean calls out, "Keep driving, don't stop!"

So that's what I do – I drive down the hill on Bushey High Street as fast as the Mini will go.

Sean's looking through the back window and saying,

"Oh God, it's Peter Smart. I know him – he's a right flash git! He's following us and it was his Capri you just hit!"

The Capri suddenly overtakes us and then cuts in front of us diagonally and, when it stops, I almost crash into it again. A young bloke about Sean's age with puffy blond hair gets out and walks over to my window. He does look like a flash git.

He says, "Trying to get away, were you?"

I can see what Sean means about him now. If I were driving a 1600 Capri, he would never have caught up with me.

"We're going to have to exchange insurance details," he says.

We argue for a while about who was at fault, but then exchange our details anyway. He gets back into his car and drives off.

"I can't stand that bloke," Sean says with a frown. "You should have driven off again, Maurice!"

"Well, now I have to try and sort the car out before my mum sees it," I say in despair.

"Take it down to my house – we can straighten it out!" Sean says confidently.

I have a horrible feeling in my stomach, thinking about how Mum will react when she finds out. I drive the car down to Roger and Sean's driveway and up to their garage. Everyone gets out. It's stopped raining, but it's dark, damp, and it's about 9:30pm. Sean pulls a carpenter's hammer out of his tool kit and starts banging the driver's side front wing from the inside. Mostly the dent comes out, but it's easy to see it was badly bent and now there're a lot of dents from the inside, too.

I say, "I'd better go home now and face the music!"

Roger and Sean say goodbye and walk slowly into their house. I'm dropping Charlie home.

"Cheer up, Maurice!" says Charlie. "It's just an accident and nobody got hurt."

"I know, Charlie, but it's my mum's car," I reply, knowing how both Mum and Dad will be about it.

I drop Charlie off at home, then head off home myself. My stomach's churning … There's no easy way to tell them what's happened. I park the car outside the house and go indoors. Mum and Dad are both in the living room watching the news. I take a deep breath before I enter the room. Dad is in his usual position sitting in his armchair with his feet up against the mantelpiece and Mum's sitting in her chair.

Mum looks around and says, "You're home early!"

"Yeah, I had a bit of an accident," I say solemnly.

"Why, what happened?" Mum says with panic in her eyes as she sits forwards.

I tell her what happened and she says, "Oh for God's sake, how could you be so stupid?"

Here we go – I'm stupid again.

"It wasn't all my fault!" I reply defensively. "He cut the corner short."

Dad looks around at me and says nothing, just shakes his head. Well, I'm a disappointment already, so what difference will this make? Mum rushes out to look at the car, but she can't see any damage. Maybe I should have said nothing?

"That's it, then, you can't use it again!" Mum says sharply.

I thought Dad would go mad, but again, when it's serious, he says nothing. I think he's happy when everyone else in the family thinks I'm stupid.

A couple of months pass and I'm still not allowed to drive Mum's car because of the accident. Sean's been going out with a girl called Jackie Somerville and they broke up last week. When we're at the club each week, she makes it obvious that she's interested in me, but I don't really want to go out with his ex. She's nice looking, though, and eventually I change my mind and ask her out. She says yes, and asks if I'll come to her house to play records on Saturday night.

"Okay, you're on – see you Saturday," I tell her and I say goodbye.

It's Saturday night, and for the first time I'm going out to see a girl instead of going out with my friends. It feels weird, but she's an attractive girl, so how could I say no?

I take a little extra time to get ready this evening, then get on my bike and head over to her house. I feel nervous, but I don't know why – she's just a girl. But as I knock on her front door, I feel a bit anxious because I don't know what to expect.

Luckily, Jackie answers the door and says, "Come on, come straight up to my room!"

She grabs me by the hand and nearly drags me up the stairs. There are two single beds in her room, teddy bears everywhere, a record player, and a chest of drawers. She sits on her bed and I sit on the bed opposite – it must be her sister's. She starts playing with her hair and lying on her bed doing funny poses, then says, "Don't you want to kiss me?"

I go over to her bed as though I do this all the time. I kiss her, then make a couple of jokes and start to talk about all the bears she has. Two minutes later, I sit back on the other bed and try to talk to her to get to know her better.

"Aren't you going to do anything then?" she asks.

"What do you want to do?" I say. "I thought you wanted to play records."

She looks annoyed with me and then rolls her eyes to the ceiling. I hear the front door open and there's a call from downstairs – her mum and dad have arrived home.

"Jackie!" her mum calls up the stairs. "Who have you got up there?"

"Um, just a friend!" Jackie shouts down.

"Well, tell *him* to come down and meet us!" her mum says.

With that, I head straight for the bedroom door and say, "Look, I'd better go."

Jackie comes down with me and says to her mum, "This is John, he's my new boyfriend."

Her mum asks me, "Oh, are you leaving?"

I say, "Yes, I have a lot to do tonight."

As I step outside the front door, her mum follows me, asking, "How long have you been with her?"

"Not long," I say. "I just got here before you did."

"No, I mean how long have you been going out with her?" she asks.

"Oh, this is the first time," I say, feeling guilty.

"Well, she's only fourteen years old, you know," she says.

I nod, then say goodbye and leave. On the journey home, I start thinking about what her mum said, telling me that Jackie's only fourteen. I was sure she was older than that; she definitely acts a lot older. I don't even know when her birthday is, but she must be nearly fifteen, surely.

It's April, 1978. I've just got back from work on a Friday evening. The sun's shining and at last it's much warmer. It's been a very hard day today – I've been building a big lorry engine with Stan, and as usual there has been no conversation with him or jokes, just work, work, work. Dad had the day off today. He's at home and Mum's been out all day somewhere. He seems to be in a really good mood this evening and actually smiles at me as I walk in.

"How was Stan today?" he asks in a warm and relaxed way.

I don't know what's happened to him, but he seems different.

I'm glad though, so I smile back and say, "He's the same as always."

Then he tells me, "I have a surprise for your mum! Come out to the garage with me, come on!"

I follow him out to the garage and he opens the garage door to reveal a sparkling light blue Triumph Toledo. It's only four years old, but it looks like it's brand new.

"Wow! It looks great," I tell him. "She'll love it.

To my surprise, he says, "You may as well have the Mini now."

"Really?"

"The wing's bent on it now anyway, isn't it?" he says sarcastically.

It's nice when he's like this. It's hard to imagine how bad he can be most of the time, but today he's like a different man.

Just at that moment, Mum arrives home and sees us both standing at the garage door. She parks and walks up the driveway.

"What's this?" she asks.

Dad still has a warm smile on his face and says, "I bought it for you."

Mum looks in awe at the car and says, "How much did that cost?"

"I got it for a good price," Dad replies.

He clearly doesn't want to tell her.

I leave them to it and go to the bathroom to try to scrub the grease from my hands and then have a bath. This has turned out to be a great week, and thanks to Dad I'll have my own car now. I'll have to ask when I can start driving it when we have dinner …

Summer's here at last, and I'm enjoying driving everywhere in my Mini. I'm still going out with Jackie, but I don't spend much time with her. I spend most of my free time with my friends. Lately, there seem to be a lot of girls who want to go out with me. Or so I keep hearing. No doubt it's because I'm the only one who has a car.

Anita's getting married this weekend coming – it's her big day on Saturday. All my friends have been invited and I'm taking Jackie, too. I'm not sure how much Anita knows about my friends, but when it comes to parties, they can be a bit wild. Hopefully they'll tone it down a bit, though, as it's my sister's wedding.

It's not long before it's the day of the wedding. I've been given the job of "usher".

Anita tells me all I have to do is give everyone a carnation and pin as they walk through the church door. Then I have to ask if they're with the bride or the groom so I can tell them where to sit. I feel like such an idiot doing this stupid job, but I go through the process anyway.

The ceremony's finished and we stand for the photographer, having the photos taken. Anita and her new husband, Dave, get into the white Rolls-Royce and all of us follow in our cars to the reception venue.

There are 40 to 50 cars following the Rolls-Royce – mostly family, uncles, aunts, cousins, and some friends. The chauffeur turns down a long driveway in Garston to where the reception is being held. But there's a problem; it's the wrong driveway. So, at the end of the driveway, he turns around and heads back up towards the main road. Now the procession of cars that's following the Rolls-Royce is still heading down the driveway and so the cars heading in are passing the cars coming out in the opposite direction. It's a joke – we're waving to the people who are following us going the opposite direction.

Eventually, we arrive at the venue. It's a disco in a hall and Dad has pre-paid the bar for everyone's drinks for the whole night. He must have more money than I thought. It's not long before all my friends are getting very drunk. Now I'm worried that everyone could get out of control and my sister will blame me. There are not many girls here our age, so everyone's asking Jackie to dance with them. She's getting really drunk, too. I have a couple of drinks myself, and when I look around, I see Jackie kissing Charlie. This is getting more and more crazy. Five minutes later and she's kissing Roger. I'm in disbelief as to what's going on. Mum walks over to me; she doesn't look very happy.

"Get rid of her, John!" she shouts. "She's a tart!" She glares at me.

I really wish I weren't here because everything's out of control. My other friends are outside drinking bottles of whiskey. Some are taking bottles of spirits from behind the bar, taking them outside and drinking them with the optics still attached. Everyone's so drunk, and Jackie has turned out to be anyone's for a tin of salmon when she's drunk.

This nightmare evening is drawing to a close and I've really had enough. I'm going to split with Jackie and I can't let my friends get away with this. I'm in so much trouble. Everyone's starting to leave. I have to virtually carry Jackie to my car. I have to take her home because I'm responsible for her. I manage to put her in the car and then I start heading down the A41 towards Bushey. I'm driving quite fast and it's raining. Jackie doesn't give a damn about what she's done tonight.

With slurred speech, she says, "I was only having a good time … What's wrong with you?"

I'm so angry that I turn and shout at her, but as I look up, I see the traffic lights have turned red. I slam on the brakes, but the car skids and we go straight through the red traffic lights. Thank God there were no cars crossing through and no police around either because I've been drinking, too.

I look back at Jackie and she looks upset. I'm still angry with her, so I say nothing to make her feel any better. I carry on driving, except more carefully because I could have killed both of us back there. I drop her off at her house and still don't say anything. I think we both know it's over between us. I'm not going back to the wedding reception. I'm driving home and going straight to bed.

30

A war with friends and a new girlfriend

The next morning, I wake up and the first thing I think about is what happened last night. God, why did I have to wake up to this? I walk slowly downstairs to see Mum and Dad both in the living room with James.

Straight away, Mum says, "Do you know what your friends did last night?"

Here we go … It's all my fault. I'm the Black Sheep, the one who ruins everything.

"I know they were behaving badly and I'm going to see them about it later," I say abruptly.

Ignoring my response, Mum says, "They took bottles of spirits from behind the bar and threw the optics on the ground outside! Why would they do that when all the drinks were paid for anyway?" she asks me.

"I don't know. I'll go and see them now, okay?" I reply in frustration.

With that, I leave the room, walk straight out of the front door, and get into my car to drive to Charlie's house first. My blood's boiling by the time I arrive at Charlie's house. I knock at the door and Charlie's mum opens it.

"Where's Charlie?" I ask her.

"He's still in bed … What's wrong?" she says, looking confused.

Without replying, I rush past her and go upstairs to Charlie's room. As soon as I see him in bed, I start demanding answers from him as to why he behaved the way he did.

"Why did you carry on like that at my sister's wedding?" I ask him.

He's half asleep and squints up at me, muttering, "Maurice, I'm trying to sleep!"

In despair, I walk out of the house and go straight up to Roger and Sean's house. Meanwhile, unknown to me, Charlie calls Roger and warns him that I'm on my way. Both Roger and Sean come out to meet me. I start demanding answers from Roger, but then Sean jumps in.

"Do you want a fight or something?" he says with his face screwed up.

"Yeah, I do. Come on then!"

"I could knock you out!" he says with clenched teeth.

"Go on then. Try it – go for it!" I say, not caring which way this goes any more.

Sean seems to be in two minds, and starts shouting at me instead.

His dad comes rushing over and grabs him, then asks,

"What's going on?"

Roger and Sean's dad is a sergeant major in the army, so I guess he must be used to this kind of thing. I tell him what happened and he tells Roger and Sean to get into his car. He then looks over at me and says, "We're going to your house now, so I think it's best you follow us there!"

I didn't want it to come to this; I only wanted them to know how upset I was about what they did. As I follow them in their VW Beetle, I can see their dad shouting at them in the car through the back window. We arrive at my house and all four of us are standing on the front doorstep while their dad rings the doorbell.

Mum answers the door and Roger's dad very politely says, "Oh, Mrs Monaghan, I'm pleased to meet you and I would like to apologise for the behaviour of my sons!"

Mum invites them in and we all sit in the living room while Roger's dad talks to Mum.

He tells her, "It was lucky I came along when I did because I stopped a fight between John and Sean – and a very bad fight, I might add!"

"Oh, not to worry!" Mum says. "It's so nice of you to come and see us about it."

Mum shows them to the front door and everyone says goodbye.

She closes the front door and says, "What a nice man Roger and Sean's dad is."

Well, he made Mum feel better about it, but I feel terrible now.

The week rolls on, and I've heard nothing from any of my friends. Nobody's called to say how bad they feel about what they did. I'm feeling sad. There was no need for it, and I feel stuck in the middle. I think they're angry with me and feel like I overreacted about it all. Maybe I did; maybe I could have handled it better, but I was hurt because they disrespected my family. Maybe I should have just told them how I felt instead of going to their houses in a rage. It's how Dad would react when he's angry, though. Maybe I'll go to the club on Saturday and talk to them about it all.

Saturday comes around after what seems to be a very long week. As lunch time approaches, I decide that I'll go up to Bushey and talk to them. As I drive along Bushey High Street, just by chance Roger, Charlie, and Sean are all walking in the other direction.

Charlie's nearest to me, so I stop my car and call out, "Charlie!"

All three of them totally blank me.

I know they saw and heard me. These are my best friends; they're my life. And they're acting as though I don't exist.

I slump back into my car and sit there for a while. If they're not even going to speak to me, what can I do to make it right? I start driving home because there's no point my staying in Bushey. I'm not welcome here any more.

On the journey home, I'm churning over the whole situation in my head. They're my friends and they wronged me. I had to show them how bad it was to do that. Now they're showing me how they feel by blanking me. I'm outnumbered. They all must agree that they're doing the right thing, so maybe I was wrong. I just don't know. None of this makes any sense to me. I arrive home and park my car, feeling really fed up. I go indoors and straight upstairs to my room. Lying on my bed, I think about the whole situation some more. They can't keep this up forever, so I'm just going to have to ride it out.

On Wednesday evening around eight pm, the phone rings. Mum answers it, then comes back into the living room and says, "It's for you, John."

"Who is it?" I ask, hoping it'll be Charlie.

"It's a girl called Tess," she replies.

Confused, I walk out to the hallway and pick up the receiver. "Hello," I say.

"My friend gave me your number. Do you want to meet up?" Tess says with a giggle.

She sounds nervous.

Disappointed that it wasn't Charlie calling, I reply, "Where and when?"

"There's a youth club at Bushey Meads School tomorrow night at seven – we can meet there," she replies.

"Yeah, okay, I'll see you there," I say.

Instantly, there's a shriek down the phone line and I have to pull the phone away from my ear. I put the phone down, thinking she screams like she's crazy excited. Oh well, now I've set a date with a shrieking schoolgirl. I suppose I may as well go now that I have no friends; it's better than staying in watching TV with Mum and Dad.

The following evening, I drive up to Bushey Meads School. This feels strange, going to a youth club where there're so many kids. Most of them are around fifteen years old. I park and walk in through the hall entrance. Looking around, I see groups of kids at different tables all chatting.

I notice a table of about six girls and one girl in particular waving to get my attention with a big smile on her face.

All of her friends look around at me. This is such a rubbish place to be. I recognise Tess; I'm sure I've seen her at a disco at the club before, but I've never spoken to her and I don't know how she got my phone number.

She runs over to me and says, "Thanks for coming – do you want to go out with me?"

She surprises me by coming straight out with it like that.

But she's a bubbly, pretty girl, with long brown curly hair, big blue eyes, and she's made me smile.

I reply, "Why not?"

She starts jumping up and down with excitement and says, "Come on, come and meet my friends!"

"Why don't we go somewhere else?" I say, feeling out of place.

"If you like, but I have to be home by ten at the latest," she says, giggling.

"Okay, well, get your coat and let's go," I say with a smile.

She gets her coat and says goodbye to her friends. They're all giggling about something, too.

I walk out to the car park with her and tell her, "Jump in the car, then."

"Where are we going?" she asks.

"How about Old Redding?"

"On a first date?" she says.

"Why not?" I ask, a bit confused.

"That place has a reputation, so I've heard," she says with another giggle.

"I know, but we can look out over the town and see it all lit up at night there. We're just going for a drink in the pub, though."

"Are you sure?" she replies with another giggle.

Oh God! I've let Barbara Windsor into my car, I think. Well, at least someone wants to spend time with me.

We arrive at the pub and I find a table by the window. We sit and talk for a while to get to know each other a bit better. Once she calms down, she's a fun person to be with and we have quite a laugh together. With the time seeming to fly, I glance at my watch and it's 9:30pm.

"We'd better get going in a minute if you have to be home by ten!" I say reluctantly.

At that very moment, who should walk over to my table but Sean. And he looks really angry. He ignores that I'm with someone and start shouting at me about what happened at his house. The funny thing is that I'm relieved about it. If he's shouting, it's way better than him ignoring me.

He says, "We could have beaten you up for what you did!"

We argue for a couple of minutes and agree to put it all behind us. As soon as he leaves, I look back at Tess and she looks shocked.

She says, "I wanted to hit him for talking to you like that."

"Forget it," I reply. Then I tell her, "We've all fallen out recently and we're good friends, really."

I drive her home and when we stop outside her house, she asks, "When can we go out again?"

"Well, give me your phone number and I'll call you," I say.

As the work week rolls on, I start thinking about my friends and I'm wondering when Charlie will call to meet up for a drink so we can sort out this argument.

It's Friday evening and I've still heard nothing – what am I supposed to do? I think I'll leave it another week and if I still hear nothing, I'll go to Charlie's house. There's no point phoning him because he probably won't come to the phone. I decide to call Tess because we had quite a good time together and there's no point sitting on my own with Mum and Dad. I call her number and her dad, Mr Robinson, answers the phone. He's quite a laid-back man and seems friendly.

"May I speak to Tess, please?" I ask.

"Just a minute," he says. Then he calls out, "Tess, it's John on the phone for you, oohwee!" in a teasing voice.

I can hear Tess say, "Shut up, Dad!" and then she says, "Hello?"

I reply, "There's a movie on tonight at the Empire in Watford. Do you want to go and see it?"

"Oh yeah," she says. "What's it called?"

"*Saturday Night Fever*, but I don't know what it's about."

"Oh cool, everyone's talking about that film," she says in her usual bubbly way.

"Okay, I'll pick you up at seven pm," I tell her, and again there's a squeal down the phone.

I pull the phone away from my ear and then hang up. I'm going to have to prepare for that next time. I get ready as quickly as I can and drive up to Bushey. When I ring the doorbell, her mum and dad both come to the front door, and they keep looking at me and making jokes. Then Tess comes out and she looks great. She's wearing a black silky top with a pencil skirt, but her wavy hair's so shiny and goes all the way down her back. Her eyes are sparkling and she looks excited. She's so much fun to be around and it's good to see someone who's glad to see me. She goes straight to the passenger door of my car and gets in, then waves at her mum and dad and tells them to go in. I get in the car before saying goodbye to her parents.

All the way to the Empire, she's chatting away about her friends, but I don't know any of them. We arrive at the Empire and she's hugging me in the queue. I'm really not used to this, but it's nice. Eventually, after a long wait in the queue, we go inside and the curtains open, ready for the film to start. She snuggles into me and this is the first real date that we've had where we're both relaxed and there's no awkwardness.

The film's really good and has a few adult scenes in it. She looks at me during one of the scenes and says, with a smirk, "I hope you're not getting any funny ideas from this film."

"No, of course not!" I say and she does her Barbara Windsor giggle.

At the end of the film, everyone starts to leave and they're talking about it on the way out.

Tess is hugging me on the way down the aisle and says,

"That's the best film I've ever seen."

"I think it was really good, too. It's getting late, so I'll have to drop you straight home," I tell her.

"Oh, but I was just starting to enjoy the night with you!" she says, then makes a sad face at me.

I smile at her and we walk through the crowd to get to my car. As I unlock the car, she walks around to the driver's side, then right up to me and says, "Thank you", in a sincere and lovable way.

"It was just a film, no big deal," I say quietly.

She moves closer and says, "No, thank you for being you."

Nobody's ever said that to me before. We kiss and she makes me feel warm inside. Then she just stares into my eyes and smiles.

"Come on, I better get you home," I say as I get into the car.

On the way home, she keeps looking over at me and rubbing my arm and leg. She makes me feel happy. This has been a really nice evening, maybe even better than being with my friends. Well, different anyway. We turn onto her road and I park outside her house. She smiles and says, "I'm late, so I'd better go straight in, or Dad will be angry."

"Yeah, I know," I say. "See you again soon."

She gives me a kiss on the cheek and then walks up the footpath to her front door. She unlocks the front door, then turns to me and blows a kiss. I'm going to keep that picture of her in my head forever. I smile and drive to the end of her road still smiling. She's a really nice girl.

As I arrive home, I remember that my car has been getting hard to start, so I park it around the corner on Sandown Road at the top of the hill so I can roll it down the hill to bump start it in the morning. It's a pleasant short walk between Sandown Road and Sandringham Road. I feel so relaxed. I put my key in the front door and open it, but there's something odd this evening. Everyone's in bed and it's only 10:30 on Friday night?

Anyway, I go in quietly and go to bed early myself.

31

A family shock

The next morning, I wake up early and I can hear Mum downstairs in the kitchen talking to Anita. I get dressed and go downstairs.

"Good morning," I say to them.

"Good morning," Mum replies in a shaky voice; she seems upset. She disregards me and carries on talking to Anita. She's telling Anita that Dad had a hospital appointment yesterday and they've done some tests. Anita's leaning against the kitchen sink by the window and Mum is standing with one hand on the draining board. I sit down at the kitchen table and listen to what they say. Mum explains to Anita what happened at the hospital, her one hand still leaning on the draining board. Then she says, "It's cancer!"

She bursts into tears, almost collapsing. I jump up to catch her, but Anita does it first.

In tears and shaking like a leaf, she says, "They say they can operate, but prepare yourself for the worst."

Still sitting at the table, I watch Mum and Anita hug each other. They're both crying. It sounds as though they're saying he's going to die. As I watch them, I feel a sense of numbness. I feel as though I'm watching a film. Surely this can't be real?

On Monday morning, I'm back to work as usual. I'm up and out quite early, and it's a sunny morning. I walk around the corner to Sandown Road where my car is parked at the top of the hill. I get into it and just sit there for a minute or two. I really can't take in what I've heard over the weekend. It's made me want to look around more and pay attention to my surroundings. I try to imagine the world with Dad gone, but I can't. I feel angry that he's made me despise him so much that I don't care if he dies.

There's a man walking his dog towards me. He's probably wondering why I'm just sitting here in my car. Okay, here goes then. Handbrake off, ignition on, open the door and start to push the car down the hill. Once the speed is up, I jump in, put it in second gear, half throttle and let the clutch up. A couple of splutters and my Mini fires into action. I close the door and I'm on my way.

I enjoy this drive into work; the sun's shining and everything looks bright and cheerful.

As I drive along St Albans Road and across the traffic lights at Horseshoe Lane, I enter the A405 and drive along the dual carriageway. There's not much traffic and the roads are clear. I pass my old school and glance over at the trees that Kevin and I planted along the perimeter fence. It makes me realise that nothing is forever. Is Dad really going to die? I start to feel a bit upset … What's wrong with me? Do I love him or do I hate him? I don't even know for sure any more.

He worked for years to provide for me as well as the rest of the family. He used to bring sweets home for me when I was little. He gave me this car. I've seen him crying over Mum like a baby and I've comforted him. He's an idiot, but I must love him because, after all, he is my dad. My head is so screwed up.

I'm near work, so I pull in and park my car around the corner from Godfrey Davies to sit for a minute and get my head straight.

As I'm walking towards work, my heart sinks – as it does every morning when I enter this place. Through the gates, past reception, and through the massive steel sliding doors into the dirty smelly workshop, I can hear the voices of the mechanics, Paul Wake and Brian Liversedge, talking loudly and laughing. I can hear Joe Christina, an Italian man, swearing and moaning about the place. He's a stumpy man who always lets everyone know he doesn't like management. They're all in the locker room. I open the dark blue painted wooden door and the voices get louder. Then the stink of barrier cream hits me and makes me want to throw up. Nobody says good morning because apprentices are not worth saying good morning to; we are all nobodies. The other apprentices don't say good morning because they've learnt not to from the skilled mechanics. There are so many reasons why I don't want to work here, but I put on my overalls anyway. They have a big Ford badge on the back and a Ford Trucks logo on the top pocket with red stripes down the outside of each arm. I am the property of Ford Motor Company. They're dark blue, of course, because everything here has to be dark blue for some reason.

Once we all have our overalls on, the first thing we apprentices have to do is empty all the bins. Paul Graves, Clive Saunders, Chris Mitchell, Graham Lazenby (whom nobody likes), and I all get started. I get my sack barrow from the corner of the workshop and wheel it over to Stan and my work bay. I glance towards Stan. He's standing there opening his toolbox, getting his tools out.

He looks up at me and the first thing he says is, "You not stripping any bloody threads today, matey, or I smack you like anything!"

Okay, well at least he's made me laugh. I stripped the threads on a wiper motor on Friday and he's still angry because he's lost bonus money because of it. I push the sack barrow underneath our overflowing bin, which is really a 40-gallon steel drum. And, surprise, it's dark blue, just like the sack barrow and the walls. Well, the walls are white from halfway up to the roof but blue at the bottom.

As I wheel the sack barrow with the bin across the workshop to the skip outside, I can hear the usual everyday sounds of this time of the morning: Ford D series diesel engines starting up and one of the mechanics, Brian Liversedge, singing the usual songs that a man with a pot belly, ginger hair, and a chubby face should not be singing – "Do Ya Think I'm Sexy" by Rod Stewart. But he sings it like he's not even joking.

All the apprentices help each other lift the heavy bins up to the skip and we empty them all.

After a long day of working with Stan, rebuilding, and fitting a truck engine, and not understanding anything he's said, it's 5:30pm and time to go home. Stan's been asking me to do things partly in English and partly in Polish. My hands are black with oil and grease, and I'm glad the day's over. I put all of Stan's tools away, cleaning them as I go.

"You work good today, matey, so you can do that every day none it!" he says.

"None it" means "isn't it". "None you" means "don't you". I have learned something.

I take my boots and overalls off in the locker room, then scrub my hands with a nailbrush using Swarfega, which stinks, but it's not as bad as the barrier cream. I say goodbye to Stan and walk through the big steel doors and out to the road. I can feel the heat from the sun and everything is bright and calm. Walking out of that old Victorian building makes me feel as though I've just been released from prison. I can see my little blue Mini parked at the side of the road and it brings a smile to my face. I jump in, start the engine, and zoom off down the road.

Driving along the A405, listening to the radio, it's like a different world compared to work. The trees are full of leaves and the sound of my engine with the radio playing makes life worthwhile. When I arrive home, James is watching TV and Dad is still at work, but he does a lighter job now, driving a forklift. Mum is in the kitchen, putting dinner on for everyone. She seems a bit happier than she was at the weekend, despite everything. Dad still works, so maybe there's a chance he'll be okay.

Just as Mum's getting ready to dish up the dinner, Dad arrives home. Even now, I still feel the tension build, as I don't know what mood he'll be in. The gates clang and I can hear his car reversing up the driveway. He opens the back door and walks into the kitchen.

"What's for dinner?" he asks Mum.

"I bought you a steak, and we have liver and mash," she says.

He seems happy enough, so we all sit together in the kitchen and have dinner. I finish as quickly as I can and go straight up to get washed and out as soon as possible. Just as I leave the table, the phone rings, so I answer and surprisingly it's Charlie.

I had almost given up on him ever calling me again.

"All right, Morris," he says.

"All right, Charlie, are you okay?" I reply.

"Yeah, I'm working behind the bar at McGinty's tonight, so do you want to come up and have a drink?" he says.

Charlie often works behind the bar at McGinty's, because his dad runs the club.

"Yeah, okay," I reply.

Very soon I arrive at McGinty's and Charlie's behind the bar serving the usual Irish drinkers, Jonny Coffee and Taxi Cab Tom. They're both in their forties and they both drink a lot of Guinness. We call Tom "Taxi Cab Tom" because he always gets so drunk, then falls over, shouting, "Charlie, call me a taxi cab!"

Charlie normally responds by saying, "You're a taxi cab, Tom!"

But then he always orders him a taxi and helps him into it.

Taxi Cab Tom is a huge man and he's very heavy. It normally takes at least fifteen minutes to get him into the taxi. He spends ten of those minutes rolling around on the pavement first. Scones for Tea in Gloucestershire is another even bigger man. You can guess why he's called that. But he's not here tonight; maybe he's in Gloucestershire.

Well, I have a few drinks with Charlie and we don't even talk about Anita's wedding. We both want to forget it. I've missed these times with him a lot. I can tell he has too; he's such a good friend to me. When everyone has left, we have a lock in and at around 11:30pm Charlie asks if I want to meet up on Saturday with the others and I agree. It looks like everything's going to be okay again.

A hard week at work passes and it's Saturday morning. I didn't go out last night, so I'm awake early and it's yet another very hot day. I've arranged to go to Wembley market with Charlie, Roger, and Sean. Charlie's brother, Anthony, is going to come with us, too.

I need some new clothes and I've got a lot of money to spend. There's a new trend, which is a bit punky – baggy jeans with a blue or white pinstripe down either leg, and furry jumpers. I'm in two minds about furry jumpers, but I'll get some anyway and some new extra tight Levi's 501s. I think I'll get some beige ones, too, and a pair of Dr Martens boots.

Within half an hour, I'm up, washed, and out through the front door. As soon as I stop outside Charlie's house, the front door opens. They all rush out and clamber straight into my car.

Sean jumps through the passenger door first. He flips the seat up to get into the back and says, "All right, Maurice?"

"Yeah, I'm all right, Sean," I say.

Charlie and Anthony jump in too and say hello, which puts a smile on my face. I'm back with my old friends again. I know Charlie's done this. He's a great friend and a bit special

– there're not many like him around and he can influence anyone just by being Charlie.

With a screech of my tyres, we're racing down the road. I turn the music up and it's Wembley here we come.

Wembley market's the best for clothes – they have all the latest stuff at cheap prices. We all make our way around the stalls and I've got everything I wanted and more. Between the four of us, we've bought so much that I can barely fit it all into the small boot of my Mini. Somehow, I cram it all in and everyone's in good spirits. We're chatting, joking, and laughing all the way back. But then, just one block from Charlie's house, there's a loud hiss from under the bonnet. My temperature gauge has gone right up and steam is pouring out from either side of the bonnet.

Sean shouts, "It's on fire!"

"I know what's happened – it's overheated!" I say.

Damn, I really don't need this.

"Let us out, it's going to blow!" Sean shouts.

"It's steam!" I shout at Sean. "It's not going to blow!" I add in frustration.

He watches too much TV, I think.

I pull over as quickly as I can, and luckily we're in Bournehall Avenue right next to an alleyway that leads to Crabtree Close where Charlie lives. Charlie jumps out as soon as I stop, while Anthony flings the seat up on the passenger side and they're out of the car like cats off a frying pan. I open the bonnet and there's steam and water everywhere.

Instantly, Anthony asks, "What's wrong with it, Maurice?"

"I don't know yet, Anthony, I've only just opened the bonnet!" I say, fed up.

"Well, you're supposed to be the mechanic!" he replies.

I look at him clenching my lips. That's really not helping.

"Well, it's leaked all the water out somewhere, but I'm going to need some more water to fill it up again to see where it's leaking from," I tell him. I turn to Charlie and say, "Can we get any water in a container from your house?"

"We should have something," he says, looking thoughtful.

"Let's go and get something, then," I say.

I'm worried, because it could have blown the head gasket, so I walk on ahead down the alleyway towards Charlie's house, keen to get some water. They're all chatting behind me, when I see a group of girls walking towards us in the opposite direction. The one in front must be the prettiest girl I've ever seen. She has brown curly hair that's so shiny, big eyes, a pretty little nose and a perfect figure. She has a feminine walk, but leads the group with such confidence. As we get closer, she sits down on the ground and, with a piece of white chalk, writes her name on the ground: "Tess".

Another Tess?

She then looks up at me as I walk past with her eyes fixed on mine. She looks shy but with attitude. There's no smile from her and not from me either. I can't take my eyes away from hers, though.

Wow! That was weird … There's something about her that's different from any other girl. I continue walking on towards Charlie's house and the others are following, but they know nothing about it. I don't think her friends noticed either. I may as well forget it, because I have a girlfriend already and I probably won't see her again anyway.

We collect a container of water from Charlie's house and walk back down to the car. The others leave Charlie and me to sort the car out. We spend the rest of the day in the blazing sun replacing a split hose that's in the most awkward place under the bonnet.

It's Thursday evening, and I'm almost home from work, I'm going to have to stay in this evening because I spent so much money on clothes and parts for my car last Saturday. It's been warm but very grey all day and it's humid. I park my car around the corner as usual, but as I walk up to the house, I see Mum's car outside and Dad's new Rover is there, too. He's rarely home before me, so I wonder if something's wrong. I walk in through the back door and into the living room. Mum's sitting on the sofa and James is in her armchair watching TV.

I ask Mum, "Is something wrong? Where's Dad?"

She looks like she's been crying. She replies, "Your daddy has to go into hospital for an operation next month for his bowel cancer and I have to go in for a hysterectomy at the same time. He's upstairs in bed. He's not well at all."

I sit down next to her and give her a hug. She starts to cry and holds onto me very tightly.

"I don't know how we're going to manage, John!" she cries.

"Don't worry about that," I say, comforting her. "Stay strong, everything will be okay," I add, with no idea what I'm talking about.

"I'll get the dinner on now," she says, squeezing my hand as she stands up. "Do you want egg and chips?"

"Yeah, that's fine, thanks, Mum," I reply.

Our house seems to have a massive dark cloud over it that never seems to go away. The only time I feel happy is when I'm out with my friends.

The next day at work, it's the same old routine. I've been working with Stan for a long time now and he never really teaches me anything. I just have to watch him and learn. I understand how hydraulic brakes work, but I'm still not sure how air brakes work.

I ask him a question for the first time ever:

"Stan, can you explain to me how the air brake system works, please?"

He looks surprised and confused, but gives me his garbled lesson anyway, saying, "Okay, driver for pumping the pedal like anything. Go down the pipes like anything and push expander on a shoe and that's that, none it. You can see, none you? For that I say, none it."

"Thanks, Stan," I reply.

He rarely says anything, so that was a good result, but I'm still none the wiser. He never jokes about anything. He never laughs and never mixes or talks to anyone. He lives on his own with two Chihuahua dogs called Mickey and Morecambe. He's 63 years old and he seems so miserable.

The working day is done and Roger told me that there's a party on at someone's house in the week. It's a girl's house in central Watford. I don't know how he knows this girl, but I think she's a sister of one of his workmates or something. Roger's training to be an electrician now. We all took up trades: a mechanic; an electrician; Charlie's training as a carpenter; Sean's also a carpenter; and Anthony's a baker. What a team.

Anyway, I'm not going to lie here thinking about things; I'm going to pick up my friends and go to this party. We can walk to the party from my house, so I'll pick them all up and leave my car here when we get back. An hour or so passes and we're all walking along St Albans Road in a great mood. I think this is the first proper house party I've ever been to. I've got my new clothes and boots on, and my hair's perfect.

I've bought myself a steel comb to put in the back pocket of my new even tighter 501 Levi's, and I have on a tightly fitted black cap-sleeved T-shirt, and I used my Brut 33 aftershave.

I still have the same brown leather jacket, though. I think we all look great and this feels exciting – it's all new to me. The evening's warm and my friends are laughing and joking all the way to Central Watford. Life really is exciting and I'm looking forward to this party. As we turn the corner near the house party, I hear that song again – "Night Fever" by the Bee Gees. It's on everywhere I go.

We arrive at the house and Roger's first in, then me and the others. The girl's happy to see us all and shows us through to the living room. There are a lot of girls all sitting on the floor of the living room. The furniture's all been moved out, except for the TV and a coffee table in the middle of the room. It's laden with bottles of spirits, but no beer. There's vodka, whisky, gin and wine. I sit down opposite Charlie and pour myself a drink of straight vodka. I've never tried it before, but there's nothing else, so what the hell? This is such a girly party, because it's mostly girls here. They're playing girly music, like "Yes Sir, I Can Boogie" and Boney M. To be honest, I'm fed up with girls – they all seem to act the same. They're all so screamy. I haven't even bothered with my own girlfriend much since I made up with my friends again. Charlie's chatting to a girl next to him and the others are dancing already. This vodka's giving me a nice feeling and the atmosphere's good. There's a girl next to me who keeps talking to me, but really, I'm enjoying watching the others dance, and I feel like I'm getting drunk. I've had two big glasses of vodka and the bottle's empty, but there's plenty of whisky and wine, so after a couple of glasses of wine I pour myself a big glass of whisky. As I pour it out, Charlie looks over at me and says, "Maurice, what are you doing?" with a frown.

He's always the responsible one.

"I'm okay, Charlie. Stop worrying," I tell him.

In defiance, I down the big glass of whisky as he watches. He shakes his head and says, "You're going to be ill, Maurice."

"Nah, I'm fine," I say.

A few minutes later, everything starts to go blurry. I try to get up to dance with the others, but fall back onto the TV and knock it into the wall. I can't even get up. I can hear a girl shouting at me. Charlie's asking, "Are you okay, Maurice?"

I can feel myself being dragged along by my friends, but I can't move any of my limbs. This is weird; I'm not in control of my body. The voices sound muffled as I'm being dragged along outside and into the garden. They lay me on the concrete outside, and I can just see the ground but can't move. I've been left alone, but I can hear muffled voices talking about me. I think the girl is arguing with Charlie.

I feel a nudge from someone's foot.

"Do you want a fight? Come on, come on then!" they're saying.

I recognise the voice – it's Micky Duggan. I'm lying on the concrete and I can't move a limb, but he wants to fight with me? I think it must be some lame plan of his to impress one of the girls, because by the time they come out of the house I'll still be lying on the floor and he'll probably tell them he did it.

I hear Charlie's voice again and Roger's with him.

"What are you doing, Micky?" Charlie asks angrily.

"Well, he wanted a fight!" Mickey says.

"He's not even conscious, you idiot!" Charlie replies.

I'm conscious, but I can't move or even speak. I don't even care, though. I feel myself being pulled up to my feet again and it's Charlie and Roger either side of me. They're saying goodbye to the girl and I'm being pulled along the road. They're good friends and I've ruined the evening by being such an idiot.

The two of them drag me all the way home and into my house.

I don't know how, but I wake up in my bed in the morning.

32

She's the one

A week later, I'm on my way to see Charlie to spend the day just hanging around Bushey and maybe go to McGinty's club and have a drink. It's a really nice Saturday – the sun's shining, and the sky's so blue with no sign of any clouds.

When I get to Charlie, he says, "Let's go to the club, but I need to drop off something at John McCarthy's house around the corner. He lives at 5 Moatfield Road – is that okay?"

We jump into the car and I pull up outside number five, as Charlie asked. I don't know John McCarthy.

"I won't be a minute," Charlie says.

He jumps out and opens the iron gate, then walks up the pathway to the front door. I mess around with my radio to try to find a better station. I find a station playing "Baker Street" – I love that song. I turn the radio up and relax back into my seat. Suddenly, this blonde girl with short hair comes shooting out of John McCarthy's house. She runs up to the passenger side of my car and opens the door. She has a beaming smile and a pretty face.

She seems excited and says, "You're John Monaghan, aren't you?

Confused, I reply, "Yeah, why do you ask?"

She says, "Will you go out with my friend, Tess McCarthy?"

"Who's Tess McCarthy?"

"She's John's sister."

"Well, I don't know John either," I say, laughing.

She laughs with me, then says, "Don't you remember when we passed you in the alleyway?"

"Oh yeah, I remember …"

"Tess was the one writing her name in chalk on the ground," she says.

Oh my God, am I really hearing this? She's asking me if I'll go out with that girl? Is she telling me Tess wants to go out with me?

I have to suppress my reaction and be cool about this, but it's hard. I give her some really stupid answers.

"Well, I'm not sure … I have a girlfriend, you know."

"Oh, please, please say yes – she really likes you," she says.

I look out at the field on the other side of the road, then turn back to her to answer her question. "Okay, but just for one week only," I tell her.

"Oh my God, she'll be so happy!" she replies, clapping her hands together. "She's in the house – I'll go and tell her."

She sprints into the house, so I guess Tess must really be in there. I can't believe I said such a stupid thing. *One week only* … What an idiot.

I can't believe my luck. I'm going to go out with the most beautiful girl in the world. What a great day this is. On the other hand, though, I'm going to have to chuck the other Tess. How can I do that? She's so nice and I don't want to hurt her. But I have to; I can't let this go by … No way. Just then, Charlie comes out of the house with a smile on his face.

He gets into my car and says, "What are you doing, Maurice, causing a storm?"

"I'm going to go out with her, Charlie," I say.

"Who, Tess McCarthy?" Charlie asks in disbelief. "What are you talking about? She's only fifteen."

"Well, I'm only seventeen and how long until she's sixteen?" I reply defensively.

"I don't know, but she's like a kid anyway," he replies.

I feel offended and frown at Charlie. I say, "What do you mean?"

"Never mind … I've known her a long time, that's all," he says. "Anyway, there's a disco on at McGinty's tonight. Do you want to go?"

It looks like he's trying to put me off her for some reason.

"Yeah, of course let's go," I reply.

I start up the car and drop him off at home, then make my way home to get ready for a night at McGinty's. Within an hour, I'm ready and out. On the way to McGinty's, I can't stop thinking. I wonder if Tess McCarthy's going to be there … I park in the carpark outside and I see Charlie walking towards the Red Lion across the road.

I call out to him, "Charlie!"

He stops and says, "All right, Maurice, do you want to go in for a drink at the Red Lion first?"

"Yeah, okay," I reply.

We have a couple of drinks in there, then make our way across the road to the disco. On the way down the alleyway to the disco, I can hear the Bee Gees song, "Tragedy". Charlie opens the door first and goes to the desk where we pay our 50p to get in. He heads straight for the bar and the others are already here. Roger, Sean, Ted, Charlie's cousin, Mark, the Duggen brothers, and Anthony.

Charlie buys a round of drinks and we start catching up. I can't help having a look around to see if Tess McCarthy's here or not. Then, suddenly, I see her and she's looking straight at me with her eyes sparkling and a cute smile. I smile back and wink at her. Everyone's chatting, so I may as well walk over and talk to her. After all, she wants to go out with me. I grab my pint of light and bitter, pouring the ale into my glass as I walk slowly over to this beautiful girl. At that very moment, the DJ puts another record on, and guess what it is? Of course, it's "Night Fever", again! All the girls in the disco let out a deafening scream and run to the dance floor to start dancing the new dance. Except Tess.

She stands there with her eyes fixed on mine. I've never seen eyes sparkle that way before – they're like diamonds and she's literally glowing with energy. I can feel the anticipation of our first words. I can feel a smirk appearing on my face; I just can't help it.

My first words to her are, "So, you must be the famous Tess McCarthy?"

"So, you must be the famous John Monaghan?" she bats back.

Oh God, I just know I'm totally in love with her already! She's wearing the latest trendy clothes. A pink-and-white punky furry top with long tassels, a white T-shirt, and tightly fitted brown corduroy jeans. Her top illuminates with the flashing disco lighting. She acts bashful but confident, and as we speak to each other, it's as though we're the only two people here. Everything else is fading into the background. I know it's cheesy, but I really do feel as though I've always known her and I can tell she feels the same.

Towards the end of the evening, at around ten pm, I hear Charlie call over to me, "Maurice, are you going to speak to us tonight?"

"Yeah, I'll be over soon," I call back.

The time flies by, and now the DJ is starting to put on some slow songs. He puts another Bee Gees song on – "How Deep Is Your Love".

Tess looks over at the dance floor and then back at me.

"Do you want to dance?" I ask her.

"Yeah, I like this one," she says.

I take her hand, we put down our drinks, and walk over to the floor. It feels so natural. She puts her soft cheek against mine and I can feel her hair brushing against my face. I can smell her sweet perfume. Everything about her is perfect.

As we dance, I want time to stand still; I don't want this to end. I know I won't have to ask if she wants to see me again after tonight. For the first time in my life, I'm feeling confident – not my fake confidence, but the real thing.

The night disco does come to a close right after our dance and again Charlie calls out:

"Maurice! It's your round!"

Tess's friend Tracy calls out straight after to say that they're leaving. Tess steps back from me, then says, "I have to go", but her eyes are still fixed on mine.

I pull her towards me and kiss her on the lips, then I pull back to look into those pretty eyes again. She looks up at me with her coy smile, then walks to one side, staring my way.

"I have to go," she says with a nervous laugh.

I call out to her as she walks away, "Pick you up on Saturday morning. There's a fair on at Cassiobury Park and we're going!"

She glances back, says "Okay", and then she's gone.

It's Tuesday evening the following week, I think I'm in love with this girl. I can't concentrate at work, making mistake after mistake, and I'm worried about Mum and also Dad. I have to call Tess Robinson to tell her I've met Tess McCarthy and I can't be her boyfriend any more. God, this feels horrible. I've had dinner and I'm lying on my bed. How do I tell her? She's so nice, but I don't and never did feel this way about her. I had better just get it over with, so here goes.

At the bottom of the stairs in the hall is our white phone on the triangular wooden phone table. Nobody's around; they're all in the living room watching *Coronation Street*. I pick up the receiver and anxiously dial Tess Robinson's number. Her mum picks up the phone the other end and says "Hello" in her usual cheerful way.

"Hello, it's John here – is Tess there, please?" I say, feeling guilty.

"Oh, hello, John," she says loudly in a teasing way. "I'll just get her for you, darling, hang on."

Tess comes to the phone very cheery and says, "Hi, are you okay?"

I feel a lump come to my throat. "Tess, I can't go out with you any more!" I say quickly.

There's just silence.

"Tess, are you there?" I ask.

"Yes, I'm still here," she replies.

"I'm sorry, but I've met someone else …"

"That's it, then?" she says.

"Yes, that's it," I reply.

Then all I can hear is a dialling tone – she's put the phone down.

I hope she's okay. I feel terrible, but also relieved that it's done.

She's too nice to mess around and she deserves better.

The next day at work, Stan is complaining to me that I'm not paying attention and keeps asking what's wrong with me. I can't concentrate; I'm so looking forward to the weekend when I can go to the fair with Tess McCarthy. I've been watching the clock all day because I'm going to call her tonight to be certain she can still come.

Eventually 5:30pm comes around and I rush straight for the locker rooms to get washed up. I can hear Stan call to me, "Oh, you can move now it's time to go home, none you? You not making any mistakes tomorrow, matey, I smack you like anything," with a few Polish words thrown in.

He can say what he likes; I couldn't care less. Within half an hour, I'm home and having egg and chips with Mum, Dad, and James. Dad's home early again, but I don't know why.

During dinner, Mum tells me, "Your daddy's going in for his operation tomorrow and I have to go in on Friday for my hysterectomy, so you'll have to look after James and make sure he's okay!"

"Yeah, okay, don't worry, I will," I reply.

All I really want to do is go and call my new girlfriend. After dinner, they all go into the living room. They all seem so sad; I'm the only one who's happy. I phone Tess and, luckily, she answers.

"It's John," I say.

"Oh hello," she replies quietly.

"Is it okay for you to go to the fair on Saturday?" I ask.

"Yes, I can," she says excitedly.

"Great, I'll pick you up around 10:30 then," I say, trying to hide my excitement.

"Yeah, see you Saturday," she replies.

I've just arrived home from work on Friday evening. There's no Mum or Dad, just James sitting watching TV. I feel really sorry for him, with Mum and Dad both in hospital. He looks upset. I ask him if he's okay and he says yes, but I can see he's not. I decide I won't go out tonight.

"Do you want fish and chips from the chip shop?" I ask him.

"Okay," he replies.

I've just been paid, so I run around the corner and get us both fish and chips and a can of Coke each. James likes to watch *Rich Man, Poor Man*, so I stay in and watch it with him for tonight.

It's Saturday morning, and I've just woken up. James is still asleep and the sun is beaming in through my bedroom window. It's so hot already and it's the day of the fair. I'm up and downstairs like a shot.

I have some tea and toast, and I'm leaving James to sleep in. I think I'll visit Mum on the way to Tess, because I want to check how she is after her operation. So long as she's okay, I'll be happy. On the way to the Peace Memorial Hospital, the town is full of people in and out of shops. They all look so relaxed in this hot sunny weather. The traffic's slow along St Albans Road, so I have time to watch people every time it stops. I try to imagine what they're thinking by the expressions on their faces. It's a bit like driving through a safari park, except they're humans instead of animals. I like to make up voices for them as I watch them, a bit like Jonny Morris does on the TV show, *Animal Magic*. When the traffic stops again for a while, I get out of my car and pull my aerial up so I can put my radio on. I switch on my radio and there it is again, "Night Fever" by the Bee Gees. After around 20 minutes in traffic, I finally arrive at the hospital.

Walking down the corridor to Mum's ward, I feel sad that she's in here, but I know she'll be okay. There are a lot of iron beds and the place stinks of bleach. I find Mum's bed and sit down next to her. She's alone and she's sleeping. She seems to sense that I'm here and partially opens her eyes to look at me.

She whispers, "Hello, John, is James all right?"

"He's okay. I bought him fish and chips last night," I say.

"Oh good," she replies and drifts back to sleep.

After a while, I decide I may as well go and come back again tomorrow. I'm on my way to pick up my new girlfriend. As I pull up outside Tess's house, I see her already outside the front with her friend, Tracy. What I didn't realise is that Tracy is Tess's brother John's girlfriend now.

Tess walks over to the window on my side and says, "Do you mind if they come with us?"

"No, that's okay, jump in," I say.

They all get in and Tess gets in next to me in the front. She looks out-of-this-world great! I can't take my eyes off her. Her brother, John, is talking to me, but I'm not listening. The colour of her blue eyes is as blue as the sea and her skin is glowing clear and perfect.

"I never knew you had blue eyes!" I say to her.

"I never knew you had blue eyes either," she replies. "My brother's trying to say something to you!" she adds, pointing to him in the back of the car.

I look around and her brother asks, "So, how long have you been going out with my little sister?

"Not long," I say.

I wink at Tess and start the engine. She looks at me with a bashful look as I screech off with a full throttle wheelspin. There's a scream from Tracy, then a "Wow" from John. Well, I have to impress them, don't I?

We arrive at Cassiobury Park and I park up on the grass. We all start to walk through the park towards the fair. Tess walks beside me, while John and Tracy walk slowly behind us. It's the first time I've been to this park, and I notice there are huge ancient trees either side of us as we walk along the path. There are so many people here and the crowd is flowing towards the fair. I can hear the music from the fair as we get closer. It's all rock 'n roll – I can hear "The Hop", "Johnny B Goode", "Rock N' Roll Is Here to Stay", then "Poetry in Motion" as we get closer. This is my kind of music, and walking towards the fair with Tess beside me is such a great feeling. I've never felt like this before. She's wearing a white cap-sleeved T-shirt and blue jeans turned up on the outside, which suits her so well.

She's cool too – no silly questions, no giggling, just times when I catch her looking at me with a little smile.

She's come back at me with a few clever answers already when I've taken the mickey out of her. I can tell she's intrigued by me, though, by the questions she asks, and I feel confident she's falling for me. Well, I think she is … I've just been paid, so straight away I'm going to blow the lot here. Straight to the fish and chip van I go and I'm leading the way. I'm starving.

"Who wants fish and chips?" I call out.

They all answer "yes, please", so I buy everyone fish and chips and we walk around as we eat.

"Come on, everyone, to the bumper cars!" I say.

We make a run for it just as they're stopping. Tess jumps into a car with me, while John and Tracy grab another one. The music changes to Elvis's "Jailhouse Rock", another favourite of mine. Tess leans in close to me and says, "You will take it easy, won't you!" I think she already knows I won't.

"What do you mean?" I ask. "Take it easy on your brother?"

Just as she replies, "I guess that was a silly question", we start moving and my only target for the ride will be her brother and Tracy.

"Hold tight!" I say.

Then I go straight for a head-on bash into John. We play chicken, but I won't give up. I follow it up by spinning them out three times. John looks a bit embarrassed, but Tracy can't stop laughing.

We get on just about every ride at the fair. John's great, too, and I really like him. We all just joke around and I've never laughed so much. But like every good day, it has to come to an end. The evening's drawing in and they're playing slower songs. They're starting to close everything down. Tess and I walk on ahead and I pull her behind one of the huge trees and kiss her. She kisses me right back like we had both wanted to do that all day. And that feeling comes back – like we're the only ones in the world right now. I can hear the music from the fair playing more faintly now, "Be My Baby" by The Ronettes.

John's voice breaks the moment: "What are you two up to?" John and Tracy are walking past us. "Don't forget she's my little sister!" he says.

It doesn't matter to either of us. Tess gives me her coy look and I have to laugh about it. Those big blue eyes, I think I know what it means to fall in love now. The evening's warm, the sky's red, the sun's setting and the music's still playing. The atmosphere's relaxed as the four of us stroll towards the car through this great park. John's talking to Tracy in a low and quiet voice as she laughs. I take Tess's hand as we get closer to the car and those blue eyes tell me she knows how I feel. This day is a day I will never forget.

I drop them all back at home, and I'm on my drive home alone, smiling to myself. This is what life is all about, not the life that I have at home where there's always something wrong. Life is about fun, love, and being with people you enjoy being around.

It's mid-October 1978, and Tess and I are together almost every night these days. As soon as I get home from work each day, I have my dinner, get cleaned up, and go straight to her house. But it's Saturday night and tonight I'm going to have a drink with Charlie. He's working behind the bar at McGinty's and I'll sit by the bar and talk to him between his serving people.

It's about ten pm and I've had a few drinks with Roger, but he's going home early tonight so I'll go straight over to Charlie at the club now. Roger prefers the Red Lion to the club, but I don't mind. I walk down the alleyway to the club and try to open the door, but it's locked. That's weird! I can hear people in there and it's too early for a lock in. I bang the door hard to make sure Charlie can hear me over the noise, but there's no answer. After a while, I get fed up and go home.

At home, I'm about to get into bed when the phone rings. I can hear Dad stirring.

"Who the hell is ringing at this time of night?" he mumbles.

"It's okay, I'll get it," I say quietly.

I run down the stairs and answer.

"Maurice, it's Charlie!"

"Charlie, why are you calling so late?" I ask.

"Maurice, the police are looking for you!" he says.

"What are you talking about?"

"Someone was stabbed in the White Hart Pub down the road from the club and they've died on the way to hospital. People have told the police that you were banging on the club door straight afterwards. Were you?" he asks.

"Yeah, I was, but I didn't stab anyone. You know I wouldn't do that!" I reply.

"Well, I don't know, Maurice, I'm only telling you what happened," he says.

"I'm going to bed now, Charlie. I'm tired and it's nothing to do with me," I tell him.

"What's wrong, John?" Mum calls out.

"Nothing, it's okay," I call back. "I have to go, Charlie, see you later," I tell him and then I hang up.

The following day, Charlie calls me with an update on what happened. Kevin McDonough, who lives two doors down from Tess, had got into a fight with two other boys because of an argument over what music should be played on the jukebox.

Kevin likes rock music and they wanted to play punk. The fight was outside and both of them were kicking Kevin and they pulled his jumper over his head. Kevin panicked, he pulled out a knife that he had on him, and stabbed one of the boys a few times.

33

Near death and a mother's love

I haven't mentioned anything about how much I smoke now. I've been smoking anything up to 40 cigarettes a day, either Benson & Hedges, or Rothmans, depending on what they have in the shop at the time. It's 57p for 20 cigarettes. Tess smokes, too, but not as much as I do. Lately my chest is feeling very tight and I get out of breath easily. I had asthma when I was little, so I shouldn't smoke at all. This week, my chest feels particularly bad and I feel tired as well.

I'm not sure if it's smoking that's causing it, or the asbestos dust from the lorries' brakes at work. Everyone blows the brake dust out of the brake drums using a blow jet. They're keeping the doors closed in the workshop, as it's getting colder, but they still blow the dust everywhere. There's a haze of dust sometimes, and you can hardly see the other end of the workshop through it.

It's Thursday evening and I'm driving home from work. I feel a bit shivery and my breathing is very tight. I feel more tired than usual, so I think I'll skip dinner and go straight to bed after my wash, because I don't feel hungry. I arrive home and Mum takes one look at me and asks, "What's wrong?"

"I don't feel well," I tell her as I walk up the stairs.

The next thing I know, I've woken up soaked in sweat. It's the middle of the night, the house is freezing, and everyone else is asleep. I get out of bed and walk slowly to the bathroom, feeling shaky and dizzy. I wash myself in warm water, but I have to go back to my bed. I've never felt so weak.

The following day, I hear Mum calling, "John, you have to get up for work. Come on, you're late!"

I try to call out to her that I'm not going to work, but my chest hurts so much that I can't.

After calling me a few times more, she comes into my room and asks, "What's wrong?"

"My chest is bad," I say quietly.

"Okay, well stay in bed today then and see how you are later," she tells me.

I nod and go back to sleep.

Around midday, I'm in the house alone. I feel terrible, and I'm still sweating a lot. It feels like I'm breathing through a straw. Everything's going hazy and my chest aches when I breathe.

This is weird ... Morning seems like it was just two minutes ago and now it's evening. I look around and everyone's in bed again. I go back to sleep again. The next thing I know, Mum's standing over me. She's talking, but I can't make out what she's saying. I don't know what time of day or even which day of the week it is. I've lost all sense of anything. There's a man standing over me ... He's putting something cold on my chest. It feels like he's killing me. I can't breathe, and I lash out at him and grab whatever it is he's pushing on my chest to get it away from me. Then I lie back down. I don't know what's going on. I can just faintly hear mumbling on the landing.

The man's saying, "I know what you think it is, but it's not. He'll be okay!"

Every so often, Mum's by my bed with water and tablets.

"Please, John, sit up and take the tablets," she says. She sounds upset.

I have no strength, but for Mum I find the strength to sit up. This is like a dream or something. I don't even feel like I'm here any more. I feel as though I'm about to die, but I must fight this for Mum. My chest feels like an eggshell. It's so difficult to move it to breathe. It would be so easy to give up.

I go back to sleep, but then there's Mum's voice again:

"John … John …" Her voice is soft and sad. It echoes in my mind … Then I feel my head being pushed up from the pillow. "Please, John, take the tablets."

I feel them being pushed into my mouth and then the water. I swallow them because I know it's my mum. The same thing goes on for I don't know how long. Sometimes I see daylight and sometimes it's dark, but there's nothing in between. I feel nothing, just darkness.

It's morning. I don't know which morning it is, but I know that it's morning because the sun's shining brightly through my bedroom window.

The first thing I notice is the colour. There's colour everywhere. My eyes start to focus and I can see everything around me so clearly. I'm alive and I feel happy to be here. I don't know how close to death I was, but I don't think you can get any closer without dying. I still feel a bit weak, but

I'm okay; I can breathe better and my vision seems perfect. It's like I've been reborn. I push back my bed covers and sit on the edge of my bed. The minute I sit up, Mum comes into my room. She looks so happy.

"Are you feeling better?" she asks.

"Yeah, I'm okay," I reply with a smile.

"You had a bad chest infection and thank God for the antibiotics that the doctor gave you," she says, looking relieved. "You should stop smoking now!"

"Yeah, I will," I reply.

The thought of smoking now is the last thing I want.

"Do you want some tea and toast?" she asks.

"Oh, yes, please," I reply.

When Mum goes down to make it, I look around my room and notice my *Saturday Night Fever* album that I bought a while back. I put it on the record player to play.

It's the only record I've ever bought and I treasure it. After a good wash, I go down to have my tea and toast. It then dawns on me that I don't even know what day it is. This is weird.

"Mum, what day is it?"

"It's Thursday," she says.

"Thursday … So I've been totally out of it for almost a week," I reply in dismay.

"I don't think you realise how ill you were," she says.

I knew how ill I was, but it's weird losing a whole week. This chest infection and almost dying from it has had a massive impact on me. So much so that I forgot to tell you that I took Tess to see the latest movie at the Empire last month – a musical called *Grease* starring John Travolta and

Olivia Newton. I didn't think much of it, because I don't like movies where people suddenly burst into song. I don't think Tess liked it much either. I liked *Saturday Night Fever* more, but they've been playing a lot of the songs from *Grease* on the radio lately too.

When Saturday morning arrives, I'm feeling much better. I'm trying to get my car started, ready for work on Monday. It's been running so badly, but now it won't even start. After spending an hour checking everything, I realise I'm flogging a dead horse. The engine has had it, and it's not worth putting a new engine in it, because it's too old and it's rusting a lot. Hardly grease lightning being a Mini. I go back into the house to tell Mum my bad news.

Mum replies, "Well, you'll just have to sort the problem out!"

On Monday, I have to get up extra early to catch the train. It's only six am, and I'm washed and dressed already. It's freezing and the ice is on the inside of the windows again. At seven am, I'm walking down Bushey Mill Lane to the train station. It's not a proper train station; it's right next to the level crossing with a wooden platform and a wooden hut shelter. It's a single-track railway and the train only has two carriages. Everyone calls it the "push me pull you" because it doesn't turn around and the front of it looks exactly the same as the back. It runs from Watford to St Albans one way, then reverses all the way back again. I have to buy a ticket on the train from the conductor. When it eventually arrives at St Albans, its noisy old diesel engine rattles and clangs, and it stops near the town at the bottom of a steep hill. I have to walk up that hill because the train would never make it, even if there were a track there. Then I have to walk across to the other side of St Albans which takes another half an hour. I'm going to have to do this every day from now on.

Catching the train every day isn't so bad, though, because it gives me time alone to think about things. As I wait for the train this mild October evening at St Albans station, I notice I'm the only passenger here, so I sit on the edge of the old wooden platform and make myself some roll-up cigarettes, placing them in my Old Holborn tobacco tin ready for tomorrow. It's calm here and I'm enjoying my own company.

I start to think about Tess. It was her sixteenth birthday last month, on 3 September 1978. It's a great birthday, isn't it, to be sixteen? You only ever have one sixteenth, and mine has come and gone, and so has hers now. It always makes me think of that song "Happy Birthday Sweet Sixteen". She really is the prettiest girl I've ever seen, just like the words of the song. Well, it's not long until my eighteenth now, and that's another special one.

I can feel the timber platform starting to vibrate. Here comes that excuse for a train. Will it make it to the platform? I stand up ready to get on board as it shudders slowly to a stop with a squeal from its brakes. As I grab the metal door handle to get on, I think it's mad that I'm the only passenger boarding here and only four people get off. There's a clang from a couple of the old steel doors and we slowly build up to almost 20mph. Everything vibrates and shudders, and the ticket conductor is on me straight away.

"Where are you going, young man?" he says in a patronising way.

"Watford," I reply.

"Yeah, very funny. Are you talking North Watford or what?"

The stupid train only goes to Watford and he knows I stop there every day. I'm just about the only passenger they have, but he acts like he's some kind of a travel agent.

"Yes, North Watford, please," I reply.

I hand him my money and he winds a ticket out of his machine that he has hanging around his neck. It has a silly winding handle that sticks out of the side of it, but he acts like he's so cool with it.

Now that I have no car, it's more difficult for me to see Tess, but rather than stay at home each evening, I have dinner, get washed, and start walking to Bushey. I can't let it stop me seeing her; she's my life now. The walk from Sandringham Road to Moatfield Road in Bushey is long, but she's worth it.

After a few days of doing this walk, I'm starting to feel tired. Tess's on school half-term holiday so I think I'll skip work and spend a few days with her at her house. I hate my job anyway, and if I lose it, I really don't care. The thought of that place gets me down. Stan's a miserable old man who barely speaks any English and has no sense of humour. The asbestos dust being blown around everywhere made me ill. The smell of the barrier cream makes me feel sick. The building reminds me of a prison. The work's hard and filthy, and I don't feel like I have any value there anyway.

After a few days with Tess, I tell her that I had better go home; I'll sort out a new car and I'll see her again soon. She's okay with it. I leave her house at around four on Friday afternoon. It's cold and grey, and the walk is long and lonely.

On this long walk, I'm thinking about how much I love her and I really do think I want to spend the rest of my life with her; I could never want anyone else. As I approach my house in Sandringham Road, I see Mum parking her car. Her face looks like thunder; she's furious about something.

"John, where have you been?" she asks with a frown.

Oh no, she's guessed that something's wrong.

"I've been to see Tess," I reply.

"Godfrey Davis have called me and said you haven't been going to work and they want to sack you!" she says.

For a second, I feel a sense of relief, but I say nothing, as I really wish they would sack me so I can get a better job.

"Luckily, I was able to talk to them and persuade them not to sack you, so you can go back in on Monday and tell them you'll never do this again!" she says.

Oh damn, why did she bother?

"Yes, okay, Mum," I say.

Sunday comes around and I'm not sure if it's by chance or if Mum and Dad have organised this, but Dad has a car that he wants to sell. He says he bought it to sell on for a profit, but tells me I can buy it from him and pay him weekly until it's paid off. It's a light blue Vauxhall HB Viva. It looks okay, but the wings are rusty at the front and someone has filled them with body filler.

The registration number is VHK 477E. It doesn't start very well, the engine rattles badly, and it smokes from under the bonnet. Well, it's my dad and it's the easiest way out of this problem, so I agree and he gives me the keys.

"Thanks, Dad," I say.

"It's not as nippy as your Mini!" he tells me.

"That's okay. I'm glad to have a car again," I say.

I jump in the car and take it for a drive straight away. It feels like a very grown-up car, not a toy like my Mini. The first place to go is Tess's house to show her my new car.

Tess is not that impressed when she sees it, but she's glad I have it so I can come and see her every day and we can go places easily again.

On Thursday 9 November 1978, it's my eighteenth birthday. I've picked Tess up in my new car and she seems really happy, with a beaming smile on her face. As we drive along, I ask her why she's so happy.

"Well, you're eighteen now," she says.

"That makes you happy?"

"Yeah, well to have a boyfriend who's eighteen is a big deal," she tells me.

I can't figure out what she means, but I smile at her and drive on. These are the best days of my life so far. Just us being together no matter what we're doing makes me feel that there's meaning to life. I can't imagine anyone else making my life feel so complete. Those old black-and-white movies made in Hollywood can be real after all … I want us to get married, have children together, make a home together, and grow old together.

The sound of her laugh, the way she holds my face with both hands while looking into my eyes, saying "I love you so much" is so special. I'm so lucky.

34

Christmas tinsel love and gifts

It's Christmas Eve, 1978, and it's pouring rain. I've just picked Tess up and I've given her her Christmas present. She wants to open it straight away because I won't be with her on Christmas Day. We're sitting outside her house in my car, and she's so excited as she rips the wrapping paper off her present. Inside is a box and in the box is a silver necklace with the letters of her name hanging from it.

Her sparkly eyes light up as she takes it from the box and holds it up on her fingers to admire it. The silver letters shine light reflected from the street lights onto her beautiful face. On the radio, a song by Boney M is playing, "Mary's Boy Child".

"I love it!" she says.

Then she turns to me and kisses me like she couldn't love me any more than she does.

"Come on, let's go – I have a surprise for you!" she says.

"Go where?" I say, confused.

"I'll show you," she replies.

She directs me from her house to a jewellers shop on Bushey High Street near the Red Lion.

"Stop right here!" she tells me.

I stop and park the car outside the jewellers. She jumps out and dashes into the shop. In two minutes, she jumps back into the car.

"Your Christmas present," she says as she hands me a small plastic bag held up by decorative handles.

She looks so excited, like she's about to explode. I take the bag and look inside. There's a black box. I open the box to reveal a black velvet bag. The bag feels heavy. I turn it upside down and empty it into my hand. It's a sparkling chrome Ronson mechanical cigarette lighter. I'm stunned. This must have cost her a fortune. The top of it is chrome and the body is stainless steel. It has a lever to adjust the flame and the top hinges around to replace the flint. I squeeze it on the side button and it ignites. The flame lights up her cute face. She looks so happy.

"How did you ever afford to buy this?" I ask her.

"I've been saving for months," she replies. "I've been paying the jeweller each week and he's kept it there for me until I made the last payment just now."

She can't contain her excitement and I can see she knows I love it.

Then she pulls out a cigarette and says, "Have you got a light?"

I laugh at that and lean across to light her cigarette with my new, very expensive lighter. I park the car in McGinty's car park and we walk into the club, stopping to kiss on the way. We walk through to the bar and I see Tess's brothers, John and Vernon, are already here. I guessed Vernon was here without even seeing him because his favourite song

"Supernature" is already playing on the jukebox. Charlie is behind the bar and the others are playing pool.

"Have you got two p?" Tess asks me.

I give the two p to her and she dashes to the jukebox. I know what she'll put on and sure enough she does – "From a Jack to a King" by Ned Miller. She loves that song, but, sadly, the Bay City Rollers too. It's funny how all the young people are here early, but by 8:30pm all of the oldies and parents start to roll in until the place is packed. It's a great atmosphere, though.

Tess loves midnight mass because she can open all of her presents afterwards when she gets home. She's such a kid.

I walk over to Charlie at the bar and buy myself a light and bitter. Tess has her usual lemonade. I hand Charlie the 50p.

After a great night, we head to the church for midnight mass and it's more entertaining than I thought it would be. So many Irish people trying to stand up and be respectful, but they're all waving all over the place because they're so drunk. Tess's brother John is asleep standing up and wobbling all over the place, then jolting as he wakes up.

The following day, Christmas dinner at home feels flat and we seem to be just going through the motions of having the traditional meal. Turkey, roast potatoes, and Brussels sprouts as always, the dinner is at lunchtime and straight after I thank Mum and tell her I'm going to see Tess.

"Can't you just be with your family for one day?" she says.

The thought of just sitting in the living room all afternoon with Mum, Dad, and James, when Tess is waiting to see me runs through my head.

"I will tomorrow," I reply.

Straight away, I grab my coat and I'm gone. When I arrive at Tess's house, I feel so different. Walking up the garden path fills my heart with warmth. I knock on the front door and Tess's mum opens it.

"Oh, John Monaghan!" she calls out with a big smile.

"Come in, come in. Tess, John is here for you," she calls out in her Irish accent.

In the background I can hear her dad, Peter, laughing and joking. He has a unique and catching laugh. He's always the life and soul of the party. Tess comes straight to me and throws her arms around me. She hugs me so tightly and her dad says in his strong Irish accent, "Will you stop squeezing him now because his eyes will pop out!"

Then he laughs so loud and everyone laughs with him. Tess looks embarrassed and pulls me over to the sofa to sit next to her.

There's tinsel everywhere. They have a huge Christmas tree and they all have paper Christmas cracker hats on. Her dad, brothers, sisters, and her uncle Frank are all in the living room, and her mum is in and out of the kitchen. They're all so pleased to see me and her mum calls out to me, "John, will you have something to eat?"

"Oh no, thank you, Petra, I've just had my dinner," I reply.

Tess told me her name was Petra as a joke when I first met her, so I've called her that ever since. Her mother's real name is Francis.

"Will you take a cup of tea, then?" she asks.

"Okay, thank you," I reply.

Peter opens a new box of Benson & Hedges and places them on the coffee table. It's a huge party box where the whole top of the box comes off to display all of the cigarettes with gold lining. It's just paper and cardboard, but it looks luxurious. "Cigarette anyone?" he says. "Go on, help yourselves." He really wants everyone to enjoy this day in his home.

I go ahead and take one and light it with my new lighter, and Tess does the same. I'm so relaxed here. Tess snuggles into me and there's laughter, food, and drink. The atmosphere is like nowhere else. If I could make this day last forever, I really would. They're the greatest people I've ever known.

January 1979 is the coldest weather I've ever known, minus fourteen degrees centigrade some nights. Vernon, Roy Hamill, a friend of Vernon's, and I have been out for a drink. There's snow on the ground, and I've been doing handbrake turns in the car for fun. We're on one of the side roads in Bushey Heath where there's a long steep hill in a residential area. Going back up the hill, the car starts to slide all over the place. The wheels will not grip, so I have to rev the engine a lot. It's too much for my old car and eventually it overheats. I submit to the fact that we're never going to get to the top and we're going to have to walk.

"That's it, we're walking from here on!" I tell them.

"You're joking!" Vernon says in despair. "We can't walk all the way home in this weather – it's freezing."

"Well, there's nothing else we can do," I reply.

As soon as we all get out of the car, we realise just how cold it is. The car is clanging as everything contracts with the massive temperature difference. It starts cooling immediately and the back windows start freezing over. It's late at night and this road is very quiet. I can see curtains being pulled slightly aside where sleepy people are in their bedrooms trying to see what's going on. We all stay quiet and start our long walk back to Vernon's house. Tess is going to be so annoyed with me. After a short while into the walk, we start laughing and joking, but by the time we get halfway back, which is about two to three miles, the talking stops. We're all totally frozen and I mean frozen. I look around at Vernon and I have to laugh. His black hair is completely white and has frozen on his head. But even worse, his black bushy eyebrows are completely white, too. I can't resist it. I quickly grab his left eyebrow between my fingers and it just snaps off.

"Ow!" he screams. "What the hell are you doing?"

I show him his white eyebrow in my hand and I'm laughing so much that it hurts. He does the same back to me and says, "Yours are white, too!" as he bursts into laughter.

We finally arrive back at his house and we all check the mirror.

"This is how we'll look when we're old," I say.

Well, it's been a bad situation but we all had such a great laugh. Roy says goodbye and braves the cold to head home. Vernon throws me a blanket, and tells me to sleep on the sofa, then heads upstairs. The log fire's still burning and it's so cosy here in the living room. A few minutes later, Tess walks into the room. Everyone else is in bed asleep.

"What have you been doing?" she whispers.

I tell her what happened as quietly as I can.

"Idiot!" she whispers in my ear, then slides in under the blanket with me.

Another fun night I will never forget.

35

Dark times ahead

It's February 1979, another dark and cold evening. I've just arrived home from work. It's been a hard day with lorries freezing up. I've spent most of the day outside trying to get them started. Mum's making dinner for James and me and telling us about Dad.

"Your daddy's very ill again. He's upstairs in bed – he's not been able to eat, so he has to go back into hospital because the bowel cancer is getting worse."

I'm sitting at the kitchen table and I watch her still cooking dinner for us and trying to go on. I know this must be hard for her, but I'm only eighteen years old and I can't face it. It's hard to watch her so sad. Dad had been training as a bus driver recently, because he thought the job may be easier. He must be trying to stay positive.

I stand up and walk over to Mum to give her a hug. She breaks down crying.

"I love you, Mum. I'll stay here with you for a while after dinner," I tell her.

An hour or so later, she seems to be a bit better.

"Will you be okay if I go to see Tess now?" I ask, feeling unsure.

"I'm okay, don't worry," she reassures me.

As I leave, I feel so much guilt, but this house always has a black cloud over it. Tess is waiting and I'm torn between comforting Mum or seeing her.

I arrive at Tess's house feeling sad, but she always lifts my spirits. I knock on the front door and Petra opens it.

"Tess, John is here," she calls out.

That's unusual, she doesn't seem her usual happy self. I step in out of the cold. Petra goes into the kitchen. I walk into the living room and everyone is watching TV. They all say hello to me, but Tess says nothing. She just stares at the TV.

"Is everything okay?" I ask her.

She doesn't respond. I guess she's annoyed about my being late. She doesn't know why I'm late, though. I'm standing in the living room doorway and still she's just blanking me, and I think I can't be bothered with this.

"Okay, if that's how it is, I'll see you later!" I say.

She doesn't even look away from the TV.

"Bye, everyone," I say, hoping for a response from her.

The family all look at Tess. There's still nothing from her, so I turn around and leave. I decide to call around for Charlie and we go for a drink in the Red Lion. He's always there when I need him and he listens to me moan about my situation. I do the same for him when he's down, but he rarely is. He's one in a million.

A week or so later, Mum asks me if I can drop James off at school. She has to take Dad to the hospital to get a bag fitted, because his insides are blocked now with tumours.

"Yes, of course I will," I say.

I'll be late for work, but I've had no time off for ages and it's important. There's a lot of snow on the ground, but eventually I manage to drive James to St Michael's and park outside the gate. James jumps out and walks quickly across the playground. Nothing much was said on the journey here. I watch him walk all the way to the main entrance. I wonder what's going through his mind. I'm late; I have to go. I put my car in reverse to back up out of the space when a man in his Austin Maxi zips in directly behind me to drop off his son. But then he just sits there. God, that's so frustrating!

I open my driver's door and call out to him, "Can you back up, mate?"

"In a minute," he replies.

The arrogance of him … He could see I was starting to back up and he's parked so close to me and blocked me in. I'm boiling over in a rage. What's wrong with everyone?

I blast my horn and start to reverse towards him a bit closer, but he ignores me. I can't take this crap from anyone at the moment and it's for no good reason – he could easily back up a couple of feet.

I snap. I drive forward one foot, then put the car in reverse. I press the accelerator to the floor, and the car's revving high on full revs. Then I let the clutch up and crash straight into the front of his car. I push his car back with my car just enough for me to get out.

He jumps out and shouts, "Bloody hell, you maniac!"

"You should have moved then!" I shout back.

"I'm going down to the insurance company," he says.

I know I've damaged my car and his, but right now I don't care.

This miserable year rolls on. Dad has been sent home from hospital and they've told Mum they can do no more for him. She's been like a soldier looking after him.

It's a Sunday morning, May 1979. The sun's shining and the sky's so blue. I wasn't out with Tess last night because she's gone to Ireland with her dad. They're staying at a place called Miltown Malbay by the sea. Her uncle lives there and he invited them to stay. We've not been getting on that well recently, so we probably need a break from each other anyway. She doesn't seem to make any allowances for how my home life is, but then she shouldn't have to.

I have to do some work on my car, because it's rattling a lot from the tappets. Mum is in the kitchen washing up, and Dad's in the living room where he has to stay all the time now because his mobility's almost gone. I don't have any feeler gauges to use on my car and I feel guilty, because I have to ask Dad if I can borrow his.

I open the living room door and he's sat there gazing towards me.

"Look at me, John, do you think I'll ever get better?" he asks

For a man who was quite big and strong, he's declined to a fraction of his former self. He's skin and bone and his cheeks are drawn in. He looks so frail and hopeless.

"Of course you'll get better!" I reply.

But we both know the truth.

"Can I borrow some tools to use on my car please?" I ask.

"So long as you put them back," he says.

"Thank you," I say as I leave the room to get the tools.

It's strange how he was worried about me not putting his tools back; we both know he'll never use them again.

It's 12 June 1979, a school day for James and a workday for me. It's seven am and I have just gone downstairs. I think Mum has been up all night and Anita's here. I open the living room door and the curtains are still closed. Mum's sitting by Dad's bedside, holding his hand. She looks over at me with sadness in her eyes and says solemnly, "I don't want you to go to work today. I don't think your daddy's going to last the day."

I walk over to his bedside and I can see he's not conscious. His breathing is shallow and he looks peaceful. Mum tells me, "Last night he sat up in a panic. The last thing he did was to call out 'Anita, John, and James', then he laid back down."

I sit down at his bedside and watch his breathing. There's silence in the room. Nobody says anything. An hour or so passes, his breathing slows, gradually fades away, then stops. His eyes slowly start to open as his body relaxes; then he starts to turn cold. I'm sitting by his bedside holding his eyes closed, I don't know what else to do.

He's dead.

Anita, James, and Mum are crying. I feel sad for them, but as much as I wish I could cry, I can't.

I will always feel a lot of guilt for not mourning the death of my father but the truth is I just feel relief. I don't want Mum's suffering to go on as it has been. I could feel her pain.

It's the day of the funeral and we're at the cemetery, a mild day and luckily no rain. The whole family, including uncles, aunts, cousins, and Granny, are here.

As we stand around Dad's open grave, they lower his coffin down into it with the priest praying. Mum has Anita and James to her left and I'm standing to her right. She's holding her hanky to her mouth, tears rolling down her cheeks.

As I watch the coffin make its way into the ground, my memories with my dad replay in my head. I see his angry frowns and disapproving glances. I hear his shouting voice with threats of hitting me. I feel the burn from being hit by him and I smell my own fear.

Why did he make everything this way?

I've known the answer to that question for some time.

He was still an angry child.

From my birth to his death, the bond between my mother and me was more than he could bare.

To my father: I forgive you.

Printed in Great Britain
by Amazon